Getting It
Off the Shelf

Westview Special Studies in Public Systems Management

Getting It Off the Shelf: A Methodology for Implementing Federal Research

Peter W. House and David W. Jones, Jr.

In 1976, the federal government spent over $10 billion on civilian research, development, and demonstration projects. The vast majority of these dollars were spent for applied research—research from which it is reasonable to expect a payoff in implementation, commercialization, or problem solving. In all too many cases, that payoff has not been forthcoming. Technologies, for example, have been brought to the working prototype state, only to "sit on the shelf."

This is only one conclusion of this important new study of the federal R&D process. Concentrating on the case of energy-saving technology, the authors explain the high frequency of implementation failure by examining the reward structure of federal R&D agencies and the limits of current methods of program planning and technology assessment. They note that federal agencies perceive their mission in terms of proving new technology concepts and developing working prototypes, but that they tend to view implementation and adoption as "somebody else's problem." The result, the authors conclude, is that R&D funds are often spent to solve problems in technology design—without regard to whether the design problem is related to a real consumer need, social problem, or product demand.

Other authors have concluded that the probability of implementation could be increased if government behaved more like business. Such a simplistic solution is rejected in this book and a technology planning and screening process responsive to the social welfare and public policy objectives of government is proposed. The basic thesis presented is that implementation concerns should drive the overall R&D process, rather than be viewed as the final stage in the development of a technology.

Peter W. House, visiting scholar at the Institute of Transportation Studies, University of California, Berkeley, received a doctorate in public administration and sociology from Cornell University. Dr. House previously was with the U.S. Environmental Protection Agency, where he served as director of the Environmental Studies Division and deputy director of the Washington Environmental Research Center in the Office of Research and Development.

David W. Jones, Jr., holds a doctorate in communications from Stanford University. He is currently an associate specialist and transportation policy analyst at the Institute of Transportation Studies, University of California, Berkeley, and has served as a consultant to the Illinois and the California Departments of Transportation, the U.S. Urban Mass Transportation Administration, the National Science Foundation, and the National Aeronautics and Space Administration.

Getting It Off the Shelf

A Methodology for Implementing Federal Research

Peter W. House
David W. Jones

with

J. Bernier   V. K. Chan
O. M. Bevilacqua   M. I. Howland
H. W. Bruck   S. A. Seminoff
R. E. Burnkrant   A. R. Zahradnik

Westview Press
Boulder, Colorado

Westview Special Studies in Public Systems Management

This book is based on research conducted under Project no. 442491-26754, "Implementation of Strategies for Transportation Energy Conservation," Office of Energy Conservation, Energy Research and Development Administration.

Library of Congress Cataloging in Publication Data

House, Peter William, 1937-
  Getting it off the shelf.

  Includes bibliographies.
  1. Power resources—Research—United States. 2. Research, Industrial—United States. I. Jones, David W., joint author.
II. Title.
TJ163.25.U6H68   333.7   77-3918
ISBN 0-89158-347-5

Printed and bound in the United States of America

To Laura Steinman,
a unique Californian

Contents

5. Public Sector–Private Sector Comparisons

6. Integrating Theory and Experience

7. Getting It Off the Shelf

Figures

Tables

Preface

This study is concerned with the implementation of federally sponsored technology R&D. It focuses on the process of technology adoption and diffusion in both the public and private sectors. The research was motivated by a growing awareness that federally supported R&D ventures frequently fail to produce a technology that is compatible with both the objectives of public policy and the dictates of the technology delivery system which produces, markets, and services products. Where the issues of implementation feasibility, market potential, and user acceptance are ignored, the implementation of technologies is left to chance. "Leaving implementation to chance" appears to be the rule rather than the exception in federally sponsored technology R&D, where many technologists take the view that "implementation is not my business." As a result, the "end product" of many federally supported R&D activities is never used; research findings "sit on the shelf" and do not reach the market for which they were intended.

In the case of energy-saving technology—the case which generated this research—it appears that too much is at stake to permit a laissez-faire attitude toward commercial adoption and technology implementation. Great sums of money are being and will continue to be expended on the development of energy-generating and conserving technologies. Because known petroleum and gas reserves are limited and in large part not under U.S. control, the issue of eminent importance is to bring the most promising alternative energy technologies into their most appropriate uses with the least possible delay. If this is to happen, research programs will have to become concerned not only with the scientific feasibility and engineering practicality of a concept, but also with the means of causing the adoption of the resulting technology in the appropriate market in a useful time frame. Unfortunately, as we shall demonstrate in the following chapters, if the research and development process were to follow the pattern of past R&D activities, the challenge of successfully developing and introducing energy-saving technologies would not be met.

In addressing the problem of implementing federally sponsored technological R&D, we have examined both public and private sector R&D processes, from inception of the product idea through final deployment and use. Implementation concerns, we would argue, should drive the overall R&D process, rather than be viewed as the final stage or last event in the development of a technology. It is our thesis that marketability and implementation considerations can and should be incorporated throughout the R&D process to increase the probability of technology adoption and diffusion and to increase the payoff from each R&D dollar.

Our analysis of technology implementation has involved three phases: conceptualization and derivation of hypotheses relating to the causes of implementation failure based on a thorough review of the relevant literature; analysis of several case studies to evaluate these hypotheses and to derive additional information concerning implementation barriers arising during various stages of R&D activities; and the development of a strategy for incorporating implementation considerations into the R&D process. Findings from the first two phases of our research are presented in Chapters 1 through 6. They provide a background for understanding what has been termed "the implementation problem." In the concluding chapter (7) we propose one strategy for ameliorating this problem.

Further research is being conducted to refine the concepts and the methodology recommended in Chapter 7. In support of these activities, a conference of federal R&D managers is being planned for the summer of this year to discuss and evaluate implementation problems and strategies for reducing their impacts on federal R&D programs. In addition, the Energy Research and Development Administration (ERDA) is considering the incorporation of an implementation strategy, based on the recommendations of Chapter 7, within their Transportation Energy Conservation Division.

This book was based upon research conducted by the Transportation Energy Conservation Group at the Institute of Transportation Studies (ITS), University of California at Berkeley. The research was generously funded through a contract with ERDA's Transportation Energy Conservation Division. Peter House and David Jones held the principal responsibility for the organization and conduct of the research. In addition, various members of the research group made considerable contributions to specific chapters:

Chapter 2: Jacqueline Bernier
Chapter 3: Robert E. Burnkrant and Victor K. Chan
Chapter 4: Marie I. Howland and Oreste M. Bevilacqua

The background analysis for the case studies was conducted by the following individuals:

Stack Gas Desulphurization: Henry W. Bruck
Jet Engine Retrofit and Noise Suppression: Victor K. Chan
Urban Information Systems: Victor K. Chan
Housing Rehabilitation: Marie I. Howland
Newtowns: Marie I. Howland
STOL: Commuter Aircraft: Marie I. Howland
Transbus: David Jones
Transportation Systems Management: David Jones
Poultry Waste Processing: Stephanie A. Seminoff
Seat Belts and Air Bags: Stephanie A. Seminoff
Operation Breakthrough: Alan R. Zahradnik
Personal Rapid Transit: Alan R. Zahradnik

The authors would like to thank the principal investigators for the general implementation project under whose aegis this study was done. Dr. Samuel Berman of the Lawrence Berkeley Laboratory and Dr. William Garrison of the Institute of Transportation Studies were in this role for their respective institutions. Mr. Henry Bruck had day-to-day management responsibility for the project for ITS. We would also like to thank Dr. David Roessner of the National Science Foundation for his support and many valuable leads. A number of people agreed to be interviewed by the research group and gave their time and their interest. This too was greatly appreciated. Moreover, the staff of the Institute of Transportation Studies provided a congenial atmosphere and first-rate support. Jim Ramsey edited the manuscript. Drawings were done by Bob Aviles and Nestor Gonzalez. Special thanks must be given to Laura Steinman, who also assisted in editing and refining the text and who, with the support of Saundra Owodunni, completed the final preparation of this report. Finally, a great debt is owed to Mr. John Brogan of ERDA who saw the need for the study and has actively supported it throughout its life.

The findings and conclusions presented in this book reflect the judgments and opinions of the authors and do not necessarily represent the view of our sponsors at ERDA or of any other federal agency. In addition, any errors or omissions are the responsibility of the authors.

1
Introduction

Emergence of Goal-oriented Research

The term "research," like the term "scientist," conjures up images of white laboratory coats, test tubes, microscopes, and other paraphernalia coupled with a detached, slightly absent-minded group of practitioners, dedicated seekers of truth unaffected by work-a-day demands. This stereotype, although overblown, does describe the researcher found in numerous laboratories, centers, and universities throughout the world. Such practitioners are scientists of our day, and their vocation and goal is basic research.

There are others who also search for truth, but success for them is more clearly defined. These researchers are goal-oriented: their quest is for a specific result. In contradistinction to their colleagues who seek knowledge for its own sake, these researchers are oriented toward the attainment of a particular goal (for example, building the original atomic bomb). Their activities are classified as applied research.

Recently the stereotype of the applied researcher has been altered to include a variant, the researcher who is expected to produce results to order. He is the on-demand problem solver.

The intellectual origins of this type are probably found in Veblen's engineer and among the advocates of technocracy in the 1930s. One might even trace the type to the utopians of a century earlier. Most of the early flesh-and-blood manifestations of this type were in the military research during World War II. Sputnik, though military in origin and early research, led to the first nonmilitary multibillion dollar research and development budget. The goal of the R&D was to put a man on the moon.

There are postulates undergirding this conception of research.

- Any reasonable, defined goal can be attained in a specified time if sufficient resources (trained manpower, money) are allocated
- Judgment of results is not confined to a small, esoteric peer group, but can be made by a larger public
- The method of dealing with problems is transferable to many endeavors, technological and other, far removed from its military origins
- In the public sector, elected officials or administrators could specify a desired product, allocate required resources, and set a period of performance with the expectation that results would be achieved
- The management techniques applicable, for example, to a construction project are also applicable to this type of R&D management

The federal response to two recent great "crises," environment and energy, have exemplified the new faith in on-demand research. With respect to the environment, goals were mandated by the Congress, and money was appropriated to purchase the technology needed to meet the standards that had been set. In the energy area, funds were appropriated to move the U.S. toward energy "independence." In both cases there was an explicit conviction that on-demand R&D could produce the desired results in specified time periods.

The nature and uses, or misuses, of on-demand R&D are not a principal concern in this study. But this conception of R&D gives rise to the implementation problem with which we are concerned and thus has to be discussed briefly. The advocates and users of on-demand research have learned, mostly through experience, the validity of the Fourth Law of Thermodynamics which states that everything takes longer and costs more. They have also learned that PERT or CPM charts are not the product of revelation, but rather are estimates made by fallible mortals.

The fact (once on-demand research has been torn from the military and space womb) that has not thus far been adequately understood is that successful R&D is not enough. The military and space organizations which gave rise to this type of research process are closed systems. The specifiers of the product are also its users. In contrast, the organizations concerned with R&D related to the environment or to energy do not include most of the users of the products of their R&D. These organizations are open systems.

To be sure, it is possible to evaluate R&D products strictly according to performance standards (does this technology "work"?). But there is a distinction between a technology "working," and its acceptance and achievement of intended effects (for example, measurable improvement of air quality or production of energy from nonfossil fuel sources). The purpose of our analysis is to clarify steps needed to insure that the R&D products not only "work" but come into widespread use.

The Energy Situation

Recent events causing governmental and public concern over availability of energy resources are well known. The oil embargo of the winter of 1973–74 demonstrated the vulnerability of the U.S. to disruptions in the accustomed pattern of supply. It also highlighted the increasing U.S. dependence upon oil imports. Resulting increases in energy costs caused real and pervasive impacts on the economy.

More recent events show that the effect of higher oil prices on our balance of payments and on the rate of inflation were less than anticipated. The implication is that the United States, if it could develop safeguards against capricious disruptions of its oil supply, could continue to import large quantities of oil at current (or even higher) world market prices without deeply disrupting the economy. The embargo and increasing dependence upon imported petroleum products (currently approximately 40 percent), far more than natural gas shortages (real or artifically created), drew attention to the American society's reliance on nonrenewable resources for most energy requirements. One result of these events is the realization that in the foreseeable future the cost of energy for all purposes will remain high and will probably continue to increase.

The Energy Research and Development Administration (ERDA), emerged as one institutional response to the energy dilemma. This agency was given the mission to perform or sponsor research and development creating alternative energy sources (including renewable ones). ERDA was also to study and evolve measures to bring about substantial conservation of energy through more efficient use of available supplies.

In contrast to other R&D mandates, however, ERDA's mandate specifically included an implementation requirement. Demonstration of feasibility and operability of the products of ERDA would not be enough. Solutions for environmental and energy problems required that the product technologies be brought successfully to market. In a recent *Business Week* article (July 1976), for example, the latest energy plan was reviewed, and commercialization was highlighted.

> As for ERDA chief Seamans, he seems content to ride out the current storm, preparing for possibly worse weather ahead. "Channelling our efforts into commercialization will be one of our most difficult tasks," he says. So far his agency has pinpointed 30 technologies that could reduce U.S. oil needs, and hence imports, in the next five years. But ERDA is only now beginning to analyze what the government's role in pushing such technologies past the demonstration stage should be, and that worries Seamans. "The success of this agency hinges on how well its products are accepted," he says.

> Although Seamans does not mention it, industry reluctance to accept new ideas is apparently a big part of the problem. "The utilities don't particularly care for commercializing solar energy," claims one ERDA official, "and the auto industry doesn't want us to fiddle with the internal combustion engine." Where does that leave the agency? "Whenever possible," says planning chief LeGassie, "it will be our job to break down the barriers to accepting innovation."

This perspective places ERDA in an interesting and unique position. The agency must engage in commercialization efforts not after its R&D projects have been completed, but before and during project development. Because this is a relatively new approach, there is little research or information on how to include implementation and commercialization considerations in program or project design.

The Problem

Many scientists and legislators see the energy crisis as a technological problem. If we are running short of energy—get more. If getting more takes time—make present use of energy more efficient. Each effort, whether concerned with the development of new sources or improved efficiency, will bring forth new engineering or scientific understanding. Such mechanical responses to the energy dilemma have the potential for easing the problem, but their utility depends upon the specific circumstances.

There is a problem with this thinking. Let us postulate a stylized model of how such decisions are made. Let us assume that we are discussing a problem which can be handled by building a device (as opposed to altering the way something is done). Figure 1-1 shows the process from problem to implementation. Significantly, a form of cost/benefit analysis is normally executed to determine whether the proposed solution will work in an abstract context. Only after the development of a prototype is serious consideration given to the process of implementation and the real world constraints imposed on it. Because the development of a prototype demonstrates the existence of a technological solution, and not whether that solution is capable of implementation, the decision to begin a program is based on incomplete information.

Moreover, if a time dimension were mapped on this model, one would find that often political interest ends at the prototype stage. Although it is difficult to demonstrate conclusively, several of the studies of implementation processes suggest the model aptly describes this situation (see Chapter 4). Several case studies performed for this study also appear to confirm the suspicion. No normative inferences about the efficiency of the current process are intended here. However, present documentation of the implementation process provides some clues for guiding more projects to successful implementation.

A few specific examples may help to illustrate gaps in the existing decision process. In the consumer area, many people have advocated the introduction of simple sounding practices based on an "energy ethic," such as turning off

FIGURE 1-1. A Stylized Model of R&D Decision Making

lights when they are not being used, lowering thermostats, or insulating buildings. An alternative proposal is to move toward marketplace criteria (e.g., "full cost" pricing to encourage greater conservation through disincentive). Other proposals have considerable faith in the rationality of man when reinforced by information and education.

There is nothing intrinsically wrong with any of the proposed strategies; however, the irrefutable evidence is that they have not worked well, suggesting that more research is needed to better understand the process of implementation. For example, more reliable rail transit seems to have a new group of advocates. This form of transportation, heavily touted as a certain winner, able to stop sprawl and reduce air pollution and energy consumption, able to solve some problems of social equity, may not be a practical solution. Studies of existing systems and those in the process of being built indicate questions of passenger safety and comfort as well as revenue problems. Recently completed systems, of which the Bay Area Rapid Transit District may be the only example, have failed to attract projected large numbers of riders. There have been no discernible shifts from auto to rapid rail. BART has succeeded in shifting bus riders but not car riders (Webber, 1976). Even the Washington, D.C., rail transit system, presently under construction, was not projected in a recent Council of Government study to have significant impacts on modal switching and will have questionable energy savings and pollution benefits when all factors are included. In addition, there is increasing evidence that large-scale rail systems exacerbate rather than contain sprawl.

In short, these rail transit strategies appear to be flawed. If plans like these (which appear conceptually sound and have considerable support but no real testing) are taken seriously by the policy level and budgets are structured to implement them, then the failure rate will certainly be higher than it needs to be.

To offset the pessimistic tone of this section, let us admit that the experience of the past is not necessarily a reliable forecast of the future and that a concerted policy thrust in a specific direction might very well be able to overcome some of the past reasons for policy failure. Still, it is imperative that difficulties be anticipated. Given competing demands and scarce resources, there is no alternative.

ERDA and other agencies have and will continue to spend millions of dollars on basic and applied energy-related research. In our view, some of these funds need to be allocated to analyses leading to the development of effective implementation strategies.

In order to deal in a fundamental way with the issue of technology implementation, a broad-based study would have to be initiated. Principal components of this study would include the analysis and evaluation of:

- the effectiveness of R&D in private industry
- government-sponsored research
- the delivery system experiences of various sectors of the economy (for example, education and health)
- perceptual studies of the mission of R&D
- the concept of "technology transfer"
- the effectiveness of information systems and techniques
- case studies of the implementation process

A study on this scale would require considerable expenditures both of money and time and might be thought to be outside the charter of any single agency. Recognizing that an understanding of the structure and interrelationships between these components is a requisite to developing a preliminary implementation program, we adopted a modified approach, scaling our efforts to the current research, which incorporated the salient issues associated with each of these component areas. (This approach is presented in a later section—study design.) Based upon the findings of this work, subsequent research can pursue those areas found to be most critical and relevant to the implementation problem.

Objective of the Present Research Project

To reiterate, there is ample indication that R&D projects carried out or supported by the federal government are seldom utilized to their full potential after they are brought to prototype stage. Although specific exceptions can be found, the underlying conception remains true. The reasons for inadequate utilization are not precisely known. One can speculate that contributing factors are inadequate and inappropriate problem definitions and a lack of concern with the implementation process (that is, the process whereby the product of the R&D reaches the intended end user).

To go beyond speculation, however, will require a detailed analysis and evaluation of the R&D process. Consequently, *the objective of this research is to examine systematically the sequence of activities necessary for conveying an R&D product, technology, or policy from problem definition to end user stage.* The research will include development of procedures for precise end-user designation (market segmentation); delineation of suitable intervention strategies; definition of procedures for estimating implementation costs; and other related activities.

To carry out this study, we shall investigate hypotheses and postulates of the following type.

- The process of R&D decision making, which includes techniques such as cost/benefit and decision analysis, is so structured that the question of implementing the research product is not considered part of the process.
- Many of the barriers to implementation are beyond the intervention capability of the responsible agency and so are passed over with a "let George do it" philosophy.
- Political rewards for elected or appointed public officials tend to be coterminous with starting a project to "solve a problem" and with demonstrating feasibility. Actual implementation is a longer-term event, is less visible, and therefore has less political payoff.
- Attempts on the part of administrators, professionals, and citizens' groups to point out serious barriers to implementation are often interpreted as obstructionist in nature.
- The preferences of business, consumers, and other public agencies at all levels of government may not coincide with preferences of the R&D performing agency. Failure to consider these preferences may lead to difficulties and adversary proceedings when implementation is attempted.
- Public agencies are not often structured to deliver their R&D products to the intended end user. If no suitable

delivery mechanism has been established (often one involving private sector participation), then the prospect of implementation failure will be greater.

A solution to increasing the effectiveness of implementation is to include its problems in the day-to-day decision-making process. This can be done by (1) developing a formal process of decision analysis that incorporates the probability of actual use; (2) developing an "impact statement" that would require (in addition to the more common technology assessment) an implementation strategy; or (3) developing a management checklist to specify what questions have to be answered before an R&D project will be funded.

In this context, a question that legitimately may be asked is whether each instance of implementation will be unique and, thus, whether efforts to deal with implementation other than on a case-by-case basis will be futile. This study has not found singularity to be a constraint.

With a goal as obvious as *using* the research funded by public money, one would expect considerable research and experience to exist in the field. As the next chapter will show, this is not the case.

Study Organization

This study is organized in the following manner:

1. The first phase focuses on the problem of implementation itself, with special emphasis on the energy question.
2. The second phase covers the areas of normal R&D processes in both the public and private sector. This phase addresses topics such as innovation, diffusion, and R&D management. Finally, there is discussion of the impact of public interest in specific areas of research on the more market-oriented side of the research and development process.
3. The third phase is concerned with several case studies of completed federal projects designed to be implemented by the private sector. The emphasis here is on questions such as: what was to be accomplished? How

was the project to be carried out? What barriers arose, expected and unexpected? Did the ones that were expected actually occur? In either case, what was done to overcome them? Finally, what ultimately happened to the project?

From an evaluation of the findings of these study phases, considerations for incorporating implementation into the R&D management system are then developed.

This work is organized into seven chapters. Chapter 1 has described the evolution of the problem and the research approach. The starting point for responding to this problem is the development of an understanding of the implementation process and the barriers to adoption and commercialization of federal R&D. This development occurs in Chapters 2 through 4 and provides a summation of the current understanding of the implementation process and of methodologies for increasing the opportunities for implementing federal research.

Chapter 2 identifies the variables that other researchers have used to explain (1) the success or failure of implementation and (2) the rate of adoption and diffusion of innovations.

Chapter 3 offers a descriptive analysis of the product development process in the private sector. It identifies stages of activity, motivation for R&D expenditures, and barriers to successful product development and sales.

Chapter 4 develops a comparable description of the policy-implementation and prototype-development process in the public sector. Once again, attention is given to roles, motivations, stages of activity, and barriers to accomplishment.

Public sector and private sector R&D processes are then compared in Chapter 5. Differences between the two sectors that seem to frustrate the adoption of publicly sponsored R&D and its successful commercialization are illuminated. Differences in role, motive, and research conduct are reviewed in an attempt to explain the failure of commercial adoption of publicly sponsored R&D. This analysis leads to a set of conceptual inferences and hypotheses which attempts to explain why the implementation of federal R&D is infrequent and difficult.

The hypotheses developed in Chapter 5 provide an initial and approximate explanation for the failure of prototype adoption and commercialization. These propositions are tested in a series of case histories focused on R&D projects in the public sector. Cases of both implementation success and failure were selected to test the validity of the propositions for explaining the failure of technology transfer from prototype to commercial product.

The sixth chapter consists of these R&D program/project case studies. The case studies provided a means for testing and evaluating the hypotheses developed in the preceding chapter, as well as an opportunity for increasing our understanding of the specific implementation barriers which may arise in the technological and engineering aspects of R&D activities.

As a conclusion, Chapter 7 draws together the findings from the study's research activities and proposes a methodology for implementation and commercialization in the R&D process.

Bibliography

"ERDA's Priorities Draw Heavy Fire." *Business Week,* 5 July 1976, pp. 58-59.

Webber, Melvin M. *The BART Experience—What Have We Learned?* Berkeley: Institute of Urban and Regional Development and Institute of Transportation, October 1976.

2
Studies of the Implementation Process

This chapter reviews the literature concerned with policy, program, or project implementation with the purpose of discovering whether prior research could provide useful insights or hypotheses. In short, what is the state of knowledge? Most of the literature, other than the theoretical, focuses on human services programs and projects conducted by agencies such as the Department of Health, Education and Welfare (HEW), the Office of Economic Opportunity (OEO), the Economic Development Administration (EDA), and the Department of Housing and Urban Development (HUD). The analysts' judgments are, on the whole, highly critical. Studies of successful program or project implementation (for example, some of the long-established activities of the Department of Agriculture and the Interior) are rare. Nonetheless, useful information can be derived from the literature. This information is summarized at the end of the chapter.

Approach

In order to review the literature on implementation, a distinction between different types of implementation needs to be made. Differences in the "product" to be implemented, policy ("software") versus technological innovation ("hardware"), lead to differences in process. In the first case, the policy follows a direct path from policy mandate to execution, but there is an additional stage of product research and development that has to occur before a technology can be implemented.

Policy implementation has only recently come into its

own as a research topic. This is not to say that policies and their impacts have not been studied; the literature is rich in case studies. The focus of studies has undergone a transition, from the descriptive documentaries of the 1950s (public housing—Meyerson and Banfield, 1955) to the normative, evaluative studies of systems analysts in the late 1960s and early 1970s (PPBS—Hatry, 1971) on to today's explanatory studies attempting to combine descriptive and normative methods for learning why problems occur. It is in this last group that implementation problems have emerged as the various studies probe to discover why policies do not succeed in their objectives.

These implementation studies, still sparse in number, deal mainly with social welfare policies. Education appears to be the area with the greatest number of studies concerning implementation (Gross, Giacquinta, and Bernstein, 1971; Murphy, 1971; Pincus, 1974; Williams et al., 1975; Bailey and Mosher, 1968; Orfield, 1969). Planning (Derthick, 1972; Levine, 1972), economic development (Pressman and Wildavsky, 1973), and mental health (Bardach, forthcoming) are other areas where implementation has taken primary focus.

These works on public policy view implementation in a variety of ways. Perspectives include: the agency role in implementation (Anderson, 1975; Jones, 1970); personal characteristics of implementors (Smith, 1973); the leverage individuals have in implementation (Gergen, 1968; Bunker, 1972); implementation as a phase of an optimal policy-making model (Dror, 1968) as well as how it relates to national planning (Gross, 1966); implementation as a series of decisions (Ugalde, 1973); and the role the political environment plays in implementation (Sayeed, 1973). In the literature that synthesizes case studies with theory, problems of implementation are explained in terms of federalism (Derthick, 1972), the complexity of joint action (Pressman and Wildavsky, 1973), and the "games" surrounding assemblage of all resources required for implementation (Bardach, forthcoming).

Implementation dealing with technology (as opposed to programs) is covered extensively in the literature. Studies have concerned the implementation of innovations by and for the private sector; public sector innovations, such as for defense and space, for use in that sector; the adoption of

innovations developed mainly in the private sector by state and local governments; and the transfer of a technology developed for use in one sector to use in another (Teflon from NASA to fry pans). While much of this literature has proved valuable as secondary sources for analysis of R&D in the public and private sectors, it is missing studies that focus on the connections between sectors and as such fails to provide a firm enough basis from which to develop a methodology to secure the successful commercialization of publicly sponsored R&D.

The literature review concentrates on three main kinds of studies. There is an overview of some of the theoretical work on implementation, followed by synopses of the recent major works on the subject. The third part will examine two of the diffusion studies that are most applicable to this research project.

Implementation Theory

The following works illustrate how policy implementation has been covered in the theoretical literature. While many authors could have been included in such a review, the representative sample will suffice to describe the state of the art for purposes of our study.

The Role of the Agency in Implementation

Charles O. Jones (1970) and James E. Anderson (1975) write chapters on policy implementation in their studies of public policy. Both stress the role agencies play in the implementation process. Anderson provides a detailed discussion of the agency and its constituency, along with major barriers to policy implementation. While Jones' theoretical treatment is not as detailed, he does give the example of implementing school desegregation policy.

In his examination of the administrative process, Anderson emphasizes three major aspects: organization, politics, and policymaking. The fact that an agency's abilities to implement policy are affected by the nature of its organization has a number of policy implications. For example, proponents of a new policy will try to place responsibility

for its implementation with an agency that is favorable to the policy objectives while opponents will try to have it placed with a less friendly agency. Also, some agencies have an internal structure that is more conducive to implementing a particular type of policy than others. Hierarchical arrangements, standard operating procedures, the "rules of the game," and agency spirit all have an effect on its implementation capabilities. However, these organizational factors do not guarantee the desired output; rather, they are similar to the mathematician's condition of being "necessary but not sufficient" for implementation.

"Administrative politics" refers to the forces in the agency's environment from which its constituency is drawn. The nature of an agency's constituency will affect its power and capacity to make policy decisions and carry policy into effect. These forces include the President, Congress, the courts, other administrative agencies, state and local governments, interest groups, political parties, the communications media, and the agency's clientele directly served or regulated by the agency. As we shall see later, one of the problems with such a broad-based support group is that each part might have its own idea of what a program should do, how it should be done, and when. The more narrowly and clearly identified the client group, the greater the chance for implementation. This clientele support for an agency is expected to be stronger if the agency's purpose is to serve rather than regulate that clientele.

The source of an agency's expertise also affects its relationship to its constituency, with experts in the physical and natural sciences usually receiving more deference than those in social sciences. (A suggested explanation is that it takes years of training and the learning of a special vocabulary to work in the "hard" sciences. Such a mystique, however, does not surround the social and policy sciences since they have extensive public exposure in the mass media and, consequently, are not protected from widespread criticism.) An agency's prestige is often transitory, however, and as conditions and attitudes change, so does the amount of power that a particular expertise can command for the agency.

Two aspects of agency functioning are considered under administrative policymaking: the characteristics of the decision process and the methods of developing policy. Ander-

son's stress is "on how agencies shape policy through the implementation of legislation." Hierarchical relationships are critical to agency decision making since they are relied upon to coordinate decisions and resolve agency conflict. The political situation and desire to maintain power are two factors that have a heavy influence on agency decision making. There are a number of ways the agency can produce policy—rule making and law enforcement, adjudication, and program operations.

While Jones briefly covers some of the same areas concerning agencies, he mainly emphasizes two dimensions of administration—agency discretion and symbolism—which affect how agencies function. Agencies have varying degrees of discretion in how they administer a policy. This discretion may have been made specific by the enabling legislation, or it may be the result of a broadly worded policy that establishes the agency's boundaries, but leaves the agency the decision on how and when to act.

Added to this concept of discretion is symbolism, which refers to how much of the policy should be applied. The policy setting of an agency can be all-important in the implementation process. To the extent that the agency's charter requires its programs be implemented, the policy level can begin to set directions to monitor and evaluate all its programs for end results rather than for project production. Unless such directives appear as agency policy, no part of the agency is going to internalize the rigor required to carry out an implementation process.

The Support Network

Implementation of national plans is discussed by Bertram M. Gross in "Activating National Plans" (Gross, 1966). His basic premise is that in order to analyze plan implementation as a process, the more traditional notion of "command" must be replaced by one of "activating." Those responsible for the plans must develop and maintain "a network of supporting groups and widespread popular acceptance." Policymakers must analyze the obstacles to implementation and adopt strategies for building the activation base, dealing with conflicts, and developing campaigns for carrying out specific aspects of the plan.

A key ingredient in Gross' activation process is the support network, which can be visualized as three concentric circles. In the center are the key activators, who are the leaders in constructing the activation base and channeling influence toward legitimizing and implementing the plan. Active allies, who occupy the middle circle, possess the power to implement or block various aspects of the plan; their support is required in the areas over which they have control. Agreement or neutrality on the part of the large number of groups and individuals in the outer circle, the passive collaborators, is vital to prevent the development of a strong opposition network.

There are limits to the groups and individuals who can be brought into the two inner circles of key activators and active allies, and "the design of a support network takes into account the differential power of people and groups." Those who sought and must be given special consideration include the national leaders, financial management agencies, major national ministries or departments, other national organizations, and political parties.

Activators have a number of ways of using their acquired influence to build the support network. These include persuasion, pressure, and encouragement concentrated on groups and individuals to "activate themselves." "The 'activation mix' is the particular combination of these various forms of influence that activators may use in any particular situation." Some methods of persuasion are: (1) in forming or presenting to the public the relevant data used to justify a particular course of action; (2) expecting people to act a certain way which is often a self-fulfilling prediction; (3) providing an example so that in following it people can identify with a person or group they hold in high esteem; (4) proposing different alternatives and advising people how acceptance will be in their interests; and (5) using propaganda. Bargaining, manipulating, and using physical force are other forms of pressure that can replace commanding. Two ways to promote self-activation are to encourage public participation in the decision-making process and to educate the public, broadening their awareness, knowledge, and abilities to make them more capable of actively participating in planning.

Activators anticipate conflict in building an activation

base and developing the activation mix. How these conflicts are handled is vital to the plan outcome, so "the implementation of national plans, therefore, may also be seen from the types of outcome that are sought and attained." Once the desired outcomes are determined (for example, victory for one group with defeat for another, or a workable compromise), the campaign strategy can be developed. Exploiting crises is one of the most effective tools, since general satisfaction with the present state does not make major changes. However, it is important to act on a crisis in a timely manner, and "the only sure way to anticipate a crisis is to bring it into being." So "crisis creation" plays an important part in implementing national plans.

Timing is a crucial factor in the activation campaign. When to start, to expand, to ease up—all must be carefully planned. Also important is the ability to maintain a positive stance, keeping up initiative by showing that some progress is being made. Advertising successes can be used to counterbalance public criticism.

This policy level task of building internal and external support for a federal R&D project is often neglected. Instead, the transfer of ideas or projects from the public to private (or public to public) sectors is classified as the job of a salesman or marketeer; the building of the prototype is that of the technician. An overall implementation strategy that matches the technology development with the demands of the constituency never materializes, and the chances of the technology's ever being implemented are reduced.

Coalition Building

Yehezkel Dror (1968) views implementation as a part of the third stage of a policy optimization model that includes meta-policymaking, policymaking, and post-policymaking. The first stage involves "policymaking on policymaking"—all the processes required to create, maintain, and govern the policymaking system. Stage two includes the steps needed for the actual policymaking. For example, establishing and making priorities for operational goals, preparing and evaluating alternatives, and predicting and comparing costs and benefits of the alternatives can be included in the policymaking stage. Once the policy is made, it enters into the post-policymaking stage for the execution and evaluation of the policy. Communications and feedback channels connect all phases of the model.

According to Dror, motivating policy execution is an essential part of post-policymaking, and "giving or withholding such motivation is a main function of political power." He stresses coalition building as the means for gathering together relevant power centers for a particular policy and discusses how coalition building should be considered for optimal public policymaking.

The probability of forming a sufficiently strong coalition depends on the nature of the policy, how power is distributed, and the structure of the appropriate institutions and their tendencies to form coalitions. Since the probability of building the necessary coalition partly depends on the policy's characteristics, the policymaking should be influenced by that probability; it should also incorporate strategies for forming those coalitions.

Values shared by those groups making up the coalitions should be taken into consideration. However, this need to satisfy diverse groups limits the clarity of the policy objectives. Even though attention to coalitions often limits policy alternatives, policymakers retain some discretion depending on (1) the number of potential coalitions, (2) the policymakers' abilities to "sell" the policies, (3) the strength of the forces that sustain the coalition, (4) the power the policymakers can exert, and (5) the other variables. Motivation for policy execution must be continuous; however, the strength of that motivation can vary depending on the phase of policymaking.

Anyone who has had practical experience in the federal bureaucracy knows that large-scale technology programs and projects often require similar awareness of varied constituencies and the need to accommodate their users. For example, within ERDA the competition for various types of energy technologies (i.e., solar, geothermal, fossil, and nuclear) forces a separate support group to form behind each energy type. These external public groups are at times useful in Congress or at the Office of Management and Budget (OMB) during budget hearings and provide a sounding board and support for specific projects or programs.

Influence

Kenneth J. Gergen (1968) defines leverage points in policy formation and implementation as the individuals able to exert influence or power over a particular policy. He presents a three-dimensional model showing how much leverage an individual would have when considering the three dimensions of issue relevance, subphase resources, and personal efficacy. The third dimension is defined as the "personality constellation or set of social capabilities" that affect an individual's leverage.

The leverage points might be assessed by the reputation/referral approach, asking "knowledgeable" persons to name those they feel are the most influential. The positions that people hold in the relevant organization might be an indication of their leverage, as might their observed behavior. Another method for assessing leverage points is to determine who are the opinion leaders and to look for demographic traits common to the most influential individuals in the society. Gergen suggests a method which involves designating the issues and the people in leadership positions, narrowing the issues to more specific subtopics, and then using survey techniques to find the leaders' positions on the three-dimensional array of issue relevance, subphase resources, and personal efficacy. This information would give a better idea of who is capable of exerting influence on policy and at what point in the policy process they will try to use their leverage.

Douglas Bunker (1972) applies Gergen's concept of leverage points to the implementation process, but construes it as a problem of social persuasion and uses a three-dimensional model to highlight the available intervention strategies. His three dimensions include: (1) issue salience or the importance of an issue to an actor; (2) power resources; and (3) agreement, the extent to which an actor agrees with an advocate of the policy in question. Once it is known where the actors fall in this array with respect to an issue, it will be relatively easy to determine what actions are necessary to obtain effective support for the issue from a particular actor.

Bunker then develops a framework for coordinating the four functional areas that impact policy evaluation: (1) administrative bureaucracies responsible for the policy; (2)

political leaders; (3) groups and individuals (such as consultants and evaluators) who provide the input analysis; and (4) constituency elites (such as community leaders and interest groups). The framework takes into account both the horizontal and the vertical relationships among the organizations involved in the implementation process.

In the case of technology, opinion leaders are often used to sanction projects as well as for professional support. Reviews from the scientific community usually favor a scientific or technological approach. The National Academy of Science, the Transportation Research Board, and the individual science advisory groups of specific agencies, e.g., Environmental Protection Agency (EPA) and National Institute of Health (NIH), are used by agencies to oversee their research. A favorable review by one of these boards, especially when led by a prestigious member, helps to make life easier for those responsible for the project. These reviews may or may not help with the implementation process, but they often mean the survival of the prototype stage.

Implementation Studies

Although implementation has not been the focal point of most research documenting the success or failure of federal programs, there have been a few recent works which focus on implementation as their central theme. In this section, two of these studies will be reviewed with an emphasis on their analyses of the implementation process and its barriers.

Implementation—Economic Development for Oakland

Implementation, by Jeffrey L. Pressman and Aaron B. Wildavsky (1973), is an analysis of the Economic Development Administration's (EDA) project to create jobs for minorities in Oakland, California. By spending $23 million in federal funds for public works and building loans, EDA hoped employers would be encouraged to hire minorities. By 1961, three years after the program was initiated, only $3 million dollars were spent, and "construction ha[d] only been partially completed, business loans ha[d] died entirely, and the results in terms of minority employment were meager and disappointing" (p. xii). The purpose of the Pressman and Wildavsky study was to learn why a program that had political agreement, adequate funding, cooperation with local officials and private groups—a program that suffered none of the major problems that are the usual explanations for why federal projects fail—was nonetheless unable to meet its goals.

Through interviews and examination of various documents, the authors traced the chronology of the EDA project and were able to gain insights into the complexities and difficulties of the implementation process. They found that what seemed to be a simple program turned out to be a very complex one involving numerous participants, a host of differing perspectives, and a long and torturous path of decision points that had to be cleared. Given these characteristics, the chances of successfully completing the program (or completing it at all) were diminished by the designers' desires for a hasty finish.

EDA had tried to simplify the implementation process by minimizing the number of agencies involved and relaxing some of the normal bureaucratic requirements. Despite this fact, the number of governmental and private units whose cooperation had to be obtained became large enough to add enormous and often unexpected complexities to the procedures. Pressman and Wildavsky state that:

> To list every participant who became involved in some aspect of the EDA program would exhaust both us and our readers. Let us agree, therefore, to oversimplify the situation. We shall restrict the participants to the EDA, the rest of the federal government, and the city of Oakland, with their constituent elements. For the EDA this would mean the initial Foley-Bradford task force, EDA operating departments in Washington, the agency's leadership after Foley, the regional office in Seattle, and the field office in Oakland. Other federal agencies that became involved included the General Accounting Office; the Department of Health, Education and Welfare; the Department of Labor; and the Navy. Participants in Oakland were the mayor, city administrators, the Port of Oakland, World Airways, and several of the city's black leaders, conservation groups, and tenants of the Port of Oakland.

Some of these participants (such as the departments of Labor and Health, Education, and welfare) become involved because they possessed jurisdictional authority over important parts of the project; others (like the Navy) entered the process when they felt their interest being impinged on; and still others (such as black people in Oakland) were intentionally brought into the program by the EDA in order to build local support for the projects (p. 94).

The participants differed in their connection with the development of the project and hence the perspective from which it was viewed. In addition, each participant had different objectives and looked on the project with varying degrees of urgency. Therefore, they did not share the same measures of success. Although the actors agreed on the "substantive ends" of the proposal, they were not congruent in their ideas for implementing it. Pressman and Wildavsky offer a number of reasons why this is a common phenomenon (pp. 99-102).

1. Participants may feel that the proposal is not compatible with other goals. For example, EDA proposed a separate airline training center, but the Department of Health, Education and Welfare (HEW), which had responsibility for skills training, was committed to the East Bay Skills Center and felt a new center would compete with the existing one for funds.
2. Even though there may be no direct incompatibility with other programs, these may be preferred to the new proposal. Many in EDA and OMB felt that EDA's focus should be on small towns and rural areas, and the large urban centers were the responsibility of other agencies.
3. Participants may be committed to a number of projects concurrently; time and manpower resources are devoted to one project at the expense of another.
4. The project might depend upon participants who do not feel the same sense of urgency as its proponents. Lack of priority status subjects the project to normal bureaucratic delays.
5. There may be disagreements concerning who is responsible for implementing the program, who the leaders are, and what the "proper organizational roles" should be.

6. Participants may differ in what they believe to be the correct way to carry out the program, both legally and procedurally.
7. People and groups may be enthusiastic about a program, but lack the political or financial resources to translate their enthusiasm into action.

The probability of project success decreases with an increase in the number of participants and decision points that have to be cleared. Looking at the public works program, and concentrating "on those major decision points that determined the course of the program or that had to be passed in order for the program to continue," Pressman and Wildavsky identify thirty of these decision points which required a total of seventy separate agreements (p. 102). Added to these were a large number of more minor decisions which nonetheless had to be cleared for program success. Even if each of these decision points had a high probability for favorable action, the large number of these points made the "ultimate probability of success" low.

This situation was complicated because EDA was trying to satisfy two objectives, public works construction and jobs for the hard-core unemployed. Thus, instead of one decision path to follow with its points to clear, there were two, creating more potential for delay and unexpected circumstances.

The problems of multiple objectives, numerous participants, and a large number of decision points had not been anticipated or planned for at the project's inception. There was a huge amount of money allocated to the program and little time to decide on how to spend it. Thus, projects were selected quickly and without sufficient forethought. Had more time been devoted to implementation considerations in the beginning, a simple route based on a sounder economic theory might have been taken. For example, subsidizing the wage bill of business enterprises instead of their capital might have eliminated many of the decision points and activities that ultimately blocked implementation (p. 147).

From the outset the emphasis was on designing the program, obtaining initial agreement at the local level, and committing the funds. All this was done quickly, with fanfare and enthusiasm by EDA leaders and by the agency's special

Oakland task force. The later steps of implementation were felt to be "technical questions" that would resolve themselves if the initial agreements were negotiated and commitments were made. But the years have shown how these seemingly routine questions of implementation were the rocks on which the program eventually foundered (p. 143).

This analysis of the Oakland Project is a major contribution to the study of implementation for it describes a project's failure in terms of agency and group inability to coordinate all the factors required for implementation. A closer look at the human elements which often contribute to blocking a program's implementation follows.

The Implementation Game

In his introduction to *The Implementation Game: What Happens After a Bill Becomes a Law*, Eugene Bardach (1977) notes several instances where a policy failed to reach its goals: EDA's project in Oakland, New Towns In-Town, Title III of the Elementary and Secondary Education Act of 1965 and Title VI of the 1964 Civil Rights Act as it applied to education, and attempts to develop a nuclear powered plane. This list illustrates "the three perils of latter-day public policy: after a policy mandate is agreed to, authorized and adopted, there is under-achievement of stated objectives . . ., delay, and excessive financial costs" (p. 3). Such failures have led to three "post-liberal heresies:" (1) a growing skepticism that we do not know how to solve our problems with liberal reform measures; (2) a doubt that government is capable of doing the job even if we know what should be done and can adopt the means to do it; and (3) a further doubt that, despite the development of a suitable governmental intervention strategy, there is no guarantee that it can be successfully executed.

In order to mitigate these problems, policies and programs should be designed "that in their basic conception are able to withstand buffeting by a constantly shifting set of political and social pressures during the implementation phase" (p. 5). However, accomplishing this goal in policy design will not guarantee implementation since the "character and degree of many implementation problems are inherently unpredictable," and some person or group must take responsibility for guiding the program through its execution. Thus, the purpose of Bardach's book is twofold: to present an analytical framework for anticipating the implementation problems, and to discuss how implementors can work to enhance the chances for program success.

Besides drawing on earlier literature concerning implementation, which is still meager (this reinforces Pressman and Wildavsky's findings), Bardach relies on his previous study of the Lanterman-Petris-Short Act (L-P-S) of 1967 to develop and assess his perspectives on implementation. This act had two goals: (1) "to restore the civil liberties of persons alleged to be mentally ill," and (2) "to substitute community-based care and treatment of the mentally ill for care and treatment in state mental institutions" (p. 9).

The analysis concentrates on the role Assemblyman Lanterman played in the passage and implementation of L-P-S; he was just as zealous in trying to make the law work as he was in seeking its passage. Lanterman had a large number of resources he could use to help implementation. As a legislator, he was able to introduce bills clarifying, amending, and strengthening the original legislation (p. 11). He was also in a strong position to get these bills passed and have the governor sign them (p. 13). His access to analytical resources was substantial, as was his political support (p. 14). Lanterman and his staff used these resources as they "intervened actively and continually in what would normally be considered administrative matters" (p. 17). He also defended the policies of L-P-S which were attacked by critics hostile to the act in principle (p. 27).

Bardach's conceptual analysis presents implementation as an assembly process for putting together a machine to carry out the policy. What goes into the machine depends on many factors—the policy, clientele participation, private services or goods providers, permits or clearances, innovations in program design, funding sources, trouble shooters, and sustained political support (p. 36). A second feature of the implementation process is the varied and often independent number of participants who control the different parts of the machine. These participants are in competition with one another over political, financial, bureaucratic, and other kinds of perquisites; and these struggles can lead to unintended, usually adverse effects on the implementation of a program (p. 37).

In comparing his conception of implementation with those found in the previous literature, Bardach finds that his analysis is not significantly different from the others, although "it does differ in certain subtle, and sometimes important ways" (p. 37). His review of the literature places each study in the context of how its author viewed the implementation process while serving as a lead-in to his own conceptualization of implementation as:

1. a process of assembling the elements required to produce a particular programmatic outcome, and
2. the playing out of a number of loosely interrelated games whereby these elements are withheld from or delivered to the program assembly process on particular terms (p. 57-58).

There are four general types of adverse effects that these implementation games can exert on the program-assembly process:

1. the diversion of resources, especially money, which ought properly to be used to obtain, or to create, certain program elements
2. the deflection of policy goals stipulated in the original mandate
3. resistance to explicit, and usually institutionalized, efforts to control behavior administratively, and
4. the dissipation of personal and political energies in game-playing that might otherwise be channeled into constructive programmatic action (p. 66).

For the purposes of his discussion, Bardach has grouped the implementation games according to their dominant adverse effect.

Those games that have the first type of impact (the diversion of resources) include "easy money," "budget," "pork barrel," and "easy life." "Easy money" is the implementation game where private sector participants try to get

more from the government in money than they give in
services (p. 66). Easy money players usually receive their
funds from government bureaus (which themselves are
involved in the "budget" game) seeking to maximize their
own budgets.

> As part of their budget game, moving money somehow,
> somewhere, and fast, even at the price of objectives, is the
> characteristic strategy of virtually every governmental agency
> which channels grants to other levels of government or to
> nonprofit institutions (p. 72).

"Funding" is similar to the "budget" game. Here the
receiver of the money tries to get as much money with as few
restrictions as possible (p. 72). The funding bureau is at a
disadvantage when playing these games because it is limited
in its monitoring capabilities. It is difficult to be specific
about the goals and how to measure their success. Even if the
funding bureau can do this, it still may not know how much
money it should pay. Also, efforts to maintain a program
will present problems of coordinating the different funding
sources.

"Pork barrel" is played by elected officials to insure that
their constituencies receive a fair portion of the funds. This
game is a version of easy money or budget that is played by
the politicians (p. 77).

Civil servants, trying to make up for their "not particularly handsome salaries and wages" by manipulating their
work environment as much as possible to suit themselves,
play a game called "easy life." Easy life is less difficult for
them to play than it is for their counterparts in private
industry who are not protected by civil service regulations
and who serve a more narrowly defined "client" (p. 76).

"Piling on," "up for grabs," and "keeping the peace" are
in the second group of games, those that deflect the implementation process away from the policy goals of the original
mandate. Often a program that is proceeding in its intended
direction is seen as a good opportunity for policymakers to
add their own objectives to it. This practice of "piling on"
often has the effect of destroying the initial progress of the
policy (p. 85). Piling on is partly a game of chance, however,
and instead of eroding public support for the program, there
is a possibility that it might enhance the original policy

objectives and increase their political support (p. 88).

Frequently these program objectives are ambiguous or poorly defined by the policy mandate. When this is the case, the various program elements are "up for grabs," and the various players try to convert them into political resources they can use to tailor the program to their own objectives (p. 90).

"Keeping the peace" is the game played by political leaders in the executive branch and bureaucrats who try to balance the opposing viewpoints on how a policy should be administered. Since the participants range from the zealous originators of the policy who seek its active and immediate implementation to those opposing the policy from its inception, the ability to keep peace becomes largely a game of compromise and one where the players can never really win.

"Tokenism" and "massive resistance" are two principal games that prevent administrators from assembling all the program elements required for policy implementation. Players of "tokenism" try "to appear to be contributing a program element publicly while privately conceding only a small ('token') contribution" (p. 99). Two variations of this game are procrastination and substitution of inferior program elements.

The basic tool allowing actors to obstruct policy administration by tokenism is a monopoly power over the resources required to carry out the policy. Administrators, in turn, can deal with tokenism by incorporating strategies into the policy design that minimize the monopoly power an actor has over any one program element. They can:

1. design the program so the resource controlled by an opponent is not critical to its success;
2. create a new monopoly over which the implementors will have control;
3. encourage competition among those who could provide a necessary resource;
4. "buy off" monopolists by adding features they desire in a package including the feature they do not like;
5. bring those whose support is necessary for successful implementation into the early stages of policy planning;

6. develop institutions that can exercise countervailing power (pp. 103-08).

The second method of obstructing policy implementation by withholding program elements is "massive resistance," which "is a means of evading the responsibility specified in the policy mandate to provide these program elements by overwhelming the capacity of an administrative agency to enforce sanctions for noncompliance" (p. 108). Bardach suggests a number of ways to prevent this from happening:

1. taking advantage of the fact that people behave in a certain way because they think it is expected of them;
2. enabling or giving to a party the resources it needs to do something;
3. providing incentives to encourage parties to act in a certain way;
4. using a deterrent system or punishments for not acting in the prescribed manner (pp. 109-24).

Overcoming tokenism and massive resistance requires the effective employment of control systems. However, control systems can be confounded by impersonal or nonpersonal forces in the social world governed by the laws of entropy. These problems are incompetency, variability in control activities, and poor coordination (p. 125). Implementors frequently handle these problems by playing the "management game"—utilizing the services of institutions whose speciality is management, such as a personnel department, auditor, and comptroller. These control techniques can and often do lead to greater centralization of functions which in turn leads to attempts at decentralization because of an inherent distrust of big government.

The final games—"tenacity," "territory," "not our problem," "odd man out," and "reputation"—do not fit neatly into any one category. However, they do appear to have the common theme of players avoiding responsibility while defending against others' games and advancing their own. These games usually lead to underperformance of the policy objectives and to delay.

"Tenacity," or the withholding of a program element until one's particular terms are met, is a "game for everyone," played by legislators, bureaucrats, interest groups, etc. Although the intention is generally not to kill the program, excessive delay and ultimate program failure may often result from playing this game (p. 148).

"Territory" is a game played by bureaus that

> can have very positive results so long as no one really wins, that is, so long as the competitive forces among bureaus with overlapping jurisdictions or similar missions generate information that enables review officials either in the legislature or at higher levels of the bureaucracy to evaluate their performance and to choose among their alternative service offerings (p. 151).

On the other hand, this competition can have adverse effects if it results in a breakdown in the interagency coordination needed for implementation.

Although agencies compete for jurisdiction and a larger share of the budget, they will often pull back when a program could impose too heavy a work load on the agency, is too controversial, or is beyond the agency's performance capabilities. This unwillingness to accept responsibility for a program is a game called "not our problem" (p. 159).

Since there is a large amount of uncertainty in the program assembly process,

> whatever other implementation games the various actors play, they normally play, at the same time, a game in which they attempt to create or maintain their option to withdraw and cut their losses while they monitor the remaining uncertainty, and in which they at the same time try to maneuver other players into foregoing their own options. This is the Odd Man Out Game (p. 164).

Players of most of these games are acting in an organizational role. When personal considerations are included as well, they play a game called "reputation" (p. 168). This game has the most significance when players try to convince others they are doing "more or better than they really are" or when they wish to enhance their personal image.

Up to this point, Bardach has been speaking of games various actors can use to cause delays or to block the implementation process. There is another set of delays, however, not falling into this game analysis that just seem to happen. These delays occur in trying to assemble the different program elements and reach collective decisions.

A program element is contributed as a result of a transaction between the "provider" and the "solicitor" (p. 181). Delays in these transactions stem from three sources. First, it takes time for the solicitors of these elements to find suitable providers. Second, once the potential providers have been contacted, they must decide whether to commit the elements they have access to and the terms of the commitment. And third, the number of such transactions is exceedingly large.

Assigning a priority status to a program might reduce some of the delays associated with these provider/solicitor transactions. Sometimes it is possible to work around program elements that are facing too long a delay, or implementors can try some of the techniques of project management used by private industry and the Department of Defense (DOD) and The National Aeronautics and Space Administration (NASA).

Because actors are reluctant to commit themselves to a project when they are not certain about its future operation or exogenous events over which they have no control (including how the other actors will perform), the collective decision process inevitably results in delay. In this process, providers and solicitors are trying to "test the future" to get a better feel for how the program will unfold (p. 211). Negotiating among the parties (communicating with one another about their expectations and hesitations) is one way to solve delays related to future testing; but these negotiations might be an additional source of delay (p. 222). The use of intermediaries and maneuvering to foreclose options have potential for reducing this delay.

Bardach, in his final chapters, synthesizes his various suggestions on how to reduce delay to propose a method for anticipating implementation problems during policy design and adoption. Basic to successful implementation is a policy that is sound in its theoretical conception.

> Any policy or program implies an economic, and probably also a sociological, theory about the way the world works. If this theory is fundamentally incorrect, the policy will proba-

bly fail no matter how well it is implemented. Indeed, it is not exactly clear what 'good' implementation of a basically misconceived policy would mean. As we have used the term 'implementation,' it should probably imply that the process of implementing the policy would reveal its defects and that over time they would be removed. The more likely event, however, is that implementation problems will exaggerate rather than ameliorate basic conceptual problems (p. 251).

The outline in Table 2-1 incorporates the awareness of implementation games into a scenario that a policy designer can use as a guide. There are limits to a scenario primarily because of uncertainties about the future. It is not known how well the different actors will play the implementation games and what their effect on implementation will be (p. 268). It is difficult to predict the behavior of the population toward which the policy is directed (p. 270). Finally, although it is easy to predict some delays, it is not so easy to know their causes and magnitude in advance.

Because of this inability to predict the future, policymakers must try to "fix the game" once it has begun. This is what Lanterman did in his efforts to implement L-P-S. Bardach sees two elements to fixing: (1) "repairing," as when Lanterman introduced bills that clarified or added to L-P-S, and (2) "adjusting" certain elements of the system of games in order to lead to a preferred outcome (p. 274).

Once again, there are problems. Game fixing can be expensive, for it requires public funds over and above what would normally be used for implementation. It also involves many covert and manipulative dealings which make it difficult to hold "fixers" accountable for their actions.

> The real problem, however, is that too few of the would-be fixers know how to do the right thing, are willing to do it if they do know how, and have the political resources to make their will effective (p. 279).

In conclusion, Bardach reiterates one of the "heresies" brought out in the introduction,

> . . . which currently threaten the ideology of liberal reform: government *ought* not to do many of the things which liberal

TABLE 2-1

Writing an Implementation Scenario

I. The Basic Policy Concept
  A. State the policy mandate you hope to see implemented.
  B. What problem(s) do you hope the policy will "solve" or ameliorate?
  C. What do you expect government intervention, as reflected in your preferred policy, to accomplish?
  D. What costs-financial and otherwise-do you expect will accompany government intervention?

II. Making an Inventory
  List, and describe briefly, the program elements that will need to be assembled. Indicate who controls these elements either directly or indirectly.

III. The Management Strategy
  A. How might your policy be designed so as to minimize the need to play the Management Game?
  B. How will your policy deal with the problems of social entropy:
    1. Incompetency?
    2. Variability in the objects of control?
    3. Coordination?

IV. Dilemmas of Administration
  A. Tokenism
    1. Which if any, of the program elements listed above do you regard as critical to the success of your policy?
    2. Are any of these controlled by interests (or persons or groups) likely to be resistant or uncooperative?
      a. Will they respond with tokenism, procrastination, or "substitutions of inferior quality"?
      b. Can you think of ways to counteract these problems?
    3. Will problems of tokenism, procrastination, and inferior substitutions be aggravated by monopoly conditions?
  B. Massive resistance
    1. What design features have you (or others) introduced into your policy to deal with massive resistance? (e.g., deterrence, incentives, etc.)
    2. How successful do you expect them to be?

V. Diversion of Resources
  A. What games will be set in motion that will, in effect, divert important resources? (Easy money? Budget? Funding? Easy Life? Pork Barrel? Other?)
  B. How might you neutralize these adverse effects? Could they be turned to the advantage of the pro-implementation party? Would design modifications be in order?

VI. Deflection of Goals
  A. What games will be set in motion that will, in effect, threaten to deflect the original goals of the mandate? (Up for Grabs? Piling On? Keeping the Peace? Other?)
  B. How might you counteract these games by altering the policy design? Any other strategies?

VII. Dissipation of Energies
  A. What games will be set in motion that will, in effect, dissipate people's energies and impede constructive change? (Tenacity? Odd Man Out? Reputation? Territory? Not Our Problem? Other?)
  B. How might these games be counteracted or prevented by altering the policy design? Any other strategies?

VIII. Delay
  A. Assembling program elements
    1. How much delay do you expect from this source?
    2. What can you do to reduce such delays?
  B. Collective decision delays
    1. How much delay do you expect from this source?
    2. What sort of negotiations do you expect to take place? Between whom? Over what? How long will they take?
  C. Would it help to:
    1. Assign priority status?
    2. Use the project management mode?
    3. "Work around" obstacles?
    4. Enlist intermediaries to help negotiations?
    5. Foreclose options by maneuvering?

IX. Fixing the Game
  A. Elite activists
    1. What officials would you like to play the fixer role? Why? What resources have they?
    2. What incentives have they to play this role?
  B. "Eyes and ears"
    1. Whom would you like to furnish the "eyes and ears"? Why? What resources have they?
    2. What incentives have they to play this role?
  C. What could be done to bring into being a viable game-fixing coalition?

Source: Bardach, 1977, pp. 264-266.

reform has traditionally asked of it; and even when, in some abstract sense, government does pursue appropriate goals, it is not very well suited to achieving them. Markets and mores are sturdier and more sensible, and government is probably less sensible and less reliable than liberal reformers have been willing to admit. The most important problems which affect public policy are almost surely not those of implementation but those of basic political, economic, and social theory. In the short run, it is essential to invest a great deal of energy in designing implementable policies and programs. For the longer run, however, it is equally essential to become more modest in our demands on, and expectations of, the institutions of representative government (p. 283).

As with Pressman and Wildavsky's book, this work by Bardach is a significant evaluation of the policy implementation process. However, for the purposes of our study, the greatest benefit to be gained from these two works is a general understanding of a process preceding the R&D that produces the technology for which we are seeking an implementation strategy. The next type of study jumps to the other end of the process, to the actual acceptance of the innovation once it has been developed.

Diffusion and Adoption

There is a large literature on the diffusion of innovations and the adoption of new technologies by state and local governments. Other innovation diffusion studies concerning information transfer among different components of the private sector (such as firms in one industry) are used in the analysis of the private sector in the following chapter and therefore will not be reviewed here.

The diffusion and adoption of innovations is a complex and confusing area of study.

Part of the confusion lies with the fact that the literature concerned with the diffusion or adoption of innovation comes from a variety of disciplines, with management and business, sociology, and psychology somewhat in the lead. Added confusion develops as we note the variety of different types of organizations under study—business corporations, federal bureaucracies, state bureaucracies, local government, schools, health organizations, social clubs, and dozens more. Due to problems of differing organizational goals, variations in the need for profit, diverse methodologies, and many other factors, it is difficult to transfer the findings concerning the diffusion of innovation in one type of organization directly to an organization with completely different structure and goals (Bingham, 1975, p. 1).

Lack of a distinct definition for the terms "diffusion" and "adoption" is one difficulty with classifying this literature. While one study might equate diffusion with the dissemination of information on a technology (Rogers, 1962), another might consider it synonymous with the actual adoption of the technology (Baer, Johnson, and Merrow, Rand Report, 1976). Ideally, the latter would be the case; however, although diffusion as defined in the first instance generally is not a problem if the technology is well in hand, the adoption of that technology is often constrained by variables other than a lack of information. For example, the local government may not be able to afford the new technology. Even when the federal government supplies 80 to 90 percent of the funds, some projects are so expensive that 20 or 10 percent is still too high an investment for the local government. A second reason diffusion may not result in adoption is a gap in the expertise required at the local level to implement the technology.

Diffusion in other studies might be used synonymously with technology transfer, which is a specific kind of diffusion. Technology transfer is classically defined as "the process whereby technical information originating in one institutional setting is adapted for use in another institutional setting" (Doctors, 1969, p. 3). Since this type of diffusion is not a major concern for the present study, it will only be looked at as a part of the R&D management process described in Chapter 4.

Studies of the adoption of a technology by a state or local government and of diffusion, when it results in adoption, could add valuable insights to our research. Two reports in particular will be looked at in depth—a 1976 Rand report on twenty-four demonstration projects (which equates successful diffusion with adoption) and a study of state and local governments' adopting technological innovations in air quality and highway safety.

Rand Study

The two major purposes of Rand's study (Baer, Johnson, and Merrow, 1976) of 24 federally funded demonstration projects were:

1. to identify major factors associated with successful and
   with unsuccessful project outcomes, and
2. to formulate guidelines for federal agencies in improving the planning, implementation, monitoring, evaluation, and dissemination of results of future demonstration projects (p. iii).

Although the projects chosen for the study may have
received some additional funding from private and other
governmental sources, they were all federally supported. All
the projects were oriented to the civilian sector; projects that
were results of technology transfer from public (defense and
space) to civilian sectors were excluded. Private sector firms
were significantly involved in the chosen technologies either
as the designated end users or as the suppliers of the innovations to adopters in the public sector.

It was estimated that in fiscal year 1974, the federal
government spent $625 million (or just over 10 percent of the
$5.9 billion that went to all civilian R&D) on demonstration
projects. These projects have as their objectives: (1) producing new information about the use of a technology in a real
world environment so potential adopters might be motivated to try it, and regulators might have better information for
formulating their regulations; (2) disseminating existing
information on a technology to make potential adopters
aware of its potential; (3) encouraging changes, both institutional and organizational, in private and public organizations to make adopting new technologies easier; and (4)
supporting a "high level national policy goal." The information supplied under the first three objectives reduces
uncertainties regarding the technical feasibility, the cost of
manufacturing or operation, public or private demand for
the technology, the effect adoption of a new technology will
have on the adopting organization and its relationships with
other organizations in its environment, and externalities
that are not included in the anticipated cost of adoption (pp.
3-5).

The Rand research team conducted three rounds of case
studies. In the first round, a conceptual framework for the
entire study was developed. Hypotheses to be investigated
came out of the second round of cases, and these hypotheses

were assessed in the third round. Eleven agencies were represented in the study, and the listing of the projects, their locations, and the sponsoring agencies is reproduced in Table 2-2.

Three distinct types of successes were evaluated for each case. The project experienced information success if it was able to significantly reduce the uncertainties (cost, technological, demand, institutional, and externalities) that were blocking the adoption of the innovation. This, of course, did not imply that adoption of the technology would follow. The information might have been sufficient to show that the innovation should not be adopted. It may not be economic; it may not readily diffuse to potential adopters; the organizational and institutional barriers may be insurmountable; and so forth. Although the information acquired from the demonstration project is a necessary condition for adoption when the uncertainties the demonstration is supposed to eliminate are impeding adoption, this increased knowledge is not sufficient to insure acceptance.

The measure of the adopter's satisfaction with the results of the demonstration project—"the reliability of the system and quality of the goods and services"—is the degree of application success. Low application success occurred when the project was unable to provide the goods or services or when there were serious problems with quality or reliability. If these problems were only minor, the demonstration was considered to have medium application success. It was high if the services or product were provided to the local users on an acceptable and reliable basis.

Diffusion success refers to the degree to which the technology has spread to other potential adopters. The project experienced significant diffusion if the technology was adopted by other users without federal intervention on a case-by-case basis. If the technology does not look as if its adoption will be self-sustaining beyond a few projects, it has experienced "some" diffusion. Little or no diffusion implies the process is unlikely to be accepted by more than one or two adopters without significant federal intervention.

The various projects were rated on the degree of success they were able to attain for each of the three categories. A high degree of information success did not always guarantee significant diffusion success, nor high application success.

TABLE 2-2

Selected Case Studies of Federally Funded Demonstration Projects

Federal Agency	Project	Location	Short Title for Reference
First Round (Develop Conceptual Framework)			
AEC/MarAd	Nuclear Ship Savannah		Savannah
EPA	Mechanized Refuse Collection (Godzilla)	Scottsdale, Ariz.	Godzilla
HEW	Computer-Assisted Electrocardiogram Analysis	Denver, Colo.	ECG
HEW	Teleprocessing of Medicaid Claims	Montgomery, Ala.	Medicaid Claims
MarAd	Shipbuilding Research, Development and Demonstration Program	U.S. Shipyards	Shipbuilding
NMFS	Fish Protein Concentrate Plant	Aberdeen, Wash.	FPC
OSW	Saline Water Conversion Plant	Freeport. Tex.	Desalination
UMTA	Dial-A-Ride Transportation System	Haddonfield, N.J.	Dial-A-Ride
Second Round (Develop Hypotheses)			
AEC	Yankee Nuclear Power Reactor	Rowe, Mass.	Yankee
AEC	Connecticut Yankee Civilian Nuclear Reactor	Haddam Neck, Conn.	Connecticut Yankee
EPA	Refuse Firing Demonstration (solid-waste-to-fuel conversion)	St. Louis, Mo.	RFD
ERDA	Synthetic Fuels Program	Various	Synthetic Fuels
HUD	Operation Breakthrough (industrialized housing techniques)	Various	Breakthrough
UMTA	Personal Rapid Transit System	Morgantown, W. Va.	PRT
VA	Hydraulic Knee Prosthetic Device	Various	Hydraulic Knee
Third Round (Assess Hypotheses)			
BU Mines	REAM (Rapid Excavation and Mining) Gun	Hope Valley, Ca.	REAM Gun
EPA	Resource Recovery from Refuse	Franklin, Ohio	Resource Recovery
EPA	Poultry Waste Processing	Durham, N.C.	Poultry Waste
FHA	Expressway Surveillance and Control	Chicago, Ill.	Chicago Expressway
MarAd	Maritime Satellite Program		Marisat
NASA/FAA	Refan Jet Engine Program		Refan
OSW	Saline Water Conversion Plant	Pt. Loma, Ca.	Desalination
UMTA	Bus-on-Metered-Freeway System	Minneapolis, Minn.	Minneapolis Corridor
UMTA	Automatic Vehicle Identification	New York, N.Y.	AVI

Source: Rand, 1976, p. 6.

Although information success resulted in a high proportion of cases with application success, this did not always hold true. The relationships among the three types of successes are summarized in Figures 2-1, 2-2, and 2-3.

The hypotheses developed in the early rounds of case studies were tested against the measures of information, application, and diffusion success. It was found that the highest diffusion success was generally linked to the following characteristics:

1. a technology already well in hand;
2. presence of cost- and risk-sharing;
3. initiative for project from non-federal sources;

FIGURE 2-1. Information Success Measured Against Diffusion Success

INFORAMTION SUCCESS	LITTLE OR NONE	SOME	SIGNIFICANT
YES	Desalination (freeport) Medicaid	ECG Dial-A-Ride (manual) Marisat Godzilla Resource Recovery Connecticut Yankee	Yankee Chicago Expressway RFD Desalination (Pt. Loma) Poultry Waste Hydraulic Knee
NO	Breakthrough Dial-A-Ride (computer) PRT FPC Savannah Minneapolis Corridor		

DIFFUSION SUCCESS

Source: Rand, 1976, p. 42.

FIGURE 2-2. Application Success Measured Against Diffusion Success

APPLICATION SUCCESS	LITTLE OR NONE	SOME	SIGNIFICANT
HIGH	Breakthrough	ECG Godzilla Connecticut Yankee Resource Recovery Dial-A-Ride (manual)	Yankee Poultry Waste RFD Shipbuilding Hydraulic Knee Chicago Expressway
MODERATE	Savannah Medicaid PRT	Marisat	Desalination (Pt. Loma)

LOW	Dial-A-Ride
	  (computer)
	FPC
	Desalination
	  (freeport)		

DIFFUSION SUCCESS

Source: Rand, 1976, p. 44.

FIGURE 2-3. Information Success Measured Against Application Success

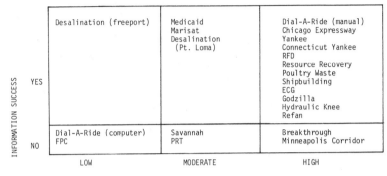

		Desalination (freeport)	Medicaid Marisat Desalination (Pt. Loma)	Dial-A-Ride (manual) Chicago Expressway Yankee Connecticut Yankee RFD Resource Recovery Poultry Waste Shipbuilding ECG Godzilla Hydraulic Knee Refan
INFORMATION SUCCESS	YES			
	NO	Dial-A-Ride (computer) FPC	Savannah PRT	Breakthrough Minneapolis Corridor
		LOW	MODERATE	HIGH

Source: Rand, 1976, p. 45.   APPLICATION SUCCESS

4. a strong technology delivery system;
5. inclusion of all active components of the technology delivery system;
6. absence of tight time constraints (p. 46).

A number of general conclusions on which recommendations for further demonstration projects could be based were drawn from the Rand study. First, the potential for using demonstration projects to significantly enhance technology diffusion is limited. Demonstration projects are usually warranted when (1) there is a medium amount of uncertainty about a technology's cost, reliability, demand, and externalities; (2) when diffusion has been hindered by a lack of information on which adopters can base their decisions; and (3) when its prospects for commercial-scale use by many adopters are unknown. Demonstration projects are not a substitute for regular R&D activities, nor are they appropriate when the private sector is able to achieve full-scale implementation without federal intervention.

Second, market pull is an important factor that must exist for diffusion to take place. There must be evidence of a need that the innovation might be able to fill. Also, the use of the technology should offer more to society in benefits than it takes in costs. The risks associated with the technology should be lowered by the time it reaches the demonstration stage, with the major technological problems having been worked out in the early research and development stages; otherwise, the project is not ready for demonstration.

A third conclusion of the Rand study refers to the difficulties attendant to large, heavily federally funded projects. A large federal investment in a project makes it "highly visible and vulnerable to political pressures." These pressures often cause the objectives to exceed the project's potential because of technological, time, and cost constraints. Additionally, the large, lengthy projects are more likely to be affected by changes in administrations, priorities, and staffing in the implementing agencies. Because of this unreal time frame to complete a project under one administration, technologies often go into the demonstration stage prematurely; demonstrations taking the role of product development cannot be used for their intended purposes.

Another related factor is whether the private sector should share responsibility for funding the project. If private industry is unwilling to share a reasonable portion of the cost and risks associated with the demonstration, this unwillingness might indicate a higher than usual risk of failure and a lack of private sector confidence in the project.

Although demonstration projects can aid in information and project diffusion, a fourth observation of the study is that the demonstration projects themselves are generally not successful at breaking down the institutional and organizational barriers to technology implementation. The three projects that did face institutional barriers—Operation Breakthrough, *Savannah*, and Shipbuilding—were "by themselves weak tools in tackling these barriers." Operation Breakthrough was not able to change the building codes and practices, labor union rules, or the general characteristics of a fragmented housing market preventing industrially built housing from showing a cost advantage over housing built with conventional methods. *Savannah*, although it was able to change foreign and domestic port entry clearance permits for a specific case, was not able to implement a new administrative procedure that could be used over time. The Shipbuilding program was able to change a number of institutional barriers; but the comprehensive program, not an individual project, acted as the change agent. The program aligned potential users and government agencies in an innovative manner to encourage shipbuilding firms to work with the technology, promote industry standards, establish a mechanism for sharing technologies among firms, attract new materials and equipment suppliers to the industry, and have central information dissemination through the project managers.

A fifth observation was that on-site project management was not usually a problem and was, in fact, very effective. The Rand investigators had anticipated that the complicated management process would impose a significant barrier to the demonstration, but this was not the case. Management difficulties that did appear were insignificant compared to other problems faced by the projects.

A final conclusion was that dissemination of information obtained from demonstration projects was not a serious problem. The authors had expected many "good" ideas to be lost in the demonstrations, but this assumption proved incorrect. Diffusion failure was not a result of a lack of information channels, but of poor results from the demonstration projects. A successful project usually enjoyed successful diffusion.

Feller Study

The Center for the Study of Science Policy, Institute for Research on Human Resources, at Pennsylvania State University analyzed the adoption of four transportation technologies: impact attenuators, transportation modeling, automatic telemetry systems, and air pollution modeling. The general focus of the research was on the characteristics of diffusion and adoption of new technologies in the public sector. A specific question addressed in the study was whether some states tended to be early adopters of technological innovations while others consistently lagged behind; and, if this was the case, what the factors were that influenced this differential adoption pattern. The researchers also hoped to learn if diffusion networks, or leader/follower relationships, existed among the different states' mission-oriented agencies (p. 1).

Through interviews with the adopting (or nonadopting) agencies in all fifty states, the authors rated the states in three classifications—early adopters, followers, and late adopters—assigning points on the basis of how the states adopted each of the four technologies. The researchers then tried to identify any common factors which influenced the adoption decision.

The authors tested the relationships between eight variables they had hypothesized would influence adoption and their actual findings. The early hypotheses are depicted in Table 2-3.

TABLE 2-3

Hypothesized Relationships between the Adoption of
New Technologies by Public Sector Organizations
and Selected Independent Variables

Independent Variables	Direction of Relationship
(1) Size of decision unit, i.e., number of members	Inverse
(2) Prestige of decision unit	Direct
(3) Professional orientation of individuals in decision unit	Direct
(4) Degree of interaction with agency personnel in states reputed to be leaders in their respective functional fields	Direct
(5) Degree of interaction with agency personnel in other states	Direct
(6) Agency resources	Direct
(7) Agency autonomy, i.e., independence of governor	Direct
(8) Professional climate of agency	Direct

Source: Feller et al., 1974, p. 24.

Their data gave little support to these hypotheses. For example, their findings regarding variable 6 (agency resources) suggested that although adoption might be inhibited by a lack of resources, adequate agency resources did not always facilitate adoption (p. 24).

The two factors that did appear to have a significant impact on adoption were federal influence and the role played by external change agents (p. 29). The federal arrangement with the state and local governments and its influence on technology diffusion are explained in terms of federalism, national legislation, and patterns of intergovernmental relations.

Under our system of federalism, the governing responsibility is shared by the three levels of government. Responsibilities are divided according to which governmental level would most logically manage a specific problem area. If a state or locality does not feel that a problem comes under its jurisdiction, it would naturally be reluctant to spend its resources on a technology designed to alleviate that problem.

Frequently, "the passage of a new highway act or air quality act [was] the critical event leading to the adoption of a new technology" (p. 31). The legislation does not usually mandate a specific technology; however, given the standards to be met and availability of products, the lower levels of government are often faced with a limited choice.

Federal agencies are often in the position to encourage state and local adoption of new technologies. Their two main leverage tools are fiscal support to reduce expenses for the lower levels of government and various kinds of technical assistance.

The external change agents that facilitate state and local adoption of technologies can be profit-oriented or nonprofit organizations. Commercial manufacturers, private consultants, and contractors are motivated by profit. Universities, private research institutes, and federal agencies are nonprofit organizations that can facilitate adoption (p. 42).

The authors present six recommendations to encourage and facilitate the diffusion of technology to the public sector.

1. The objectives underlying development of technologies to be utilized by the public sector should be clearly delineated. These objectives (an increase of productivity in the public sector, the transfer of federal R&D to the civilian sector, and the enhancement of overall economic growth and national technological leadership) can be mutually reinforcing and can also differ. The motivating force behind the public adopters and the product manufacturers should be better understood. In addition, more should be known about the organization, marketing channels, and marketing practices of firms that supply products to the public sector.

2. The federal government should create a "performance gap" by promoting standards and objectives (and possibly technologies) for the states to follow. Such a performance gap would result from federal legislation that requires a state to do something that it was previously not doing. This

recommendation is based on the assumption that

> the creation of a market through legislation would induce firms to develop products that will satisfy the new performance standards. Although limited in the number of technologies studied, our investigation does reinforce evidence supporting the importance of market demand in determining the efforts that manufacturers will put into a given product line.

3. Activities to evaluate new technologies should be supported by federal agencies. This would help to alleviate the risk associated with adoption for state and local governments which cannot afford the burden of being the testing ground for new products that might fail.

4. Federal agencies should continue to support mechanisms for technology transfer, most importantly the means by which state and local officials can obtain the results of evaluative studies on new technologies.

5. The marketing strategies used by industries that provide goods and services to the public sector should be investigated. Product innovation in the private sector should be included in these studies.

6. The final recommendation is "that increased attention be devoted to the implementation phase of the innovation process" (pp. 52-62).

Summary

This chapter has reviewed the literature on implementation to determine how a study on commercializing the technologies produced by research and development fits in with the state of the art. Since we found no studies directly related to this topic, other types of implementation literature were reviewed.

The first group of studies, public policy works including implementation in their discussions, although useful for the policymaker, has little direct application for the commercialization of federal R&D. Awareness of how the implementing agency functions, how to build support networks and coalitions, and the use of influence to enhance or impede implementation—all are prerequisites for policy implementation to be considered in the early stages of policymaking if a policy is to become a viable program. However, these prerequisites are the "given" variables for our research project, the factors which transferred the policy objective of achieving energy conservation into an intensive program of research and development. How to insure that the products of the R&D are actually used is beyond the scope of the theoretical literature investigated here.

While the case studies that focus on policy implementation contribute a significant amount (and hopefully will encourage further research), they have limited application to our study. They concern translating a policy into a program and do not deal at all with the complex process of commercialization. There is some potential for drawing analogies between policy and technology implementation. For example, the problems of complexity experienced by EDA's project in Oakland could serve as a warning to avoid including too many participants in the commercialization process; or Bardach's implementation scenario might be adapted and used as a guide for a technology commercialization methodology. But for the most part, a study on technology implementation can draw little from this literature.

It is the literature on diffusion that can provide the most insights for our research since this work touches on some of the areas relevant to our study. For example, many of the findings of the Rand study on diffusion could be applicable to implementation of federal R&D if it is decided that demonstration projects should be used to reduce the uncertainties associated with a new product and enhance its commercialization.

- Demonstrations should not be used as a substitute for R&D. Before going into a demonstration, the main technological problems should have been solved. The chief benefit to be gained from demonstrations is the reduction of uncertainties of cost, reliability, demand, and externalities.
- There should be some evidence of market pull for the technology—a perceived need that the innovation might fulfill—for it to be accepted by the intended end users.
- Since large, heavily federally funded demonstration

projects are more visible and easily subjected to criticisms, particularly in the early stages where technological problems may occur, it is important that the project's goals do not exceed its potential.

- Measures should be taken to minimize rigid time constraints, particularly those imposed by the potential of changing administrations every four years.
- The extent to which the private sector is willing to share the costs of the demonstration should be used as indication of its potential for successful commercialization.
- If the demonstration is of a technology to be used by a state or local government, then substantial local involvement in project management should be encouraged (pp. 52-62).

While the Feller study on adoption does not have the same kinds of specific recommendations that can be incorporated into a commercialization methodology, it does note several points also found in our research, particularly the need for more attention to implementation characteristics. There is a large gap between the research on federal R&D processes (which have been throughly documented) and the commercialization of the products developed under public support of R&D. The present study begins to fill in the gap.

Bibliography

Albert, James G. "Defining the Policy-Making Function in Government: An Organizational and Management Approach." *Policy Sciences* Vol. 5, No. 3 (September 1974), pp. 245-255.

Anderson, James E. *Public Policy Making.* New York: Praeger Publishers, 1975.

Baer, Walter S., Leland L. Johnson and Edward W. Merrow. *Analysis of Federally Funded Demonstration Projects: Final Report.* Prepared for ETIP, U.S. Department of Commerce. Santa Monica, Calif.: Rand Corp., 1976.

Bailey, Stephen E. and Edith K. Mosher. *ESEA: The Office of Education Administers a Law.* Syracuse, New York: Syracuse University Press, 1968.

Bardach, Eugene. *The Implementation Game: What Hap-*

pens After a Bill Becomes a Law. May 1977 version. Cambridge, Mass.: M.I.T. Press, forthcoming.

Bingham, Richard D. *The Adoption of Innovation by Local Government.* Milwaukee, Wisconsin: Office of Urban Research, Marquette University, 1975.

Bunker, Douglas R. "Policy Sciences Perspectives on Implementation Processes." *Policy Sciences* Vol. 3 (March 1972), pp. 71-80.

Derthick, Martha. *New Towns In-Town.* Washington, D.C.: The Urban Institute, 1972.

Doctors, Samuel I. *The Role of Federal Agencies in Technology Transfer.* Cambridge, Mass.: M.I.T. Press, 1969.

Dror, Yehezkel. *Public Policy Making Reexamined.* San Francisco: Chandler Publishing, 1968.

Duffy, N.F. and P.M. Taylor. "The Implementation of a Decision." In William T. Greenwood, ed., *Decision Theory and Information Systems.* Cincinnati: South-Western Publishing, 1969.

Dye, Thomas R. *Understanding Public Policy.* 2nd ed. Englewood Cliffs, N.J.: Prentice-Hall, 1975.

Feller, Irwin, Donald C. Menzel, and Alfred J. Engel. *Diffusion of Technology in State Mission Oriented Agencies.* University Park, Penna.: Center for the Study of Science Policy, Institute for Human Resources, 1974.

Gergen, Kenneth J. "Assessing the Leverage Points in the Process of Policy Formation." In Raymond A. Bauer and Kenneth J. Gergen, *The Study of Policy Formation.* New York: Free Press, 1968.

Gross, Bertram M. "Activating National Plans." In Lawrence, J.R., ed., *Operational Research and the Social Sciences.* New York: Tavistock Publications, 1966.

Gross, Neal, Joseph B. Giaquenta, and Marilyn Bernstein. *Implementing Organizational Innovations: A Sociological Analysis of Planned Educational Change.* New York: Basic Books, 1971.

Hatry, Harry P. "Status of P.P.B.S. in Local and State Governments in the United States." *Policy Sciences* Vol. 2 (1971), pp. 177-189.

Hirshberg, Alan and Richard Schoen. "Barriers to the Widespread Utilization of Residential Solar Energy: The Prospects for Solar Energy in the U.S. Housing Industry." *Policy Sciences* Vol. 5, No. 4 (December 1974), pp. 453-

468.

Jones, Charles O. *An Introduction to the Study of Public Policy.* Belmont, Calif.: Wadsworth Publishing Co., 1970.

Levine, Robert A. *Public Planning: Failure and Redirection.* New York: Basic Books, 1972.

Lindblom, Charles E. *The Policy-Making Process.* Englewood Cliffs, N.J.: Prentice-Hall, 1968.

Meyerson, Martin and Edward C. Banfield. *Politics, Planning, and the Public Interest.* New York: Free Press, 1969.

Murphy, Jerome T. "Title I of ESEA: The Politics of Implementing Federal Education Reform." *Harvard Educational Review* Vol. 41 (February 1971) , pp. 35-63.

Orfield, Gary. *The Reconstruction of Southern Education: The Schools and the 1964 Civil Rights Act.* New York: John Wiley & Sons, 1969.

Pincus, John. "Incentives for Innovation in the Public Schools." *Review of Educational Research* (Winter 1974).

Pressman, Jeffrey L. and Aaron B. Wildavsky. *Implementation.* Berkeley: University of California Press, 1973.

Rogers, Everett. *Diffusion of Innovations.* New York: Free Press, 1962.

Sayeed, Khalid B. "Public Policy Analysis in Washington and Ottawa." *Policy Sciences* Vol. 4, No. 1 (March 1973), pp. 85-101.

Schick, Allen. "A Death in the Bureaucracy: The Demise of Federal PPB." *Public Administration Review,* March/ April 1973, pp. 146-156.

Smith, Thomas B. "Policy Roles: An Analysis of Policy Formulators and Policy Implementors." *Policy Sciences* Vol. 4, No. 3 (September 1973), pp. 297-307.

Stone, Alan. "The F.T.C. and Advertising Regulation: An Examination of Agency Failure." *Public Policy* Vol. 21, No. 2 (Spring 1973), pp. 203-234.

Ugalde, Antonio. "A Decision Model for the Study of Public Bureaucracies." *Policy Sciences* Vol. 4, No. 1 (March 1973), pp. 75-84.

Williams, Walter, ed. *Special Issue on Implementation. Policy Analysis* Vol. 1, No. 3 (Summer 1975), pp. 451-569.

3

Innovation in the Private Sector

This chapter will present a general description of the innovation process in the private sector. The specific activities carried out in pursuit of successful innovation differ considerably among companies and industries. The success which companies have realized in pursuit of new products differs as well. However, intensive study of the innovation process of many of the most successful innovators has led to the identification of a stylized sequence of events that carries a new idea through development and on to commercialization. An understanding of the private sector innovation process is considered a necessary precondition to the development of effective strategies for private sector implementation of federally funded research and development. Whether this statement is accurate or not, a careful analysis will uncover criteria employed in the private sector decision-making process which suggest primary considerations in attempting to implement a public sector research product in the private sector.

Clearly, there are major differences between public and private organizations, and many of these have been reviewed (Rainey, Backoff, and Levine, 1976). Differences include goals pursued and whether there is unanimity in determining these goals. A major guiding goal of business is to achieve a satisfactory (or better) rate of return. In contrast, there is little agreement regarding goals pursued by public organizations. These goals tend to be more complex and numerous and, yet, less clearly stated.

Innovation and the Innovation Process

Freeman (1973) defines innovation as "the technical, industrial and commercial steps which lead to the marketing of new manufactured products and to the commercial use of new technical processes and equipment" (p. 228). He points out that the crucial defining aspect of innovation is "the commercial launch of a new product or system" (p. 228). A new good, service, or process, then, is the output of an innovation process.

We may proceed further by distinguishing between product innovation and process innovation. Product innovation is the sequence of activities which culminates in the commercial realization of new marketable goods and services. Process innovation refers to the activities leading to the advent of new methods and added efficiencies to reduce the cost of producing existing items (Kamien and Schwartz, 1975). General Motors, for instance, may develop a new, more efficient method of producing its automobiles and incorporate this process innovation into its assembly line. In accordance with preceding chapters, we are concerned with product innovation: the sequence of activities leading to the commercial realization of a new marketable good or service.

Innovations vary considerably in terms of their newness. Lazer and Bell (1973) clarify innovations as being adaptive, functional, or fundamental (Table 3-1). Adaptive innovations are minor modifications or changes in already existing products. A new brand of cigarettes or detergent is an adaptive innovation. While these innovations represent the least change, they are the most frequently encountered new product entry. They require the least research and development expenditure and the least change in marketing strategy on the part of the "innovating" firm. They also tend to have the least impact on the market. As a result, the profit potential from these new products tends to be less than the profit potential of the other two types of innovation.

Functional and fundamental innovations more readily fit the commonly held concept of innovation. These are new products which apply a new method to perform an old function or incorporate new ideas to perform new functions for the customer. The former type of innovation is considered "functional," while the latter is identified as "funda-

TABLE 3-1

Classification of Product Innovations by Type of Innovation

Fundamental	Functional	Adaptive
	Characteristics	

Requires:
  Absolute newness
  No substitutability
  Habit change
  New process
  New markets
	Substitutability
	Improved product or
	  process
	New or changed
	  production
		New in minor aspects:
		  e.g., weight, color,
		  design, package
		Much substitutability

May require:
  New skills
  New resources
  New consumption
    patterns
  New distribution
    systems
	Change in consumption
	  patterns
	New or changed distri-
	  bution systems
		Limited production
		  change
		No changes in con-
		  sumption pattern
		No change in distri-
		  bution required
		Greater convenience

	Examples	
Missiles Dehumidifiers Airplanes Televisions Lasers Computers	Clothes dryers Electric knives Electric sharpeners Automatic dishwashers Jet planes	Flip-top box Filter and mentholated cigarettes New brands
	Marketing	

Create primary
  demand
Create new consump-
  tion habits
New production
  facilities and/or
  processes
Overcome resistance
  to change
Gain acceptance
	Create selective demand
	Change consumption
	  habits
	New or changed
	  production
	New service facilities
	Extend markets
		Meet competition
		Extend markets
		Create selective demand
		Specialize product for
		  market segments
		Differentiate product
		Create image of newness

Source: Lazer and Bell, 1973, p. 181.

mental." Both require increasingly large changes in the customers' behavior. As a result, they not only have greater risk associated with their introduction, but they also frequently require increasingly major changes in marketing strategy. The profit potential associated with these ideas tends to be much greater than the profit potential associated with adaptive innovations.

Moving across categories from adaptive to functional and then to fundamental innovations, one observes an increasing R&D expenditure and an increasing risk of failure. A part of this added risk is a function of the added R&D expenditure, but it is also a function of the increasing difficulty associated with forecasting activities. Moving across these categories, however, one observes an increasing impact on the economy and an increasing profit potential for the firm.

The Importance of the Innovation Process

Products have been found to follow a life cycle which proceeds from introduction in the market through a period of rapid growth, leveling off as the product reaches maturity, and then decline (Booz, Allen and Hamilton, 1968; Wasson, 1971). This pattern exhibited by the product's sales revenue is shown in Figure 3-1. Associated with the product life-cycle revenue curve is a net profit curve reaching a peak at or near the end of the growth stage and then declining. In order for firms to maintain their profitability, they must have new products entering the market as their old products reach maturity.

FIGURE 3-1. Basic Life Cycle of Products

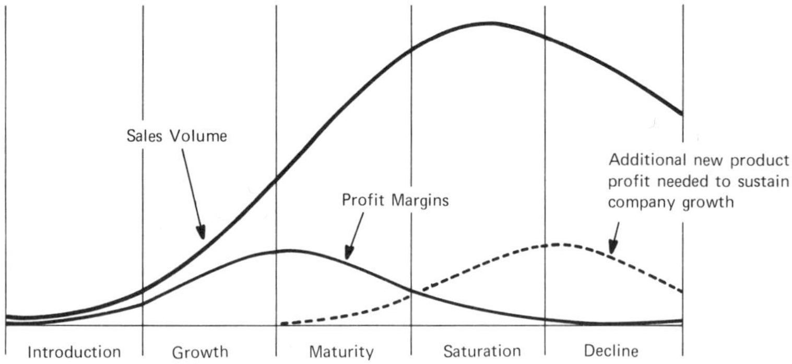

Sales Volume

Profit Margins

Additional new product profit needed to sustain company growth

Introduction   Growth   Maturity   Saturation   Decline

Source: Booz, Allen & Hamilton, 1968.

According to Booz, Allen and Hamilton (1968), an average of 75 percent (individual industry figures ranged from 46 percent to 100 percent) of the expected growth in sales revenue in 111 industries was anticipated from new products (the figures are for the period 1963 to 1967). Not surprisingly, firms derive substantial profitability from their research and development effort. It has been estimated that "industry earns an average 30% rate of return per year on R&D spending—about twice the return that companies get from their capital investments" ("The Silent Crisis in R and D," *Business Week*, 1976, p. 90).[1] The economy at large profits enormously from R&D expenditure. "Fully one third of the growth in GNP has come from technological process" (p. 90).

In view of the high profitability of R&D and its necessity to both the firm and the economy, one would expect a substantial and growing commitment to research and development by both the private and public sectors of the economy. Yet, governmental R&D expenditures are rising exceedingly slowly. From 1967 to 1975, governmental R&D expenditures (adjusted for inflation) shrank by 3 percent while nongovernment spending rose 1.9 percent per year ("The Silent Crisis in R and D," *Business Week*, 1976, p. 90). The private sector contribution to the total R&D expenditure rose from 42 percent in 1963 to 61 percent in 1973. It is expected to remain at approximately 60 percent in 1975 ("Where Private Industry Puts Its Research Money," *Business Week*, 1976).

The bulk of the federal funding has been concentrated in only a few industries. In 1973, 92 percent of federal funds went to five leading R&D performing industries: aircraft and missiles, electrical equipment, chemicals, machinery, and motor vehicles (National Science Foundation [NSF], 1975). Only in the area of energy is federal R&D support increasingly dramatically. "Federally supported energy-related research and development in industry increased by 26 percent in 1973 over 1972, from $224 million to $282 million" (p. 8).

The R&D spending picture is more bleak if viewed as a percent of net sales. Total R&D expenditures went from a high of 4.6 percent of net sales revenue in 1964 to 3.2 percent in 1973. Research and development spending by the private sector remained constant at 2.0 percent of sales (pp. 51-52).[2] Private sector spending on R&D was 1.8 percent of net sales in 1975 ("Where Private Industry Puts Its Research Money," *Business Week*, 1976). A breakdown of private sector spending by industry in 1975 is shown in Table 3-2.

TABLE 3-2

Private Sector R&D Expenditures - 1975

Industry	R&D Expenditures (Millions)	% of Sales	% of Net Income (After Taxes)
Aerospace	$ 825.3	3.2%	136.0%
Appliances	67.1	1.2	89.6
Automotive	2508.3	2.7	137.9
Beverages	14.5	0.3	4.0
Building Materials	208.4	1.2	27.8
Chemicals	1317.4	2.6	39.4
Conglomerates	499.1	1.5	48.7
Drugs	1157.6	4.7	51.2
Electrical and Electronics	11345.1	3.0	81.5
Food	243.2	0.5	14.3
Food and Lodging	0.3	0.1	2.0
General Machinery	288.1	1.7	40.5
Instruments	695.6	5.4	68.6
Leisure Time	62.2	1.7	93.2
Metals and Mining	204.2	1.2	33.3
Miscellaneous Manufacturing	480.1	1.8	43.4
Natural Resources Fuel	715.2	0.4	8.3
Office Equipment Computers	1707.0	5.6	60.8
Oil Service and Supply	137.2	1.2	16.8
Paper	98.2	0.8	12.0
Personal Care Products	242.8	1.6	27.6
Publishing	2.1	0.2	3.6
Service Industries	48.8	0.3	12.1
Special Machinery	349.6	2.4	42.7
Steel	105.9	0.6	10.9
Textiles, Apparel	30.3	0.4	26.4
Tire and Rubber	319.4	1.9	69.2
Tobacco	20.0	0.5	10.1
Telecommunications	235.3	1.9	19.9
All Industry Composite	14515.8	1.8	38.2

Source: "Where Private Industry Puts Its Research Money," Business Week, 1976.

The rapid growth in R&D spending realized in the 1950s and early 1960s has been totally eliminated.

From 1953 to 1961, R and D expenditures, adjusted for inflation, increased at an average rate of 13.9% a year for government and 7.7% for nongovernment according to the National Science Foundation. From 1961 to 1967, government funded R and D increased 5.6% a year and private R and D 7.4% ("The Silent Crisis in R and D,) *Business Week*, 1976, p. 90).

The slowdown in the rate of growth of R&D spending indicates that we may expect a slower rate of growth in the GNP in the near future.

Failure

Even with the commitment of large sums of money to the development of new products, the failure rate of newly introduced products is high. Booz, Allen and Hamilton (1968) found that an average of only 67 percent of the products reaching commercialization were successful; 23 percent were doubtful, and the remaining 10 percent were failures. What the authors mean by failure, however, is unclear. Definitions vary as do the resulting failure rates. Buzzell and Nourse (1967), in their study of the food industry, found that 17 percent of the introduced products were subsequently withdrawn from the market as failures. Given the percent of products withdrawn after test marketing or introduction (39 percent), the percent rated "moderately" or "extremely" unsuccessful by their sponsors (42 percent), and the percent failing to break even within two years (44 percent), the authors conclude, that, "if a single figure must be used to characterize the rate of failure among new processed food products, it appears that approximately 40% should be classed as failures" (p. 170). Hopkins and Bailey (1971) found that approximately 40 percent of the new products introduced by consumer product manufacturers "failed in some important respect to meet original expectations" (p. 20). Industrial goods manufacturers incurred a failure rate of approximately 20 percent while the failure rate in the service industry was between 15 and 20 percent. When these failures were combined across industries, they yielded a median failure rate of "slightly more than 20%" (p. 20). While Booz, Allen and Hamilton found that failure rates were fairly constant across industries, Hopkins and Bailey found marked discrepancies with rates considerably higher for consumer goods manufacturers than for industrial products manufacturers.

Many reasons have been given for the frequent occurrence of product failures. Most of these reasons revolve around the link between product characteristics and customer desires. Tauber (1973) suggests that products fail if they do not satisfy an unmet need or solve a problem (p. 62). Based on a survey of over 150 advertising and manufacturing executives, Angelus (1969) concluded that the major reason for new product failure was the lack of a real difference from the consumer's point of view. He goes on to point out that "unfortunately, the difference in most cases is important only to the manufacturer and not to the consumer" (p. 85). Buzzell and Nourse (1967) found that all those products which had "substantial, visible differences from existing products in taste, form, preservation or other physical attributes" were successful (p. 170).

Hopkins and Bailey (1971) elicited the principal causes of product failure from 125 members of the Conference Board's Senior Marketing Executives' Panel. The responses they obtained are itemized (p. 20).

Cause of Failure	Percent of Companies Citing
Inadequate market analysis	.45 %
Product problems or defects	.29
Lack of effective marketing effort	.25
Higher costs than anticipated	.19
Competitive strength or reaction	.17
Poor timing of introduction	.14
Technical production problems	.12
All other causes	.24

These reasons for failure were not much different from one industry to another. Furthermore, they were very similar to the results of a Conference Board survey conducted six years earlier.

By far, the most frequently cited cause of product failure was inadequate appraisal of the market in advance. The disappointing sales of two new metal-working machines, for example, were attributed by a spokesman

> to the fact that advanced research on the products was conducted purely as an engineering exercise, without reference to opinions and evaluations from sales and marketing personnel. A net result was the design and manufacture of machines that exemplified engineering's concept of the ultimate in engineering achievement and not the products that were most marketable. These machines were without suffi-

cient user advantages to overcome the lead of competitive products, in view of the fact that the highly engineered products necessarily had to command higher prices (Hopkins and Bailey, 1971, p. 21).

Effective innovation requires both engineering and marketing expertise. It "depends in an important way on R&D being integrated with marketing" (Mansfield and Wagner, 1975, p. 189). Emphasis on one of these aspects of innovation to the exclusion of the other will likely adversely affect the developing product and retard its eventual market acceptance.

Further insight into the determinants of successful innovation is provided by the results of a recent study.

> Successful attempts were distinguished frequently from failure by greater attention to the education of users, to publicity, to market forecasting and selling . . . and to the understanding of user requirements. The single measure which discriminated most clearly between success and failure was 'user needs understood.' In our view this should not be interpreted as simply, or even mainly, an indicator of efficient market research. It reflects just as much on R and D and design as well as on the management of the innovation. The product or process had to be designed and developed and freed of bugs to meet the specific requirements of the future users, so that 'understanding' of the market had to be present at a very early stage (Freeman, 1973, p. 242).

In summary, it appears that product failure results from the development of a new product and marketing strategy which is not sufficiently consistent with the desires of the market. This failure to achieve a sufficient match between product characteristics and market desires may come about in several ways. It may be the result of confusing the company's assumptions about what they think customers desire with the actual desires of those customers. It may be due to insufficient marketing research to determine what the customers want and to repeatedly check the developing product's consistency with these wants. It may be due to inadequacies in the research which bias the information derived from it. It may be due to misinterpretation. It may be the result of technical inability to provide a product with the desired characteristics. However this failure occurs, the results are the same: those products which fail to provide a sufficiently close match with the desires of the markets fail to achieve the hoped-for success.

Formalization of the Innovation Process

An outcome of the trade-off between the severe risks of innovating and the extreme importance of innovation has been the development of a formal systematic treatment of the innovation process. Based on examination of "several hundred companies' new product activities," Booz, Allen and Hamilton (1968) reports that "there is a basic approach to the management process of new product evolution that is sound for companies in most industries" (p. 7). While the total business community does not formally embrace the process, it is based on the actual practices of companies that have most successfully managed their new product activities. The process may be described as a number of distinct steps beginning with the generation of an idea in what Booz, Allen and Hamilton calls the exploration stage and proceeding through screening, business analysis, development, testing, and ultimately commercialization. Other writers add a concept development and testing stage between screening and business analysis (for example, Kotler, 1976). The process is charted in Figure 3-2.

As the idea proceeds through stages of the process, it is specified more clearly and modified to improve its fit with market desires and company requirements. Figure 3-3 portrays this action sequence in the form of a Program Evaluation and Review Technique (PERT) chart and identifies a number of activities associated with the various stages in the innovation process. PERT is frequently employed in new product decision making to schedule activities in a way which will lead to their coordinated and timely completion. The activities circled in the key and charted in bold lines represent the critical path. Any change in the time or scheduling of these activities will alter the final completion date of the project. Those tasks not on the critical path are endowed with some "slack" time whereby leeway is permit-

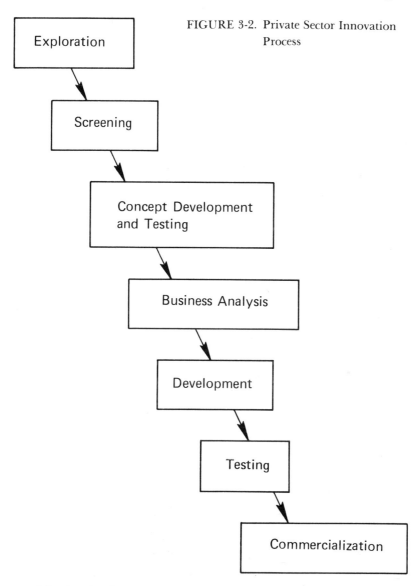

FIGURE 3-2. Private Sector Innovation Process

ted in beginning or finishing without affecting the final completion date. (See Hough, 1970; and Booz, Allen and Hamilton, 1968, for further discussion of this tool.)

Each succeeding stage in the innovation process, with the possible exception of testing, is increasingly costly to the innovating firm (Booz, Allen and Hamilton, 1968). Clearly,

FIGURE 3-3. Innovation Process

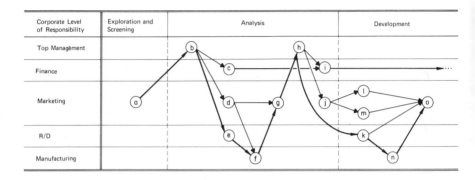

Key to PERT Chart

Exploration & Screening
  a. Continuing market audit discovers a new customer need, starts proposal preparation.

Analysis
  b. Top management approves the study proposal.
  c. Finance records budget and starts budgeting controls
  d. Marketing starts preliminary market investigation.
  e. Research and development starts preliminary technical investigation.
  f. Manufacturing starts preliminary cost study.
  g. Marketing in cooperation with research and development and manufacturing starts general evaluation of a new product.
  h. Top management approves new-product program and budget.
  i. Finance records new budget and starts budgetary controls.
  j. Marketing starts detailed plan and schedule.

Development
  k. Research and development starts prototype development and drawings.
  l. Marketing starts determining product packaging, units/case, price, and discounts.
  m. Marketing starts determining distribution, introduction plans.
  n. Manufacturing starts setting up prototype production and production plans.
  o. New product committee starts reevaluating product.

Source: Pessemier, E.A. New Product Decisions, 1966.

a direct relationship exists between the length of time a product idea remains under consideration and the expenditures incurred in the processing of that idea. As a result, it is important to eliminate as quickly as possible those ideas which will not ultimately become successful new products. Most ideas, therefore, are eliminated during screening.

FIGURE 3-3. (continued)

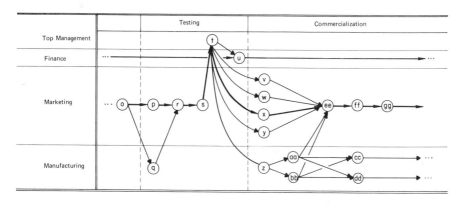

Key to PERT Chart

Testing

p. New product committee starts plan for test-marketing prototype.
q. Manufacturing starts prototype production and new cost estimates.
r. Marketing starts test marketing.
s. Marketing starts evaluation of test results.
t. Top management approves proposal and budget.
u. Finance records new budget and starts budgeting controls.

Commercialization

v. Marketing starts developing advertising strategy, media plan, and copy.
w. Marketing starts developing final product packaging, units/case, price and discounts.
x. Marketing starts developing final plans for distribution and introduction to trade.
y. Marketing starts developing final plans for introduction to sales force.

z. Manufacturing starts acquiring production equipment and planning facilities, and equipment installation.
aa. Manufacturing starts ordering materials.
bb. Manufacturing starts training manpower (production personnel).
cc. Manufacturing starts production.
dd. Manufacturing starts building up inventory.
ee. Marketing starts series of conferences with sales force.
ff. Marketing starts conferences with dealers.
gg. Marketing starts full-scale marketing by breaking consumer advertising.

Fewer ideas are eliminated in each succeeding stage. Figure 3-4 shows a decay curve for ideas. The curve is characteristic of the process.

In practice, it is difficult to determine just where the innovation process begins and where it ends. For instance, Myers and Marquis (1969) report that "a substantial number

FIGURE 3-4. Mortality of New Product Ideas

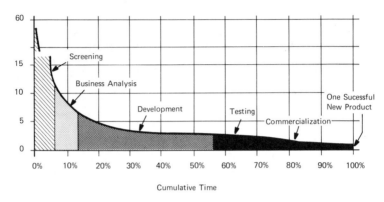

Source: Booz, Allen & Hamilton, 1968

of the innovations studied did not originate in the firm under study, but had already been developed by another company and were then adopted by the firm in question" (p. 19). The authors employ the example of an extruded asbestos cement window which was developed from a process widely used in the industry. They point out that "the change from stainless steel to cast iron head inserts was simply the adoption of a component used by most competitors in the engine industry" (pp. 19-20). In fact, many product ideas seem to evolve out of other inventions, innovations, or technological breakthroughs. Knowledge of these processes or products, recalled from other contexts in the presence of a specific problem, is frequently the stimulus which leads to major new innovations. The following scenario concerning the advent of the high-speed paper-feed device for printers illustrates this point.

One day Dr. Able was listening to a colleague tell of the difficulties that were cropping up in the clutch mechanism of the electromechanical document feed-in device which was being developed. He recalled an article he had read years before in a professional journal in which the author described a hydraulic pump and motor used as a control device for a DOD application. The article was fairly specific and included photographs of the device. Dr. Able thought that something like this device could replace the clutch that was so troublesome (Myers and Marquis, 1969, p. 12).

There are similar vagaries associated with the delineation of the end of the innovation process. Most studies, including the present endeavor, consider commercialization as marking the end of the process. However, successful products go from introduction to a period of rapid sales growth, followed by a period of fairly stable demand, and ending with the products' decline and ultimate extinction (see Figure 3-1).

In summary, innovations seem to evolve. They frequently are based on ideas stimulated by the recall of a technological breakthrough in some seemingly unrelated area. The knowledge of some new device or finding of basic research, when paired with a specific problem, can and frequently does result in the formulation of a new and better problem-solving idea. It is this idea which may eventually become a major new innovation.

Organization

The innovation process involves a large commitment in numbers of personnel from a variety of fields. Substantial input is necessary from product researchers, production specialists, marketing specialists, and financial analysts (to mention only a few). Frequently, the inclinations and orientations of these individuals are at odds. For example, while the production specialist desires a standardized, easily mass-produced product, the marketer would like a product which is uniquely tuned to the desires of each customer group for whom the product is being designed. At the same time, the product researcher desires a thoroughly researched, technically superior product, and the financial analyst wants to minimize research and development expenditure. Although clearly oversimplified, these trade-offs are illustrative of the types of conflicts likely to surface at various points in the innovation process. Organizational requirements for effective direction and coordination through the stages of the innovation process are in Table 3-3.

TABLE 3-3

Requirements and Organization of New Products Departments

Requirements for Effective Direction and Coordination of Product Evolution	Organizational Provisions Needed to Meet These Requirements
Exploration Phase	
1. Areas of company interest (in terms of potential products) clearly stated and widely understood.	A single executive charged with the specific responsibility to focus and coordinate searches for new opportunities in technology and markets.
2. Full and programmed coverage of all productive sources of ideas.	Specialized personnel, free of responsibilities for present products, to conduct supplementary exploration of unrelated markets and technology in a neutral environment.
3. Complete capture of all ideas for proposed products to assure that each is considered.	A central collection station to record and process all ideas and the data supporting them.
Screening Phase	
1. Standards for the measurement of proposed product ideas against company product policy.	Authority to determine the criteria and method by which each idea will be judged.
2. Complete and careful consideration of each idea by the persons best qualified to judge each screening factor.	Authority to select screening participants and to secure formal replies to specific questions.
3. Evaluation of ideas for their commercial value prior to committing development funds and manpower.	Skilled personnel to secure the data necessary for early commercial evaluation and to summarize all facts and opinions as a basis for deciding the disposition of each idea.
Proposal and Development Phases	
1. A management commitment of willingness to accept and utilize a product before development is begun.	Formal construction and authorization of a concrete development proposal, in business terms: a product of stated characteristics by a specific date, at an approved development cost.
2. Continuing liaison and agreement between marketing, R&D, other departments, and top management during the development phase.	Direction of the interdepartmental relationships required during development; preparation of regular summary status reports to top management.
3. Complete and realistic evaluation of the performance characteristics and market acceptance of the product developed.	Impartial review and audit of all new product data developed prior to top-management decisions based on these data.
Test Marketing Phase	
1. Opportunity to exploit all products developed, even if judged unsatisfactory for further commitment of company resources.	Perspective and personnel to acquire or dispose of products outside established company channels.
2. Complete and careful programming and control for test marketing, product testing, and early production.	Coordination and guidance of committee work and the preparation of progress reports to top management.
3. Complete and realistic appraisal of product, production, and market testing results.	Perspective to help establish evaluation criteria and review results impartially.

Source: Johnson, 1962, p. 365

A number of organizational structures have been suggested for incorporating the new product function (cf. Hopkins, 1974; Kotler, 1976). Although appropriate structures are available, a few basic organizing principles emerge. First of all, the nature and size of the tasks involved and their time and monetary implications for the firm require that top management be directly responsible for the new product function. Second, the innovation function should be divorced from concern with a specific product or product type. This frees it from a product orientation which all too often results in a tendency to view innovations as product limitations or revisions. Third, it must allow for substantial interdepartmental coordination.

The new product venture team is used to provide this interdepartmental coordination while closely guiding the new product through the innovation process (cf. Hill and Hlavacek, 1972). Specifically, the team guides a new product idea from screening to commercialization and is typically set up by drawing people from the various functional departments of the company. According to Hill and Hlavacek, team participants are typically drawn from engineering, production, marketing, and finance. Once the team has been set up, these people work full time on the new product idea until they are reassigned or until the team's mission is completed. They typically report to top management. The team allows the coordination of specialized knowledge from a variety of disciplines, because its members represent these various disciplines. As such, the project benefits from the specialized knowledge of different functional units without incurring the resistance from factions and interdepartmental rivalries which may otherwise slow and perhaps stifle the project.

The innovation process traditionally begins with "exploration" and ends with "commercialization." We will now turn to a detailed treatment of this innovation process, followed by a consideration of the process by which the newly introduced innovation is diffused through the market. The chapter will end with a discussion of the barriers to implementation which manifest themselves at various points in the innovation and diffusion processes.

The Innovation Process

Exploration

The initial stage in the innovation process is generally identified as "exploration" or "idea generation." This is treated as an ongoing activity of the firm, very frequently involving the management of idea flows within the organization as well as the establishment of specific procedures designed to generate ideas. The major sources of new product ideas are customers, company researchers, competitors, and company salesmen. According to a comprehensive study of the innovation process in the food industry, most ideas come from sources within the firm (Buzzell and Nourse, 1967). This is supported by the Booz, Allen and Hamilton (1968) study, which cites percent of new product ideas internally generated, with marketing and research and development contributing 60 percent of these.

At this stage in the innovation process (in contrast to each of the remaining stages), the emphasis is on building up large numbers of ideas. Little consideration is given to the quality of the ideas. Nevertheless, guidelines and directions are frequently provided by people whose task it is to elicit ideas. The characteristics of a good idea can frequently be given some substance at this stage. Fundamentally, a good idea is one which may enhance customer satisfaction by, for instance, permitting him to perform some task more readily or improve his performance on the task. Thus, from the very beginning of the innovation process, primary emphasis is placed on the end user.

Attention is directed at tasks the company's customers and potential customers perform within the company's area of interest as well as at goals they seek to accomplish in the performance of these tasks. The consistency of the final product with these criteria within the innovation process will ultimately determine the product's success or failure in the market.

The proper organization for the flow of ideas within the firm is a crucial determinant of this stage's effectiveness. This includes designation of idea collection points, establishment of comprehensive idea collection procedures, coverage of selected outside sources of ideas, and motivation of company personnel and customers to facilitate idea flows. A number of techniques have been employed to generate ideas, including morphological analysis, brainstorming, analysis of product use systems, and analysis of customer activities (see Kotler, 1976; Boyd and Massey, 1972).

Screening

During the screening stage and each succeeding stage in the process, the emphasis is on quickly eliminating those ideas which are not likely to result in marketable products. Because the company's expenditure on a new product idea is directly related to the amount of time the product remains under consideration, a considerable incentive is provided for rapid elimination of unsuitable ideas.

The screening stage quickly rules out unsuitable ideas. While many screening devices or guidelines have been suggested and vary considerably in detail, they must permit a rapid assessment of an idea's consistency with corporate goals and resources. Ideas are generally compared with a set of fixed decision rules or criteria that facilitate speed review.

A number of checklists have been developed to permit an efficient screening of product ideas (see Table 3-4). For example, a large materials processor employed a device which permitted a rating of nine criteria, each on a five-point bipolar scale labeled from very good to very poor (Kline, 1955). The patterns obtained from the ratings were used to assess suitability of product ideas. Others (e.g., Harris, 1964; O'Meara, 1961; Richman, 1962) have suggested a quantitative rating procedure in which numerical scores are assigned to the scale positions on bipolar scales, such as the very good to very poor scale mentioned above. If we were to employ this scale, for example, we could assign a value of "1" to "very poor," "2" to "poor," and proceed in this fashion to "very good" with an assigned value of "5." One such scale would be provided for each idea. Screeners would then rate an idea on these scales by assigning a numerical score to each criterion in accordance with the idea's standing on that criterion. The score assigned to each criterion would be weighted by its importance, and each project idea could be given a single score representing a weighted average of the criterion scores. This procedure is similar to the one proposed by Richman (1962) described in Table 3-4.

Table 3-4 describes methods for systematically evaluating and comparing project ideas. Generally, those ideas emerging with high overall ratings are advanced to the concept development and testing stage where they are more clearly specified prior to being subjected to detailed analysis. Product ideas which emerge with intermediate ratings are subjected to further screening. Ideas which emerge from screening with uniformly low ratings are dropped.

Over half the ideas generated in the first stage of the

TABLE 3-4

Criteria Employed in the Screening of New Product Ideas

Screening Criteria	Scoring
Kline (1955)	
1. Sales volume	An idea is given a rating on each
2. Type and number of competitors	criterion from "very good" to "very
3. Technical opportunity	poor." The pattern of the ratings
4. Patent protection	is used to determine whether or not
5. Raw materials	to proceed with the idea.
6. Production load	
7. Value added	
8. Similarity to major business	
9. Effect on major products	
Richman (1962)	
1. Company personality and goodwill (.20)	An idea is given a numerical score
2. Marketing (.20)	for each criterion on a scale which
3. Research and development (.20)	varies from 0 to 1.0. The score
4. Personnel (.15)	is related to how the idea fits
5. Finance (.10)	with respect to program policies,
6. Production (.05)	resources, and other constraints.
7. Location and facilities (.05)	Each criterion source is weighted by
8. Purchasing and supplies (.05)	the relative weight shown in paren-
	theses and summed to yield a single
	score for the idea.
O'Meara (1961)	
1. Marketability distribution channels, product lines, quality/price relationships, number of sizes and grades, merchandisability, effects on sales of present products.	Five separate indices are developed. The first four indices are derived in a manner similar to that employed in Richman. The first four derived
2. Durability: stability, breadth of market, cyclical variation, seasonal fluctuation, exclusiveness.	scores are totaled to yield a single derived "intangible factor index."
3. Productive ability: equipment necessary, production knowledge and personnel necessary, raw material necessary.	This index is compared with the pay-back index. These latter two indices are used as a basis for making the
4. Growth to potential: place in market, expected competitive situation, expected market growth.	final screening decision.
5. Payback index: a function of probability of commercial success, sales units per year, selling price per unit, cost per unit, years before likely competitive entry, additional capital expenditures, production development costs.	
Richman (1964)	
1. Financial aspects: return on investment, estimated annual sales, new fixed capital payout time, time to reach estimated sales volume.	An idea is scored on each criterion from -2 to +2 according to the idea's perceived potential on that
2. Research and development aspects: research investment payout time, research know-how, patent status.	criterion. The pattern of the scores in each major category is assessed in order to make the final
3. Competitive position: market development requirements, promotional requirements, product competition, product advantage, length of product life, cyclical and seasonal demand.	screening decision.
4. Production and engineering aspects: required corporate size; raw materials equipment, process familiarity.	
5. Marketing and product aspects: similarity to present product lines, effect on present products, marketability to present customers, suitability of present sales force, market stability, market trend, technical service.	

innovation process are rejected at the screening stage (Booz, Allen and Hamilton, 1968; Kotler, 1976). Checklists, or other similar devices, are employed to contribute some degree of consistency and objectivity to the screening process while maintaining the speed which is an essential aspect of the review at this stage. Formal screening criteria do not eliminate the need for informed managerial judgment. They divide a complex problem into its component parts and make it possible for the screening decision to be made on the basis of specific criteria which the company has determined to be central to the successful implementation of the idea. The checklists in Table 3-4 clearly show that the idea must be consistent with the firm's goals, objectives, and orientation and that it must have clearly favorable profit potential to be viewed positively by the organization. While checklists, rating scales, and other formal decision criteria are frequently employed to assist in making these decisions, they are rarely followed without scrutiny and even scepticism. Projects which may show up poorly on a formal screening device may be advanced to the next stage in the process if they score highly in an important dimension or if, for some other reason, management's faith in them persists.

The criteria employed to screen product ideas may be viewed as barriers to the implementation of a research project, for an idea will be difficult to implement when perceived to be inconsistent with these criteria. The following barriers to the development and ultimate commercialization of new product ideas may be derived from the materials provided in Table 3-4.

1. The company's major business direction and orientation
2. The firm's human resources
3. The firm's current marketing strategy
   a) similarity to and effect on present product lines
   b) suitability of present product lines
   c) suitability of present distribution system, and
   d) market ability to present customers
4. Financial objectives and requirements
   a) capital requirements
   b) net profit margins
   c) rate of return on investment
   d) growth potential
   e) cyclical and seasonal fluctuation
5. Technical feasibility
   a) likelihood of producing the good or developing the product
   b) acceptibility of estimated R&D time frame
   c) anticipated R&D expenditure

It is also important to determine at this stage whether

adequate supplies of raw materials will be available in sufficient quantity to make the idea economically feasible. According to Gordon Canning, Jr., Vice-President at the New York consulting firm of William E. Hill and Company, one of the first things they now do "is to pinpoint what raw materials a product needs and determine whether we can get them now, five years from now and at what price" ("The Two Way Squeeze on New Products," *Business Week,* 1974 p. 30).

In summary, screeners rate an idea on a number of factors, and these ratings determine whether the idea will be dropped or advanced to the next stage in the process. An idea which is consistent with the firm's major business direction and orientation will be more readily accepted than an idea which is inconsistent with this direction and orientation. An idea which can be marketed in the same way to the same markets is more likely to be accepted than one which requires new marketing techniques to reach new markets. An idea which requires little capital investment and minimal developmental costs and which is likely to yield substantial net profit is more likely to be accepted than an idea which does not have these characteristics.

Concept Development and Testing

Those ideas which survive the screening phase of the innovation process are subjected to further development into specific product concepts. A product concept may be viewed as the total meaning of the product, the perception or image that the company wishes to develop from its idea. Thus, it is a much more specific and complete version of the comparatively nebulous idea which initiated the innovation process. For example, the development of a two-seated sports car may be an acceptable idea for the Ford Motor Company to pursue. In the concept development and testing stage, this idea is given further meaning. The company must decide specifically for whom the car is to be designed (i.e., they must identify the market for the car). They must determine the major unique benefits or combination of benefits which the product is to provide. The combination of benefits which is appropriate follows directly from the desires of the market. These decisions about the market and the product should lead to a fairly complete, specific concept which places the firm's product uniquely in the market.

A number of techniques have been employed to assist in the development of product concepts. Multidimensional scaling has been used to determine how people perceive the products available to them (cf. Green and Wind, 1973; Klahr, 1970; Silk, 1969). This frequently points out "holes" in the market; that is, desired combinations of qualities which are not currently available. Other techniques such as conjoint measurement (cf. Edwards, 1957) have assisted marketers in determining product-attribute combinations of qualities likely to be desired by substantial numbers of consumers. In all cases, these techniques provide information about products from the point of view of potential customers and not from the point of view of the manufacturer. This is an important consideration, for it is the customers' perception of the products available to them that will ultimately determine their buying behavior regarding those products.

The product concept, or several alternative product concepts, are tested before further analytical and developmental resources are committed. In this testing process, a sample of consumers representing the market is given a complete description of the proposed product. Frequently, alternative product concepts and currently available products are pitted against one another to determine the relative merits of the new idea. Subjects are questioned to see whether they understand the product concept (i.e., to see whether their perception of the product matches the product concept), believe it satisfies their needs, and react favorably to it ("Market Testing Consumer Products," *The Conference Board*, 1967). Kotler (1976, p. 209) lists the following questions which should be answered by the concept test.

1. Is the concept clear and easy to understand?
2. Do you see some distinct benefits of this product over competing offerings?
3. Do you like this product better than that of its major competitors?
4. Would you buy this product?
5. Would this product meet a real need of yours?
6. What improvements can you suggest on various attributes of the product?

According to Arthur Pearson of Bristol-Myers:

> Although a concept test is undertaken primarily to determine
> whether or not the concept is worthwhile from a development
> point of view it should also help build the framework for our
> volume estimates and bench marks to be used later in evaluat-
> ing test market results. That is, the concept test should make
> possible a first rough forecast of the product's 'trial' or
> 'acquisition' curve, a curve showing the percentage of con-
> sumers who purchase it for the first time ("Market Testing
> Consumer Products," *The Conference Board,* 1967, p. 57).

The concept test, then, provides a vital check to determine
if the company's expectations about the product concept are
consistent with the reactions of the market. Beyond this, it
provides a check on the validity of the firm's beliefs about the
desires of the market. Usually, as a result of this testing,
further refinements are made in the product concept. The
output of this stage is a "blueprint" or detailed description
of the product which is to be produced in the development
stage of the innovation process. It also yields further information about the product's market potential which will be
used in the business analysis stage to provide estimates of
profitability.

Business Analysis

At this stage in the innovation process, the idea is subjected to a thorough business analysis. This analysis is carried
out to project future sales revenue, net profit, and rate of
return on investment for the proposed new product (Kotler,
1976). Although business analysis is identified as a distinct
stage in the innovation process, it should be noted that this
analysis will continue through the subsequent stages, and
forecasts will be revised as new information is accumulated.

A variety of analytical approaches has been suggested for
use at this stage of the innovation process. A number of
marketing scholars (Pessemier, 1966; Kotler, 1976) suggest
that firms begin by assessing the market potential of the
product idea. This may be accomplished by identifying each
group of potential customers for whom the product is to be

developed. The evaluators then complete a detailed set of price-volume estimates and outline the type of pricing, distribution, and promotional strategies which appear reasonable, given the market. For each group or market segment, an annual sales revenue is projected over a period of at least five years. This should lead to estimates of sales revenue per year derivable from the project as well as associated expenses. This information is included with projections of the cost of producing the good to yield estimates of net profit figures over a period of years. Given an estimate of the capital investment required for this project, the firm is able to estimate the rate of return on its investment.

In a recent survey involving ninety-six of the nation's largest manufacturing firms, the most frequent reason given for the deletion of product ideas was poor anticipated sales (Hise and McGinnis, 1975). The company responses describing the reasons for rejecting ideas are as follows:

Expected future sales volume	68%
Return on investment	56%
Future market potential	34%
Costs exceed revenues	29%
Excessive executive time	11%
Product malfunctioning	8%
Prior competitive entry	6%

In addition to factors mentioned here, payback is frequently given major consideration. Cash flows are related to the cost of the investment to determine the number of years required to recover the investment. General Motors, for instance, chooses those projects which seem to offer the best payback ("How GM Manages Its Billion-Dollar R&D Program," *Business Week*, 1976). Other firms reduce future cash flows to their present value by applying a discount rate that allows for risk and a desired return on investment.

Whatever decision criteria are employed in the analysis phase of the innovation process, the objective is to select projects on the basis of their projected profitability to the firm and to reject those projects which do not exhibit sufficient potential profit. Those projects which receive sufficiently favorable estimates are passed on to the development stage.

Development

Those product concepts which are successfully passed from the business analysis phase are developed into actual physical products in the development stage of the innovation process. As may be seen by reference to Figure 3-4, this stage generally occupies a considerably longer period of time than any other stage in the innovation process. Furthermore, the expenses incurred are much greater than those incurred in any of the preceding stages. It is, therefore, desirable to eliminate as many weak ideas as possible before beginning product development.

This portion of the innovation process may itself be broken down into a number of distinct steps. Patrick (1959) has identified the following sequence of activities.

1. *General Approach.* A means of accomplishing the task is set forth.
2. *Detailed Approach.* The general approach is broken down into individual parts for the purpose of assigning groups according to their area of speciality and responsibility.
3. *Experimental Program.* Design data is obtained from simple models.
4. *Preliminary Design.* A layout of the product with all the component parts is made.
5. *Stress Design.*
6. *Final Design.* Product appearance is given particular attention with respect to materials used, heat treatments, protective coatings, and decorations.
7. *Model Shop Work.* A crude working model, accurate to all functioning details, incorporates all the final design features.
8. *Model Testing.* A complete performance test is given.
9. *Prototype Design.* Changes dictated by model tests are incorporated into the prototype design.
10. *Prototype Fabrication.*
11. *Prototype Testing.*
12. *Production Design.*

13. *Release for Production.*
14. *Liaison with Production.*

At first, research and engineering efforts focus on the development of an initial rough prototype which will demontrate the product's feasibility and provide the firm with a basis for making more accurate forecasts of total development costs. The time required for this work varies considerably with the magnitude of technological change required. Some products may proceed through this phase of the development process in less than a year's time. Other projects, such as the development of a new automobile engine, may require ten or more years and the expenditure of over $20 million (Jet Propulsion Laboratory, 1975).

At Westinghouse, a "breadboard" is defined as "a model constructed to demonstrate the feasibility of a new principle" (Herwald, 1972). This model provides the firm with a basis for making more accurate forecasts of total development costs. As a result, the cost of developing the breadboard becomes a major determinant of whether or not the project will be continued. On the basis of their past experience, Westinghouse has found that the prototype development cost will range anywhere from five to ten times the cost of the breadboard model. Furthermore, full scale production models cost from ten to one hundred times the breadboard model. If these figures yield estimates of total development costs which are significantly above those initially projected for the project, they will clearly impact on the profitability projected for the new product idea. They may, in fact, result in the project's discontinuance.

After the satisfactory completion of the breadboard model, work begins on the development of a full-scale preproduction prototype, representing the company's idea of the product as it will be produced. This phase may cost from two to seven times the cost of the preceding step and may vary in duration from a few months to five or more years.[3]

The product is subjected to repeated evaluations as it progresses through these developmental stages. Cost estimates are revised as new information becomes available. This data is employed to readjust estimates of the product's profit potential. Product testing is conducted to insure that the product meets performance, manufacturability, durability, and serviceability criteria. Customer reactions to the developing product are solicited in order to provide information on ways the product may be changed to provide a better fit with market desires. The results of this evaluation and testing determine whether development should be continued or revised. Typically, refinements and other changes are made on the basis of these tests.

The sequence of activities involved in product development and the changes resulting from testing are illustrated by R. G. Hennessey of Fairchild Camera and Instrument Corporation. The firm was in the process of developing a plastic film cartridge to facilitate the handling of educational film. The cartridge was to be used in 8-mm film projectors designed to accommodate the encapsulated film load. Hennessey articulated the development of this product.

> At this stage the task-force setup included primarily research and development capabilities. The breadboarding investigation then concentrated on feasibility of the fully automatic technique within broad parameters already determined by the preliminary market survey. For example, it was not sufficient that the machine merely permit automatic loading of film contained in a cartridge. Realizing that the individual cartridge must be reasonably priced, we required in addition that it be nothing more than a plastic shell containing no mechanism. Moreover, a five-year old must be able to handle it with safety and ease.

> By the spring of 1962, feasibility on a breadboard basis had been demonstrated, and by summer of the same year a working model in prototype form was being shown to many of the same educators who had been contacted in the initial survey. This phase made use of the existing machine on a combined laboratory testing and demonstration schedule. It might, for example, spend two days on the road and four days in the lab, since it served as the springboard to the next generation and both performance and utility could be investigated only by this dual evaluation process. There was very little exposure of R&D personnel to potential users except through survey reports. This was not a philosophical decision but was made necessary by the fact that the engineering personnel were preoccupied with the second-generation unit.

The features and characteristics of the new unit were affected as much by comments from the field as by laboratory engineering testing. By the fall of 1962 the initial prototype was replaced in the field survey by the second model, and it was then reworked to reflect a third-generation design. Feedback continued and the design was again reworked, so that by the end of the year we had actually a fourth generation suitable for freezing of the development phase. So significantly different were all these versions of the machine that the final model was designated as Mark IV and will continue to bear this name in its production form (Marting, 1964, p. 257).

In addition to the actual development of the physical product, several other simultaneous activities should be taking place. Packaging and branding will be determined at this stage. A complete marketing plan will also be produced prior to the conclusion of this stage. The plan will provide a specification of how to price, promote, and distribute the product. At the conclusion of the development stage, the firm will have in its possession a complete physical product and a plan of action specifying how the product will be marketed.

As noted earlier, business analysis continues to play a major role throughout development. Frequently, cost estimates, which were used in pricing and profitability assessment, must be revised as a result of the further information made available. Forecasts are revised in accordance with the additional information provided by developmental experiences. These revised forecasts provide the basis for deciding whether to continue with development or to drop the project.

Market research is conducted during this stage in order to accomplish several goals. First of all, product tests are conducted to determine how the prototype is perceived by the potential customers for whom the product is being designed. The output of this research will guide technicians in the actual development of the physical product and enhance the likelihood that this work will remain consistent with the desires of the market. Second, research is conducted to determine which brand name is most consistent with the characteristics of the product and the image the firm wishes to project. Third, research is frequently conducted to assess the market's reaction to the package which will contain the product. Fourth, if advertising is to play a role in the planned promotional program, proposed advertisements are pretested. Fifth, research may be conducted in order to obtain reactions to and test effects of the proposed pricing strategy.

A number of factors are related to the successful passage of a project through this stage in the innovation process. The clarity of the initial specification of the characteristics desired in the product and their conformity to market desires are crucial determinants of the project's success. The more clearly the product is specified and the more consistent this specification is with market desires, the more likely it will be successful.

Projects which can be accomplished by applications of known technology are more likely to be developed successfully than projects which require technological breakthroughs during development. Due to the added uncertainty regarding the latter requirement, such projects have more risk associated with them. As a result, they are more likely to be dropped prior to development unless the added profit potential offsets the negative effects of the added risk involved in development. This is one of the reasons most new products tend to be minor innovations.

Effective management of the development stage requires that facilities, manpower, and capital requirements be planned in advance and provided as they are needed. The product's durability, manufacturability, and technical performance characteristics must be continuously monitored and evaluated according to previously determined objectives. A continuing assessment of the developing product's cost, market potential, and profitability must be planned in advance and carried out.

These and numerous other activities required during development require contributions from many individuals with widely varying backgrounds. Engineering requirements, market demands, and their financial implications are primary determinants of project success. Expertise must be contributed from each of these areas. Furthermore, these contributions must be coordinated and integrated into a cohesive product and associated marketing plan. This calls for establishing multidisciplinary development groups to bring together expertise from engineering, finance, marketing, and production (cf. Hill and Hlavacek, 1972).

Testing

By the time a project enters the testing stage, the product has been fully developed and an action plan is available specifying how that product is to be marketed. The product and its associated marketing strategy then undergo a period of testing designed to provide a final check on the project's potential profitability.

The thoroughness and duration of this testing vary considerably depending on the product and market characteristics under consideration. The most complete test of a product's potential is provided by what is called "test marketing." It involves the actual full-scale introduction of the product in a small number of isolated markets which reflect the makeup of the ultimate market for the product. In each of these markets, the product is distributed, promoted, and priced in accordance with the previously formulated marketing plan. Customer response is assessed by examining company sales figures and by marketing audits of sales at the wholesale and retail levels. Market surveys are employed to obtain more complete information regarding the effects of the promotional program and the characteristics of the product. This data permits the company to project the product's sales revenue and rate of return from actual market experience. It also gives further insight into possible product and marketing shortcomings. This enables the firm to take corrective action or scrap the project altogether prior to full-scale introduction.

Not all companies engage in full-scale test marketing before commercialization. Test marketing is an extremely costly procedure and represents a time commitment varying from less than six months to more than two years. In addition to the large required test market expenditure, the required time delay can represent a substantial cost in terms of lost opportunity for sales which would otherwise be generated. The delay also gives competitors an opportunity to introduce nationally a similar product before the innovating company's product is out of the test market. The extreme cost of test marketing and the added delay involved have led many companies to substitute a simulated test market for the more time-consuming and costly procedure of the test market. In the simulated test market, the purchase situation is reproduced within the confines of the laboratory, and the researcher assesses customer reactions to the alternative products available to them. Subjects are exposed to promotional materials similar to those planned for use during full-scale product introduction. Yankelovich claims that his simulations cut 85 percent of the test market time and 95 percent of the cost ("Marketing Observer," *Business Week,* 1974). He indicates that he is able to produce a 95 percent accuracy rate on market shares of products later introduced.

Other firms omit test marketing altogether, but rely instead on a detailed assessment of customer reaction to the product. Samples of potential customers are given the product and asked to try it out. After having used the product, these potential customers are asked to assess its strengths and weaknesses relative to other similar products. These product use tests provide further information about the product's merits, and the results are used to predict future sales volume. However, they do not address the nonproduct aspects of the proposed marketing strategy. As a result, the eventual market acceptance remains more uncertain than it would if a market test were actually conducted.

Test marketing is rarely conducted for major industrial products. Here, the markets are much smaller, and frequently the potential customers comprising a market are known to the company. As a result, the final testing takes on a more informal posture. Frequently, salesmen or other company representatives try the product out on a number of prospective buyers. The feedback they receive determines whether the company will proceed to market the product, drop it, or revise it.

It is common in industrial marketing for a few potential customers to work closely with the innovating firm as a product idea is being developed. They are able to provide valuable input which will ensure that the developing product is consistent with their needs. Potential customers are often willing and anxious to try the new product under actual operating conditions. The feedback they provide determines whether the company will move immediately to commercialize the product or make further design changes and seek a reappraisal.

This approach to new product development should make product failure less likely. The close working relationship between customer and producer ensures that a close fit will be obtained between market desires and product characteristics. Customers who have played a major role in determining the characteristics of the developed product would feel some degree of commitment to purchase the product. Furthermore, they are much more familiar with the product and its benefits than they would ever be if exposed to the product for the first time at introduction. For these reasons, they would be the first to adopt the product. Their experience can then be used to reduce the risk for other adopters.

In summary, the crucial objective of the testing stage is to provide a final, more precise check of the product's marketability. The demand for the product is assessed, either through test marketing or a more limited testing procedure. This permits a further revision of the sales potential and profitability estimates initially made in the business analysis stage. Those products which perform satisfactorily are commercialized. In many cases, testing reveals weaknesses that can be easily corrected prior to commercialization. The result is a more predictable and successful product introduction.

Commercialization

This final stage in the innovation process concentrates on last preparations for and introduction of the product. This stage continues until the project is a going commercial success accepted into the established organizational structure and requires finalizing the product and the marketing plan. This last stage includes the company's investment in whatever fixed plant and equipment are required to produce the good in the required volume. The company must commit substantial resources to training and motivating its own sales force as well as the sales forces of whatever middlemen it will utilize in the distribution of the product.

A critical task during this stage is obtaining an adequate supply of raw materials. The introduction of Glamorene

Products Corporation's new product "Drain Power" was held up for several months due to lack of chlorinated fluorocarbons ("The Two Way Squeeze on New Products," *Business Week*, 1974). Potential supply problems should be pinpointed in the innovation process and taken into consideration as an added risk factor. However, at this stage the company should have firm access to sufficient quantities of scarce materials to satisfy the demand anticipated after introduction.

Production capacity for the new product must be fully developed to enable the firm to supply its distributors with sufficient quantities of the product to satisfy the expected demand. When other goods (or other new goods) are consumed in conjunction with the use of the new product, these goods also must be available in adequate quantities. When Kodak was unable to supply the film packages which were to be used in their instant color photograph cameras (models EK4 and EK6), retailers withheld the cameras from sale until adequate supplies of film were forthcoming ("Slow Deliveries Dog the Kodak Instant," *Business Week*, 1976).

Products have been described as proceeding through life cycles beginning with the stage of introduction (e.g., Wasson, 1971). Here, the objective is to develop widespread awareness of the product's benefits and obtain the initial trial by those who will be the first to adopt the product. The promotional program is designed to provide this awareness. Marketing expenses at this stage are at a very high level in order to move the product as quickly as possible into a period of rapid, sustained growth. In the food industry, marketing expenditures averaged from 40 to 50 percent of sales during the first year of distribution (Buzzell and Nourse, 1967).

New products are generally not initially introduced nationwide. Most companies usually begin in key (large metropolitan) markets and spread out gradually as the product's growth and firm's resources warrant. For instance, Proctor and Gamble extends distribution outward from test markets as production capacity becomes available until, after six months or a year, distribution is nationwide (Vanderwicken, 1974).

Innovators and Adopters

Throughout the preceding sections of this chapter, we

have focused on the workings of the innovation process. There are two additional aspects of innovation. First of all, the distinguishing characteristics of firms having the strongest commitment to innovation will be considered. These firms would be most receptive to innovation contributions by governmental agencies. Furthermore, if we can identify the characteristics most compatible with innovating firms, the fostering of these characteristics may lead to greater emphasis on innovation in the private sector and a higher rate of technological progress.

A second aspect concerns determining the rate at which an innovation is adopted by its market. Innovations vary in the length of time required for them to be diffused through the market. The identification of those factors leading to rapid diffusion should provide insight into characteristics of innovation likely to expedite the adoption process. The earlier consideration of these characteristics should lead to more rapid diffusion of innovations.

Innovating Firms

There has long been concern with characteristics most conducive to innovation. Among the more well-known positions regarding the relationship between innovation and market structure is Schumpeter's (1950) contention that there is a direct relationship between market concentration and innovation expenditure. According to this view, firms with monopoly power have excess profits available with which to innovate and are forced to innovate in order to maintain or enhance their present position. A related position is taken by Galbraith (1952) who maintains that bigness per se is necessary for innovation to occur. He maintains that the large sums required to innovate are available only to the very large firms.

Despite the notoriety of these contentions, there is little evidence to support the conclusion that greater concentration and size lead to greater emphasis on innovation. In fact, the evidence indicates that increasing concentration beyond some threshold level (varying by industry) fails to increase the emphasis placed on innovation and probably acts to reduce it.[4] Worley (1961) noted a tendency for research and development intensity to rise and then fall as firm size increases. Williamson (1965) found that as the industry concentration ratio exceeds 30 to 50 percent, the four largest firms account for less than their share of research and development. Kamien and Schwartz (1975) summarize the literature in this area. "The bulk of the evidence indicates that among firms engaged in R&D, relative effort tends to increase with size up to a point and then decline, with middle size firms devoting the most effort relative to their size" (p. 3).[5]

If we turn to the effectiveness of R&D, it appears that small- to medium-sized firms have more efficient R&D programs than larger firms (Kamien and Schwartz, 1975). This is clearly pointed out in Comanor's (1965) study of the pharmaceutical industry. Mansfield (1968) found, similarly, that R&D spending per innovation was lower in small- and medium-sized firms than in large firms.

It appears, then, that the relationship between firm size and innovation is a nonmonotonic one. Innovation effort increases with firm size up to a point which varies from industry to industry. With increasing size beyond this point, innovation expenditure relative to firm size either fails to increase or declines. This would indicate that the firms which may be most receptive to governmental R&D input may be the medium-sized firms in the concerned industries. Yet, if smaller firms are not making innovations relative to their size because of lack of resources, then these firms may be most receptive to governmental input tied to financial assistance. This concentration on smaller firms would be beneficial in view of the evidence indicating that these firms may be more efficient users of R&D money. Furthermore, the provision of more money to these firms rather than to larger firms would seem likely to increase competition rather than enhance concentration. These conclusions, although highly tentative, are interesting in view of evidence indicating that past governmental research support has tended to concentrate on larger firms.[6]

Diffusion of Innovations

The rate of adopting innovations, when plotted as a

function of time, takes the form of a normal curve. As a result, when the cumulative rate of adoption is plotted against time, the resulting curve takes the form of an ogive (see Figure 3-5). Mansfield (1968) found this pattern in his study of diffusion rates in the bituminous coal, iron and steel, brewing, and railroad industries. Griliches (1957) found a similar pattern in his study of the adoption of hybrid corn.

The time required for an innovation to diffuse throughout an industry tends to vary considerably. The modal pattern found by Mansfield (1968) was that 20 years or more elapsed before an innovation was adopted by all the major firms in the industry. He found, however, cases where innovations were adopted by all the major firms in less than ten years. Such variation across innovations leads naturally to questions about conditions which determine the period of time required for diffusion of the innovation.

A number of factors may affect the speed with which an innovation will diffuse through an industry. These factors may be grouped into three broad categories: (1) the structure of the industry; (2) the characteristics of the innovation; (3) the nature of the social and economic environment.

First, with regard to industry characteristics, a nonmonotonic relationship may be anticipated between the concentration and speed with which an innovation diffuses through that industry. Mansfield (1973) found that the effect of concentration is frequently not significant; but when it is, beyond a threshold level, less concentration is preferable to more concentration. "Although a certain amount of concentration probably promotes the rapid use of new technology, increases in concentration beyond a moderate level probably do more harm than good" (Mansfield, 1973, p. 204).

A number of factors are operating simultaneously. On the one hand, sufficient resources must be available to permit adoption of innovations (especially capital-intensive innovations); this favors some degree of concentration. Romeo (1975) pointed out that one of the reasons large firms may adopt innovations more rapidly than small firms is that large firms have greater resources available. Communication networks are probably better developed among firms in concentrated industries, a factor which directly relates to

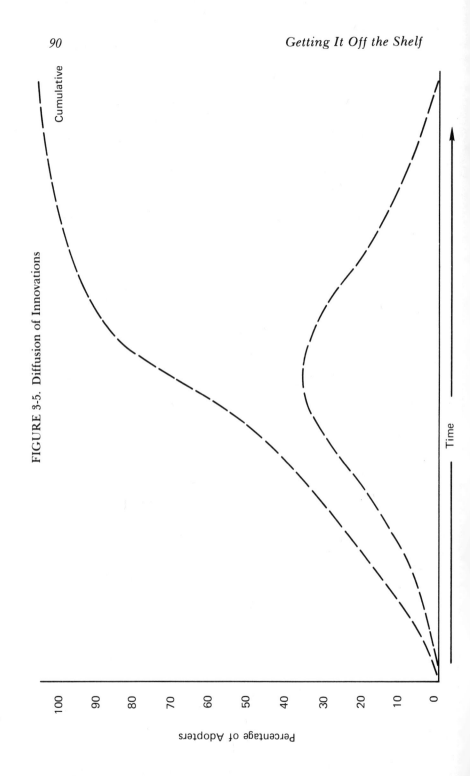

FIGURE 3-5. Diffusion of Innovations

diffusion speed (Czepiel, 1974). On the other hand, more competitive (and hence less concentrated) industries seem to have greater incentive to innovate in order to beat or maintain competitive parity with other firms in the industry; this favors less concentrated industries.

The characteristics of a product are the most direct determinants of the diffusion rate. One of the findings has been that innovations which will have a strongly favorable effect on profitability will diffuse more rapidly than innovations which have only a weakly favorable effect on profitability (Parker, 1974; Mansfield, 1968). If average profitability is held constant, the rate of diffusion tends to decrease as the variance in profitability increases (Mansfield, 1973). Innovations which require only a small investment diffuse throughout an industry more rapidly than innovations which require a large investment—given the advantage inherent in the innovation (Mansfield, 1973).

These findings, although obtained primarily from research on process innovations, are consistent with the preceding sections of this chapter. People are motivated to attain their goals whether the goals relate to profitability or more personal strivings. Clearly, a major goal of business is to receive a high rate of return on its investment. It is not surprising, therefore, to find a direct relationship between the rate of return from an innovation and the rate that innovation diffuses through its market. Similarly, it is not surprising to find an inverse relationship between profitability variance and fast rate of diffusion. Variation in profit provides a measure of the certainty with which an adopter can anticipate a high profit from the innovation. However, the rate of diffusion will be directly related to the magnitude of the reward derivable from the innovation and the certainty that adoption will lead to this high reward.

Environmental factors will also affect the rate of diffusion; the most important are probably economic and social. Social factors are defined as the orientation and disposition of society and social groups within the society. Innovations which are inconsistent with the beliefs and desires of social groups or require or imply large social change will be resisted more strongly than innovations which are consistent with the beliefs or desires of social groups or require or imply only little social change (Graham, 1956). If an innovation poses, or is perceived as posing a direct threat to a group within or related to the innovating industry, the proposed change will be resisted. This happened in the 1950s when many work groups feared their jobs, work-related satisfactions or both, were being threatened by automation (Philipson, 1962). Yet, the active support of involved social groups will hasten the rate of adoption (Blackman, 1974). These groups can generate public interest in the innovation by disseminating information about the benefits of the good or service. They can also use political pressure to facilitate the passing of favorable legislation.

Economic conditions will affect readiness to purchase the product, especially new durable goods and industrial goods requiring substantial investment. These goods would be expected to be responsive to economic conditions. Mansfield points out that most applications of new techniques do not occur at the peaks or troughs of the business cycle; applications are most frequent when firms are operating at 75 percent of capacity (Mansfield, 1973).

Although we have provided an exhaustive review of the literature, we have presented some factors which affect the diffusion rate of an innovation, as well as characteristics and conditions affecting the market's readiness to adopt a new innovation.

Barriers to Implementation

Throughout the preceding sections of this chapter, decision criteria and project/market characteristics were identified which are important determinants of new product success. If projects depart from "desirable" or "optimal" criteria, then the likelihood of these projects being successfully introduced is diminished. These inconsistencies with or departures from desirable characteristics are barriers to implementation which must be overcome in order to successfully introduce a new product. Next, we define more explicitly these barriers and the avoidance of these barriers.

It is in the interest of the innovating firm to introduce products with as few barriers to implementation as possible. The determinants of project success can be included as decision criteria and employed as early in the decision-making process as possible. Thus, the firm can screen out, prior to incurring massive developmental costs, those projects unlikely to succeed. It can also design into the product those features which will make success most likely.[7]

The barriers may be divided into several categories: market, organizational, technical, and environmental.

Market Barriers

Market barriers stem from and are directly related to the innovation's potential customers. Any idea is generated for a set of actual or potential customers, whether or not these customers are explicitly identified. If the idea is to be developed and successfully implemented, then large numbers of customers must exhibit a strong interest and ultimately buy the product. As a result, the factors which underlie and determine purchase become important considerations to study before committing resources to the actual development and probable commercialization of the product.

As emphasized before, a product idea to be successful must be capable of satisfying needs of potential customers. That is, the proposed product must permit potential customers to realize their goals and grant value to it. This goal attainment potential and the value derived from it must be perceived by the customers for whom the product is designed; it is not sufficient for the value to be clear to some third party who believes that the potential customers need the proposed product. Furthermore, this demonstrated value must be high not only in an absolute sense, but be high relative to the competitive offerings already on the market.

Several conclusions about the desired characteristics of a project likely to be successful follow.

- *Market identity*. The market must be identifiable.
- *Market size*. The market must be sufficiently substantial to make innovation economically feasible.
- *Contribution to goal attainment*. The product must stimulate its potential market so that the market identifies the product as one that satisfies its needs.
- *Price*. It must be possible to price the product at a level which will yield incremental value over current offer-

ings.

- *Communications.* The potential product's benefits must be readily communicable to the market.
- *Value.* The market must see the product as offering incremental value over and above competitive offerings.
- *Intention.* The market must intend to buy the product at its projected price in sufficient numbers to warrant development.

Considerable attention is devoted to these criteria throughout the innovation process. Initially, an idea will be formulated to help satisfy a need or attain some goal presumed to be important to an identifiable market. This idea is given further consideration in the screening process. During concept development and testing, the idea is developed into a concept designed to provide certain attractive characteristics to give it a competitive advantage. The concept is tested by its actual presentation to a sample of the market. In the analysis stage, estimates of market potential and market share are directly dependent on the extent to which the product is perceived as offering incremental value. These estimates along with behavioral intention are checked repeatedly through the development, testing, and commercialization stages.

To the extent that projects depart from standards set for these criteria, implementation will be difficult. These departures represent barriers which the project must surmount in order to generate sufficient demand for a satisfactory or higher return.

The consistency of the proposed idea with the firm's current marketing programs provides the framework for a second set of market-oriented barriers. Knowledge about the desires and habits of a market and about how and where to effectively communicate and distribute to that market is not quickly gained. As a result, innovations directed at the same or similar markets to those in which the company is already operating are preferred over innovations which are inconsistent or different from the firm's current products and are to be promoted and distributed in different ways. The criteria may be summarized as follows.

- Consistency with current markets
- Compatibility with current product mix

- Similarity of promotional demands with current promotional strategy
- Similarity of distribution system with current distribution strategy

These considerations also have financial and technical implications. If an innovation calls for new promotional and distribution strategies and for knowledge of other markets, it requires the input of additional resources in both manpower and developmental costs. Furthermore, lack of knowledge about the market means that the risk is higher and projected earnings will, as a result, be discounted at a higher rate. These requirements all represent barriers to the implementation of innovations directed at new and different markets.

Financial Barriers

Financial barriers are treated in the screening stage where ideas are checked to determine their suitability with regard to company resources, net profit margins, return on investment, growth, potential, and susceptibility to cyclical or seasonal fluctuations. During the analysis stage, when the continued viability of the project is contingent on the projected return to be derived from the idea, financial barriers become more critical.

The following financial considerations arise in the screening and analysis stages.

- Market potential
- Company resource limits
- Available marketing expenditures
- Market share
- Net profit requirements
- Growth potential
- Susceptibility to seasonal and/or cyclical fluctuation
- Fixed investment requirements
- Cash flow requirements
- Development cost limits
- Return on investment
- Payback period

These barriers remain critical through the duration of the project. As a project progresses through development and testing, changes in standing on these financial criteria determine whether the product will be dropped during the later stages or proceed through the innovation process. Ultimately, these revisions determine whether the product is removed from the market during or after a full-scale introduction.

Organizational Barriers

Organizational considerations include the company's goals, objectives, and orientation. Also included are structural factors affecting the interrelationships among various functional units in the organization. These structural factors ultimately affect readiness to innovate and carry ideas smoothly through the innovation process.

Major innovations will almost invariably bring about changes within the company which will be resisted by some and welcomed by others. These changes result from the redistribution of power within the firm.

Among criteria which may be included here are:

- Company goals and objectives
- Company reputation
- Organizational structure
- Morale
- Power distribution
- Threat of change

Company goals, objectives, and image/reputation guide the firm in setting priorities and allocating resources. If a project departs from or is inconsistent with these orientations, then it may be confronted with a substantial barrier to implementation. Projects viewed as inconsistent with company directions are screened out early in the innovation process. Thus, an outside agency seeking private sector implementation of its idea should choose companies whose orientations are compatible with the idea under consideration.

Organizational arrangements for managing and carrying out the innovation process are crucial to its success. As noted earlier, top management control or authority over the project is necessary to facilitate the interdepartmental cooperation group flexibility required to achieve project success. Successful innovation requires the expertise of people from engineering, finance, marketing, and production. This calls for establishing a multidisciplinary group to guide a project through the innovation process to successful commercialization. This team approach permits the firm to bring together and profit from the necessary contributions from many individuals with different backgrounds and interests and increases the possibility of a balanced approach incorporating marketing and engineering considerations. As pointed out by Freeman (1973), this balanced approach is more likely to lead to success than an approach concentrating on one aspect of innovation to the exclusion of the others.

Environmental Barriers

Environmental considerations are being used as a repository for uncontrollable external factors such as economic conditions, legal and political environment, current social conditions, and raw material availability. Although the firm has no control over these factors, it must operate within the confines of the constraints imposed by them.

Favorable economic conditions, such as an expanding economy, make the commitment of resources to innovation more likely than unfavorable economic conditions. Similarly, economic conditions affect the rate of adoption following commercialization. Unlike other criteria considered here, this criterion is not project-specific. Unfavorable economic conditions will present a potential barrier to all projects.

External resistance to the firm is generated by special interest groups and members of the firm's distribution system. Social groups who view the innovation as a threat will apply pressure to slow or stop the innovation. Members of the firm's distribution system will resist adding a new product to their already overextended lines. These forms of external resistance represent barriers to be anticipated and minimized or removed in order to maintain a smooth progression through the innovation process and a rapid diffusion through the market.

Social barriers are closely related to legal and political

barriers, for it is frequently through the political process that social groups seek protection. Legal action resulting from this political pressure can adversely affect the readiness of the firm to innovate and the ease with which diffusion follows innovation.

The availability of raw materials and supplies frequently plays a major role in determining project success. As noted earlier, formal consideration is increasingly being given to resource availability during initial screening. If the availability of raw materials and supplies necessary for full-scale production is uncertain, then the likelihood of project success is diminished.

The barriers considered here follow from the preceding sections of this chapter, but are not the only barriers which could be derived. An adaptation of a list developed by Farmer and Richman (1968) includes additional barriers that merit consideration (see Table 3-5). Barriers are divided into two major categories: internal barriers to the firm (endogenous) and barriers which originate externally (exogenous). While many constraints, such as growth potential and purchasing power, have been treated earlier, other more general influences are presented which play a role in determining the ease with which a firm can carry out innovation within its organization.

Implications for Public Sector Innovation

Implications for public sector innovation may be derived from assessing the private sector's innovation process. Although these and other implications will be developed in more detail in a subsequent chapter, some of them will be briefly presented in the following paragraphs.

The description of the innovation process contained in the preceding sections contributes to an understanding of business concerns and interests regarding the activation of programs and the commitment of funds to innovation. If governmental agencies hope to successfully motivate businesses to voluntarily implement projects initiated in the public sector, then the concerned public agencies must appeal directly to the forces guiding business innovation decision making. In other words, they must "sell" the

TABLE 3-5

General Barriers to Implementation

External Constraints -- Exogenous Barriers	Internal Constraints -- Endogenous Barriers

A. Economic
  1. General framework: organization, form, structure
  2. Financial structure and standing: monetary/fiscal
  3. Stability: flexibility, growth potential
  4. Organization of capital structure of markets
  5. Market size: purchasing power
  6. Factor endowment: land, labor, capital
  7. Social overhead capital: power resources, water communication network, transportation, housing, etc.
 	
B. Social and Attitudinal
  1. View toward managers and management
  2. View toward authority and subordinates
  3. Interorganizational cooperation
  4. View toward achievement and work
  5. Class structure and individual mobility
  6. View toward wealth and material gain
  7. View toward rational, predictive methodologies
  8. View toward risk taking
  9. View toward change
 	
C. Legal-Political
  1. Relevant legal rules of the game, degree of enforcement, reliability, etc.
  2. Defense policy: anti-trust competition, fair-trade, patents licensing. etc.
  3. Political stability
  4. Political organization: philosophies, pressure groups, bureaucratic extent, etc.
  5. Flexibility of law and legal changes: predictability and certainty.
 	
D. Educational
  1. Educational level
  2. Special management development program
  3. Attitude toward education: training, etc.
  4. Education match with requirements
 	
E. Technological
  1. Complexity
  2. Support elements necessary: maintenance, repair parts, etc.
  3. Compatibility with existing system: timing, product similarities, etc.
	A. Financial
	  1. Debt structure
	  2. Venture capital limitations
	  3. Prior commitments to other projects
	  4. Credit standing (Moody index, Dun & Bradstreet rating)
	  5. Stockholder dividends
	
	B. Organizational
	  1. Size of organization
	  2. Form or structure of the organization
	  3. Functions and roles not clearly defined
	  4. Bureaucratic inertia and biases
	  5. Resistance to change
	  6. Flexibility of structure to external pressures and demands
	  7. Organizational slack
	  8. View toward authority
	  9. Internal motivation devices
	  10. Technostructure (a la Galbraith New Industrial State)
	  11. Communication patterns and links
	  12. Chain of command (explicit/implicit)
	  13. Managerial impediments
	  14. Organizational efficiency, efficacy and adaptability.
	
	C. Educational
	  1. Level of education of employees
	  2. Educational programs available
	  3. Training programs
	  4. Learning curve characteristics
	
	D. Technical
	  1. Age of production equipment (obsolescence, failure, etc.)
	  2. Complexity of manufactured product
	  3. Materials involved may require special handling (toxic, etc.)
	  4. Requirements for safety regulations
	
	E. Managerial
	  1. Planning and innovation of objectives and goals
	  2. Control of operations
	  3. Organization and activities
	  4. Staffing and personnel
	  5. Direction, leadership, and motivational considerations
	  6. Marketing policies pursued
	  7. Production and procurement
	  8. Public and external relations

Source: Farmer and Richman (1968)

program by appealing to the interests and motivations guiding the individuals in charge of the firm's innovation function. The same criteria that are stressed in business project decision making should be considered when seeking business support.

The key motivator of business action is project profitability. If the public agency can show profit potential exists and that profit can be realized by the implementing firm, then the agency will obtain the ready cooperation and support of business. Favorable profit projections, then, are a powerful stimulus which can and should be used to motivate business action.

The voluntary private sector implementation of public sector projects may be obtained most readily by initially designing a favorable profit potential into these projects by maximizing the connection between project characteristics and market demand. Early assessment of the market will provide information necessary to achieve this connection and evidence to support the availability of a ready demand for the proposed good or service.

Technical R&D and production expertise is then required to show that the product is feasible and to provide estimates of developmental and final production costs along with estimates of required incremental investment. This material, in conjunction with information about market demand, should permit estimates of return on investment realizable from the project's implementation. This evidence can be used to directly encourage private sector involvement, or it can be used by the public agency as a basis for committing funds for product development.

If profitability estimates are not sufficiently favorable, several alternative courses of action are open to the public agency. First, project changes could be made to enhance profitability estimates. These changes could be aimed at increasing product benefits and perceived value(s) associated with the project concepts or aimed at reducing projected costs by (1) eliminating or reducing extraneous or marginally beneficial characteristics or (2) developing and planning more economical production processes. Proposed changes could attack simultaneously both determinants of profitability. Whichever approach is taken should result in an improvement in the proposed return derivable from the innovation by directly varying the characteristics of the project.

A second, less direct alternative is available. A public agency could provide financial assistance to alter a project's financial implications, directly supporting some aspect(s) of the proposed project. For instance, the agency could fund a part of the firm's developmental efforts. Alternatively, the agency could absorb risk by guaranteeing the return of development costs or the realization of some minimal rate of return on the firm's investment in the innovation. However, the type of financial assistance provided must increase the firm's profit projections, or the effort will not be successful.

A third, more coercive alternative would be to encourage legislation to force use of the proposed product. The effects of mandatory seat belt installation in automobiles testifies to the power of this type of alternative in achieving the adoption (but not necessarily the use) of innovations. While this alternative may, at certain times, be required and should be maintained as an option, it could be sought too often as a way of surmounting barriers to implementation; it should not be permitted as a substitute for use of an innovation strategy designed to achieve the voluntary adoption of innovations.

A final alternative which is always available is, of course, to drop the project. Although preceding paragraphs illustrate the seeking of private sector implementation prior to development, the principles equally apply to the seeking of private sector implementation after development. If the public agency hopes to achieve voluntary private sector support, it must appeal to and affect those factors guiding business decision making.

A major strategic implication of preceding sections of this chapter is that successful innovation requires a balanced effort that brings together the contributions or orientation of marketing experts and technical R&D experts. The literature repeatedly indicates that one-sided emphasis on marketing or on technical R&D reduces the likelihood that the innovation process will lead to a successfully commercialized product. Mansfield (1973) reached the conclusion on the basis of his study of technological innovation that "coupling of R&D, on the one hand, and marketing and production on the other, is of enormous importance" (p. 206).

One way to achieve balanced effort incorporating both marketing and technical R&D considerations is to establish multidisciplinary venture teams with members reflecting expertise in these areas. The venture team concept discussed earlier seems to be applicable to public agency research activities. Individuals from several disciplines are brought together to work on a project. After their services are no longer needed, they return to the work group with which they are normally associated. Successful innovation requires the coordinated contribution of many individuals with divergent backgrounds. A public sector adaptation of the venture team concept would provide a vehicle for smoothly carrying out this multidisciplinary effort.

There is an additional implication of the preceding sections; physical product development takes place relatively late in the innovation process. Preliminary market and technical screening and project analysis represent smaller expenditures than would be required to develop the product. They provide estimates of a project's success prior to the larger magnitude of resource commitment required during development. As a result, the firm can revise or drop projects with serious weaknesses *prior* to the commitment of development resources, so that developed projects will be successful and the resources expended for ultimately unsuccessful projects will be reduced. This procedure would seem applicable to research in the public sector; the market and technical factors affecting implementation by the private sector could be assessed before committing funds to development. The agency would thus provide developmental funding to only those projects likely to be successful. Yet, the assessment would provide further insight into the form that the developing product should take and in this way would make costly postdevelopment revisions less likely.

Several implications follow from innovation in the private sector. However, there are fundamental differences between private and public sectors. They do not have the same function, continuous goals, or capabilities and do not (and cannot) act exactly the same. The conclusions of this chapter apply to the public sector only if there is convergence between the goals of public policy and private profit.

Notes

1. Also reported are findings by Griliches, Terleckyj, and Mansfield which are in substantial agreement with this estimate.
2. R&D spending by the private sector rose from 2.0 percent of net sales in 1964 to 2.2 percent in 1970 and declined back to 2.0 percent in 1973.
3. The development of the Otto engine preproduction prototype took about five years to complete (Jet Propulsion Laboratory, 1975).
4. There is some evidence to indicate that in industries

which are capital-intensive the threshold is higher than in industries which are not capital-intensive (Kamien and Schwartz, 1975).

5. Effort is measured in terms of R&D expenditures. There is a strong direct relationship between R&D spending and innovational output (Kamien and Schwartz, 1975).

6. "Of the $8.2 billion federal R&D total in 1973, 83 percent went to companies of 25,000 or more employees. These same firms represented two-thirds of company R&D funds. . . . Over three-fourths of all industrial research and development in 1973 was performed by the 100 companies with the largest R&D programs. These same companies accounted for 93 percent of federal support and 71 percent of company-financed R&D activity" *(Research and Development in Industry 1973,* 1975, pp. 3 and 6).

7. Success means the realization of a satisfactory rate of return on an industry's investment in the products. There are other criteria for success applicable to the public sector.

Bibiliography

Angelus, T.L. "Why Do Most New Products Fail?" *Advertising Age,* 24 March 1969, pp. 85-86.

Blackman, A.W. "The Market Dynamics of Technological Substitution." *Technological Forecasting and Social Change,* Vol. 6, 1974.

Booz, Allen and Hamilton. "Management of New Products." Booz, Allen and Hamilton, Management Consultants, 1968.

Boyd, H.W., Jr. and W.F. Massy. *Marketing Management.* New York: Harcourt Brace Jovanovich, 1972.

Buzzell, R.D. and R.E.M. Nourse. *Production Innovation in Food Process: 1954–1964.* Boston: Harvard University, 1967.

Comanor, W.S. "Research and Technical Change in the Pharmaceutical Industry." *Review of Economics and Statistics* Vol. 47, 1965, pp. 182-190.

Czepiel, J.A. "Word of Mouth Processes in the Diffusion of a Major Technological Innovation." *Journal of Marketing Research* Vol. 11, 1974, pp. 172-180.

Edwards, A.L. *Techniques of Attitude Scale Construction.*

Englewood Cliffs, N.J.: Prentice-Hall, 1957.

Farmer, R.N. and B.M. Richman. *International Business: An Operational Theory.* Homewood, Ill.: Richard D. Irwin, 1968.

Freeman, C. "A Study of Success and Failure in Industrial Innovation." In B.R. Williams, ed., *Science and Technology in Economic Growth.* New York: John Wiley & Sons, 1973.

Galbraith, J.K. *American Capitalism.* Boston: Houghton Mifflin Co., 1952.

Graham, S. "Class and Conservatism in the Adoption of Innovations." *Human Relations,* Vol. 9, 1956, pp. 91-100.

Green, P.E. and Y. Wind. *Multiattribute Decisions in Marketing: A Measurement Approach.* Hinsdale, Ill.: Dryden, 1973.

Griliches, Z. "Hybrid Corn: An Exploration in the Economics of Technological Change." *Econometrics,* Vol. 25, 1957, pp. 501-522.

Hardin, D.K. "A New Approach to Test Marketing." *Journal of Marketing,* Vol. 30, 1966, pp. 28-31.

Harris, J.S. "The New Product Profile Chart. Selecting and Appraising New Projects." *Chemical and Engineering News,* Vol. 39, 1964, pp. 110-118.

Hennessey, R.G. "The Accelerated Program: From Idea to Product *Faster.*" In Elizabeth Marting, ed., *New Products, New Profits.* New York: American Management Association, 1964.

Herwald, Seymour W. "Building the Prototype Model." In A. Edward Spitz, ed., *Product Planning.* Princeton, N.J.: Auerbach, 1972.

Hill, R.M. and J.D. Hlavacek. "The Venture Team: A New Concept in Marketing Organization." *Journal of Marketing* Vol. 36, July 1972, pp. 44-50.

Hise, R.T. and M.A. McGinnis. "Product Elimination: Practices, Policies and Ethics." *Business Horizons,* June 1975, pp. 25-32.

Hopkins, David S. *Options in New Product Organization.* New York: The Conference Board, 1974.

Hopkins, D.S. and E.L. Bailey. "New Product Pressures." *The Conference Board Record* Vol. 8, June 1971, pp. 16-24.

Hough, Lewis. *Modern Research for Administrative Decisions.* Englewood Cliffs, N.J.: Prentice-Hall, 1970.

"How GM Manages Its Billion-Dollar R and D Program." *Business Week,* 28 June 1976, pp. 54-58.

Jet Propulsion Laboratory, California Institute of Technology. *Should We Have A New Engine,* Vol. 2, August 1975.

Kamien, M.I. and N.L. Schwartz. "Market Structure and Innovation: A Survey." *Journal of Economic Literature* Vol. 3, 1975, pp. 1-37.

Klahr, D. "A Study of Consumers' Cognitive Structure for Cigarette Brands." *Journal of Business* Vol. 43, 1970, pp. 190-204.

Kline, C.H. "The Strategy of Public Policy." *Harvard Business Review,* July–August 1955, pp. 91-100.

Klompmaker, J.E.; G.D. Hughes; R.I. Haley. "Test Marketing in New Product Development." *Howard Business Review,* May–June 1976, pp. 128-138.

Kotler, P. *Marketing Management: Analysis, Planning and Control, Third Edition.* Englewood Cliffs, N.J.: Prentice-Hall, 1976.

Lazer, W. and W.E. Bell. "The Concept and Process of Innovation." In E.J. Kelley and W. Lazer, eds., *Managerial Marketing: Politics, Strategies and Decisions.* Homewood, Ill.: R.D. Irwin, 1973.

Mansfield, E. *The Economics of Technological Change.* New York: W.W. Norton & Co., 1968.

Mansfield, E. "Determinants of the Speed of Application of New Technology." In B.R. Williams, ed., *Science and Technology in Economic Growth.* New York: John Wiley & Sons, 1973.

Mansfield, E. and S. Wagner. "Organizational and Strategic Factors Associated with Probability of Success in Industrial R&D." *Journal of Business,* Vol. 48, pp. 179-198.

"Marketing Observer: New-Product Market Testing." *Business Week,* 3 August 1974.

"Market Testing Consumer Products: Experiences in Marketing Management, No. 12." *The Conference Board,* 1967.

Marting, Elizabeth, ed. *New Products—New Profits. Company Experiences in New Product Planning.* New York: American Management Association, 1964.

Myers, S. and D.G. Marquis. *Successful Industrial Innovations: A Study of Factors Underlying Innovation in Selected Firms.* Washington, D.C.: National Science Foundation, 1969.

O'Meara, J.T., Jr. "Selecting Profitable Products." *Harvard Business Review* Vol. 39, January–February 1961, pp. 83-89.

Parker, J.E.S. *The Economics of Innovation.* London: Longman, 1974.

Patrick, Lawrence M. "The Effect of Engineering Responsibility." In Elizabeth Marting, ed., *Developing a Product Strategy.* American Management Association, New York, 1959.

Pessemier, E.A. *New Product Decisions: An Analytical Approach.* New York: McGraw-Hill Book Co., 1966.

Philipson, M. *Automation: Implications for the Future.* New York: Random House, 1962.

Rainey, H.G., R.W. Backoff, and C.H. Levine. "Comparing Public and Private Organizations." *Public Administration Review* Vol. 36, 1976, pp. 233-244.

Research and Development in Industry, 1973. Washington, D.C.: National Science Foundation, 1975.

Richman, B.M. "A Rating Scale for Product Innovation." *Business Horizons,* Summer 1962, pp. 37-44.

Romeo, A.A. "Interindustry and Interfirm Differences in the Rate of Diffusion of an Innovation." *The Review of Economics and Statistics* Vol. 57, 1975, pp. 311-319.

Schumpeter, J.A. *Capitalism, Socialism and Democracy.* Third Edition. New York: Harper and Row, 1950.

Silk, A.J. "Preference and Perception Measures in New Product Development: An Exposition and Review." *Sloan Management Review* Vol. 2, Fall 1969.

"Slow Deliveries Dog the Kodak Instant." *Business Week,* July 26, 1976, p. 43.

Tauber, E.M. "Reduce Product Failures: Measure Needs as Well as Purchase Interest." *Journal of Marketing* Vol. 37, July 1973, pp. 61-70.

"The Silent Crisis in R and D." *Business Week,* 8 March 1976, p. 90.

"The Two Way Squeeze on New Products." *Business Week,* 10 August 1974, p. 130.

Vanderwicken, Peter. "P and G's Secret Ingredient." *Fortune,* July 1974, p. 75.

Wasson, C.R. *Product Management: Product Life Cycles and Competitive Market Strategy.* St. Charles, Ill.: Challenge, 1971.

"Where Private Industry Puts Its Research Money." *Business Week,* 28 June 1976, pp. 62-84.

Williamson, O.E. "Innovation and Market Structure." *Journal of Political Economy* Vol. 73, February 1965, pp. 67-73.

Worley, J.S. "Industrial Research and the New Competition." *Journal of Political Economy* Vol 69, April 1961, pp. 183-186.

4

Technological Innovation in the Public Sector

The fundamental question being addressed in this study is, "Why is federally sponsored research underutilized (i.e., why is there an implementation problem)?" This chapter will address this question from the public sector viewpoint and will investigate the character of federal R&D expenditures, the process of R&D management, and the barriers and contravening forces which act to frustrate the implementation process. Consistent with our effort to develop procedures for increasing the effectiveness of federally sponsored R&D projects, this chapter will provide an assessment of the interaction between the R&D management process and the context within which the R&D is conducted. This assessment will in turn provide a basis for understanding those situations in which policy intent and program capabilities are mismatched, and the implementation failure that follows.

Motivation for Public Sector Investment in R&D

The principal incentive motivating the private sector to innovate is profitability. On the other hand, the public sector has adopted a policy of supporting R&D efforts which are consistent with social and national interest. In general, the government's policy toward R&D involvement is influenced by the philosophy that product development is primarily the domain of the private sector, and therefore the R&D conducted by federal agencies should not supplant or compete with private efforts, but rather focus on technology development.

Prior to the commitment of R&D resources, the private

sector conducts an assessment of project costs and the market potential, and thereby the risk associated with an involvement in a particular R&D venture. Clearly the private sector investment model is neither appropriate nor suitable to all public sector goals. This gives rise to the incidence of underinvestment in private sector R&D within certain categories of goods and services considered to be of common interest, e.g., health care, social welfare, and defense. Consequently, the government has assumed a major commitment to supporting R&D efforts in those areas where the private sector does not actively venture. This philosophy is clearly reflected in a speech made by former President Lyndon Johnson.

> Under our system of government, private enterprise bears the primary responsibility for research and development. . . . But the Government can help. It can plan and fashion research and development . . . which is beyond the responsibility and capability of private industry (HUD, 1968, p. 23).

The explicit implication is that the federal government will not conduct research that would otherwise be done by the private sector, but instead would assume responsibility for research projects that fall into one of the following broad categories.

- R&D in support of social welfare programs
- R&D supporting local government implementation efforts
- R&D for the military and space programs
- R&D supporting and supplementing private investment seeking profitmaking products in high risk ventures
- R&D supporting federal efforts to regulate the private sector

Understanding and recognizing this public sector R&D orientation is basic to assessing the structure and character of the federal R&D process and its apparent inefficiency in producing deliverables evaluated within the context of private sector R&D. Simply stated, the public sector has traditionally conducted its R&D under a different set of operating constraints and objective functions. Perhaps a justification for this posture can be found in the fact that the public sector, and specifically the federal government, views itself as providing the role of a catalyst or facilitator in local government and private sector R&D activities.

A review of the historical patterns of federal R&D expenditures will further illustrate innovation product/process bias within the public sector.

Patterns of Federal Involvement in R&D Activities

An overview of the character and trends of federal expenditures for R&D provides a background for understanding the evolution of federal R&D from defense- and space-dominated activities to activities involving both military and space as well as civilian projects. What was once an effective R&D process for implementing military and space projects must now be altered to fit the needs and goals of civilian-oriented projects.

During the twenty-two-year period between 1953 and 1974, federal expenditures for R&D increased rapidly. Dollar spending rose by a factor of six; real spending increased by more than a factor of three ("National Patterns of R&D Resources 1953–1974," National Science Foundation, 1974, p. 30). With respect to the distribution of R&D funds, national defense programs have always been the principal recipients of federal R&D funds. During the early to mid-sixties, funding of the space program reached its peak on a proportionate basis. During this period, civilian R&D played a small role. By 1974, civilian program spending, which initially comprised less than 9 percent of the total federal R&D expenditures, had grown to more than 33 percent.

Reviewing more recent information relating to the funding of federal R&D by function, it is possible to ascertain the manner and extent to which the character of public sector R&D is changing. Federal obligations for R&D in 1976 were estimated to reach $21.7 billion. The distribution of this money among the principal functional categories is shown in Table 4-1.

While defense- and space-related activities still account for the majority of federal R&D spending, their relative role has

TABLE 4-1

Distribution of 1976 R&D Expenditures
by Functional Category

National Defense	52.5%
Space	13.4%
Health	8.8%
Energy Development and Conversion	5.9%
Environment	4.6%
Science and Technology Base	4.0%
Natural Resources	3.8%
Transportation and Communications	3.3%
Education	1.5%
Income Security and Social Services	0.7%
Economic Growth and Productivity	0.6%
Area and Community Development, Housing, and Public Services	0.6%
Crime Prevention and Control	0.2%
International Cooperation and Development	0.2%

Source: National Science Foundation, August 1975

continued to decrease in significance. Figure 4-1 shows the trends in federal spending between the years 1969 and 1976 for defense, space, and civilian R&D programs. Taken together, funds for national defense and space R&D programs have declined during the period between 1969 and 1976 from 77 percent to 66 percent while civilian programs have increased their share of total federal R&D funds from 23 percent to 34 percent. Figure 4-2 illustrates the trends in distribution of federal R&D expenditures for selected civilian programs during this same period. The fastest-growing functional areas, in terms of average annual growth rates over a seven-year period are energy (21.5 percent), environment (17 percent), and natural resources (12.0 percent). These annual growth rates can be compared with those of national defense (4.5 percent) and space (-3.6 percent).

While any attempt to assign R&D funds into any specific set of categories is prone to misrepresentation, these figures are effective in demonstrating the relative focus of R&D expenditures and how this focus has changed over time.

FIGURE 4-1. Trends in Federal R&D Spending

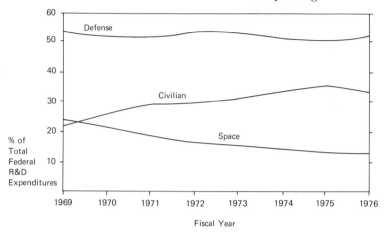

Fiscal Year

FIGURE 4-2. Trends in Principal Civilian R&D Programs

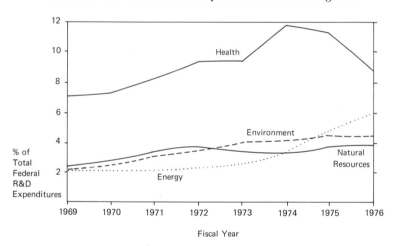

Fiscal Year

These changes support two assertions regarding the nature of the federal R&D process. First, the R&D management process as it exists today was conceived and has evolved from an era of national defense and space program management. As such, it has become a system which is suitable to the development of limited production, specialized, highly reliable, and timely components. Secondly, and perhaps more to the point, is the fact that with the advent of the expanded orientation of federal R&D efforts, this defense/space-based process is not necessarily appropriate and possibly not capable of dealing with contemporary civilian programs.

This latter point deserves further clarification, for much of the controversy surrounding the public sector civilian R&D activities turns on this point.

Melvin Webber (1972) has suggested an interesting typology for sociotechnical problems: there are "tame" problems and there are "wicked" problems. The problems that scientists and engineers generally focus upon are considered to be tame. Tame problems can be characterized as involving clear objectives and a basis for determining whether or not the problems have been solved and whether the solution is feasible.

In contrast to tame problems, wicked problems are "ill-defined, and they rely upon elusive political judgment for resolution." Government research involving social or policy planning most often falls into this latter category.

Webber argues that the classical R&D systems approach of the military and space programs, while appropriate for solving tame problems, is inadequate for resolving wicked problems. While it may be possible to organize tame problems into the discrete phases characteristic of the systematic approach, understanding and formulating a wicked problem must be preceded by some assessment of what constitutes a possible solution or set of solutions. It is only after this point that information can be gathered to help develop an understanding and context for the problem. When dealing with wicked problems, "one cannot first understand, then solve." Approaches to resolving wicked problems through R&D must involve "a model of planning as an argumentative process in the course of which an image of the problem and of the solution emerges gradually among the participants, as a product of incessant judgment, subjected to critical argument" (Webber, 1972).

Attempting to confront the series of contemporary, wicked civilian problems of air quality, energy, health, and social welfare using a science-based model can unfortunately lead to short-sighted and even ineffective R&D programs. This seems most likely to occur when problem definition is preempted by the early pursuit of a candidate technology or technology system as the "obvious solution." The resolution of "wicked" problems, Webber argues, is almost never obvious and almost invariably involves the necessity of planning for a sociotechnical system rather than the design and demonstration of a technology per se. Consequently, it would appear that the shift in R&D focus will impose new requirements for devising a modified R&D management process to deal with the unique character of civilian policies and programs.

The following sections will present an exposition of the R&D management process as it is currently conceived and demonstrate the nature and extent to which barriers and external forces intercede to render the process ineffectual.

The R&D Management Process

We will now turn to a paradigmatic description of how a government policy is transformed into a technological or programmatic solution. This innovation process, referred to here as the R&D management process, consists of four stages: organizational mandate and appropriation, program planning, project management, and technology transfer.

Throughout the following presentation of the R&D management process, a single federal agency or department will be used as the unit of analysis. It is within this organizational framework that the process activities are subdivided into a sequence of events that translate broad policy statements into technologies and programs, refined to achieve national objectives. These events, which are idealized to permit a more manageable analysis, are shown in Figure 4-3.

As can be seen from Figure 4-3, the federal R&D management process is typically initiated through an organizational mandate which contains provisions for a grant of authority and fiscal appropriations. These mandates provide the agency with the charge and the organizational means for responding to stated policies. Although outside the normal day-to-day management of research and development programs, these mandates provide the boundary conditions within which the research program managers operate.

In the next stage of the R&D management process, program planning activities transform mandates into narrower

FIGURE 4-3. Conceptualization of the Federal R&D Management
Process Activities

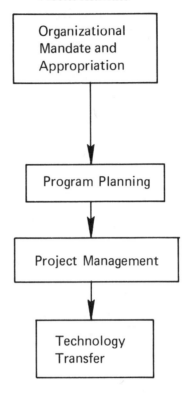

and better-defined objectives called programs. Program
planning includes the determination of organizational objectives and their priorities, the conception and incubation
of new program ideas, and the reassessment of objectives and
priorities.

Once program agendas have been determined, projects are
selected, designed, and executed. It is at this stage that
broadly stated policies are transformed into technological or
process concepts which will be used to meet mandated
objectives. The research execution phase will commonly
involve prototype construction and testing.

The final stage involves the transfer of the developed
technologies or concepts to either the public or private
sectors. Technology transfer is accomplished through various forms of information dissemination, including demon-

stration projects. The purpose of technology transfer is to familiarize potential users with the end products of federal R&D as a vehicle for facilitating the dissemination of completed technologies or processes out of the federal sector and into the local private sectors.

In the following subsections, each of the four R&D management process stages will be described and assessed in greater detail.

Stage 1: Organizational Mandate and Appropriation

The first stage of moving a formalized policy toward a deliberate action response involves the specification of an agency mandate and a grant of legal, financial, and political authority. Mandates are usually the result of congressional or executive actions leading to the creation of a new agency or the redirection of an existing agency or one of its departments. The extent to which the mandate and accompanying powers are well defined, uncontested, and promoted with political, financial, and legal support will directly affect the implementation of programs within the agency. For example, the original mandate charging the Environmental Protection Agency (EPA) with the responsibility to implement the provisions of the Clean Air Act failed to clearly specify the enabling powers (e.g., enforcement authority and the limits of the act). Consequently, the agency reverted to the courts for interpretations of the mandate and limits of the agency's powers.

In this regard, there is typically a positive correlation between congressional and executive backing and the speed and effectiveness with which policies are transformed into technologies. In addition, strong political support for an agency or program implies the availability of a wider range of intervention strategies once technologies are ready for implementation.

Legislative Action Leading to a Program Mandate

In addressing the question of "how" policy programs evolve, it is necessary to consider the legislative actions which lead to the formulation of a mandate. First, it should be recognized that legislative action has the tendency to be crisis-responsive rather than anticipatory; it can be better explained as a reaction to problems rather than as a pursuit of objectives. The way Congress responds to and attempts to resolve problems and crises sets the tone for agencies which must operate within their directives to meet the mandates set.

The character of the reaction is influenced by some enduring "rules of play" in the legislative arena.

- The need to geographically and equitably distribute benefits such as jobs, expenditures, and other payoffs from public spending.
- The need to respect the "established turf" or "spheres of influence" of major players. This means charting a path which respects:
  a. the boundaries between the public and private sectors
  b. the boundaries between federal, state, and local bureaucracies
  c. the spheres of influence of competing congressional committees and executive agencies
- The desire to see early and visible payoff. This contributes a "project" orientation to many federal programs. Projects are susceptible to the divvying-up requirements of legislative process.
- The need to balance the claims of special interests which are traditionally adversaries and/or competitors—labor and management; growth interests and environmentalists; and urban and rural interests.
- The need to balance claims advanced by competing cabinet-level agencies. In each house of Congress, the role of legislative staff, majority party leader, and committee chairman is critical. Outcomes in each house are subject to modification in negotiation with the other house and with the executive branch.

The characterization which best describes this process is one of bargaining and balancing. The game called politics and power, as it is played, involves calming some and pleasing others in order to maintain and improve a public career (Breslin, 1975, p. 34).

The end of this stage sets the arena in which individual agencies and their component parts play. Usually these players have considerable latitude in which to accomplish some very general objectives. Seldom are the means for meeting goals set out, and even when they are, the management discretion is substantial. After all, the individuals who make up Congress are elected for two or six years depending upon the house; and within the confines of their longevity as members of the legislature, they are only able to devote limited amounts of time to any one program. By necessity, then, as well as traditionally by law, these duties are assigned to the executive branch and to the specific agencies and programs therein.

Stage 2: Program Planning

Program-planning activities of the federal R&D management process translate the organizational mandate into narrower, better-defined problem areas comprising a program agenda. While the agency's staff plays the central planning and decision-making role, they are forced to accommodate demands from outside the agency. For example, at the former Office of Planning, Research and Evaluation (PR&E) of the Office of Economic Opportunity (OEO), program planning was "ordinarily an internal activity, with the external community only involved in certain steps" (Wirt, 1975). The process at OEO contained the following stages: (1) problem identification; (2) generation of basic program ideas and analysis of these alternative solutions; (3) generation and analysis of model programs; and (4) redesign of model programs. In order to carry out these steps, the OEO staff conducted in-depth policy-oriented research to develop a thorough understanding of their field and to "probe for fundamental relationships that helped in identifying basic problems" (Wirt, 1975). A separate external group contributed to the process by conducting evaluations of the PR&E experiments and other federal programs.

A second example demonstrating the influence of agency staff over program planning is excerpted from an interview with Robert Cannon, a former R&D administrator for DOT. He stated that program objectives were determined by the staff during a several-day retreat. The final program agenda was derived from the staff's collective opinions about the ideal urban transport system and what was lacking to achieve it. Cannon's explanation is supported by Arthur D. Little's observation that "since the R&D has been under Urban Mass Transporation Administration (UMTA), UMTA administrators have been the source of major policies" (1976, p. 40).

Program Selection and Evaluation: The Internal Process

When conducted internally, the process an agency's professional staff follows in generating and selecting programs typically incorporates some or all of the following four considerations (Wirt, 1975).

- The likelihood of achieving congressional, presidential, and constituency support
- The contribution to achieving the organization mandate
- The contribution to a balanced portfolio
- The availability of staff

Of these, the likelihood of achieving support is perhaps the most important. Clearly, programs depend upon fiscal resources, resources to which legislative and executive branches hold the purse strings. In conceiving programs, research managers are careful to balance legislative desires with agency orientation. Prudence would suggest that the R&D manager not develop a program that would jeopardize support from the funding bodies.

With regard to the remaining selection factors, particular attention will also be paid to the concept of providing a balanced program portfolio. In order to avoid proposing a program which has only a narrow-based support, it is necessary that the research programs reflect balance between the type of research to be conducted, the geographical representativeness, and the constituency-relevance.

In considering those factors which influence the formulation of research programs, one cannot understate the significance of the extent to which personal and organizational incentives motivate agency administrators to translate an organizational mandate into a workable and acceptable program agenda. Personal idealism, professional ethics, opportunities for advancement, and appreciation of a challenge are incentives to individual efforts. Similar survival and reputational motives might be ascribed to organizations as well. The development of imaginative, cooperative, and successful programs can enhance the general mission of the parent agency. As a consequence, payoffs and incentives play a crucial role in the direction and shaping of program planning. Since these payoffs do not necessarily arise from the end user's adopting products of federal R&D, there is no pressure for incorporating end-user needs into this stage of the R&D management process.

The evaluation of program agendas is an equally complex process. The absence of objective evaluation criteria and the reluctance of the agency administration to risk losing funds reduce incentives to actively evaluate and alter program objectives and priorities. Directors of line divisions know that if they suggest giving any existing program a low priority, it will likely be lost forever. In a year of budgetary squeeze, they will not get a new program to take the place of the discarded one, so they hang on to what they have (Bartlett and Jones, 1974, p. 64). It is this fear of losing budgetary allocations which inhibits program reassessment and readjustment and which consequently permits the continuation of programs that would not otherwise be implemented.

Congressional and Executive Influence in Program Planning

While the individual agencies' principal responsibility is to select and carry out research programs, Congress and the executive offices will guide, oversee, and monitor the R&D activities of these agencies. Congressional or executive policy guidance encompasses the hiring and appointment of agency professionals who will develop the R&D programs. They are likely, for example, to hire professionals with compatible values and politics to administer the programs.

While this practice can occur, there are other more formalized and direct procedures through which the Congress and the presidency have opportunity to exercise control over R&D activities. Two of the most influential control mechanisms are the Office of Management and Budget (OMB) and congressional oversight committees.

Federal R&D agencies are required to submit their yearly

budgets to OMB for approval whereupon OMB usually attempts to make across-the-board budget cuts to insure planned federal expenditures do not exceed budget targets. At the same time, OMB can cut individual programs or redirect expenditures. This annual activity gives OMB the power to play an evaluative role and to influence R&D priorities. OMB is therefore in a prime position to encourage programs that indicate a likelihood of successful implementation and to eliminate those that do not. Rarely, however, do they take advantage of this power. Traditionally, OMB "does not envision its role as that of a translator of national ends; instead it sees itself primarily as a manager of programs, not as a chooser among programs" (Barber, 1966, p. 112). Frank L. Lewis and Frank G. Zarb, when at the Office of Management and Budget, stated that "OMB has not in the past performed a major role in the conduct of evaluation studies, nor does it do so currently. . . . At this point in time, OMB takes the position that each agency head is primarily responsible for managing the programs under his jurisdiction" (Lewis and Zarb, 1974, p. 312).

Once OMB has approved the agency budget, it is delivered, along with the other agency budgets, to Congress where it is subjected to additional levels of control authority. Within Congress, specific committees and subcommittees are organized to oversee individual-agency R&D efforts. The House Committee on Atomic Energy and the Senate Committee on Aeronautical Space Sciences are examples.

Within each committee or subcommittee, the chairperson has significant powers with respect to influencing the outcome of any specific R&D program within the committee's control. The chairperson has influence to insure sustained support for an agency's R&D activities.

In addition to the legislative committees, which have the responsibility of authorizing programs and specifying dollar ceilings, the actual budget requests are approved or denied by the appropriations committees. The activities of the appropriations committees are limited to considering an R&D agency budget within the perspective of the total budget, and rarely do they or the oversight committees intervene in the program objectives or priorities.

Each of the congressional committees is enjoined by law to exercise "continuous watchfulness" over the agencies within their jurisdiction. Although this includes the power to influence program objectives and priorities, the committees rarely intervene in these areas. In the words of one source, "Congress ladles out the money for research without really knowing whether there is technical justification for the requests and without being in a position to evaluate the consequence of its actions" (Barber, 1966, p. 7).

There appear to be several reasons why committees and subcommittees hesitate to get involved in an agency R&D management process.

- The effectiveness of the science-related committees and subcommittees is hindered by the general lack of technical knowledge or experience of the committee members. Senator George McGovern has stated that "the Congress (and people) who are civilians occupied with other concerns have a formidable task in even thinking up the right questions to ask about the lexicon of AMB, MIRV, AWACS, ILMS, AMSA and the rest" (Murphy, 1971, p. 496).
- In some cases, Congress has difficulty obtaining information because it is classified or covered over by agencies that suspect it will be used against them.
- Except in cases where there is clear public sentiment against a particular project, e.g., Supersonic Transport (SST), or the B-1 bomber, there are no political rewards to be accrued from intervening in an agency's R&D management process. On the other hand, there are definite costs associated with meddling.
- In general, Congress is satisfied that the R&D agencies are doing an adequate job of selecting priorities in the absence of publicized conflict or controversy. When this is the case intervention is considered unwise and unnecessary.

Both Congress and the White House offices are only half-heartedly interested in seeing that an agency complies with policy mandates and objectives (which include the implementation of successful programs and projects). Both institutions have the power to influence individual R&D programs and projects. The oversight and budget planning processes are useful ways of controlling the general R&D

program of an individual agency. However, this power is rarely exercised.

Stage 3: Project Management

The project management stage involves the continuous process of generating, selecting, and executing the projects which comprise an R&D program. The major and most recent work in this area came from John G. Wirt's *R&D Management* (1975), a study of R&D in thirteen federal agencies. Much of the following section is drawn from his work.

Project Generation and Design

Project generation and design consists of creating project concepts and preparing proposals in response to program objectives. It is at this point that policies begin to be translated into technical solutions. The major source of project generation and design generally is the internal agency staff. For example, in the National Cancer Institute (a division of the National Institute of Mental Health), new projects are generated by an internal work group. Project inception, however, may also come from contractors through participation in annual conferences, from solicited and unsolicited proposals conceived by extramural investigators, or from scientists who may or may not be associated with the program.

Proposals for projects and project designs may also originate from the potential manufacturers. For example, manufacturers were key participants in the National Academy of Engineers study which provided the documented need for the Transbus Program. Manufacturers also participated in studies and government hearings in developing the California Steambus Program (Milbergs and Quick, Jr., 1976, p. 27).

Once a project has been conceived, be it the result of an internal or an external process, the next step in the project's synthesis is the project design. Project design effectively consists of the specification of a set of operating performance characteristics which the desired technology is expected to achieve. This design orientation stems from the fact that the principal objective of federal R&D projects is the proof of the operating feasibility of new technological concepts.

It is not obvious exactly how the project performance criteria for individual projects are set; however, some evidence suggests that a form of "maximization model" is used. The majority of the people who design projects in the federal government are technically trained. Consequently, there is a tendency to specify a maximum technical performance within certain technical constraints as the project objective. In addition to the technical constraints (which are an integral part of the project design specification), project time and cost constraints are established as part of the project's design. However, operating costs, production costs, and time controls are not typically incorporated in the project design. For example, the objective of Urban Mass Transportation Administration's (UMTA's) paratransit research is to develop a vehicle which maximizes fuel savings. Design constraints include strict pollution emissions specifications and vehicle design standards; but production cost constraints do not enter into the project design.

Agency technicians argue that "effectiveness" in "maximizing performance" is dependent upon a project's budget. Moreover, with larger budgets, technology performance, and consequently the ability to satisfy the policy mission, could be improved. This suggests, then, that federal R&D is pursued in a context where the critical variables are research budget and technology performance specification. Consequently, the management structure within which the design engineer or research technician operates seems to provide incentives for maximizing both the overall budget and the performance criteria which, in turn, affects the technology's unit cost for an R&D project.

It can be hypothesized that this set of incentives is unacceptable in terms of the eventual marketability of the prototype technology. A marketable technology is likely to satisfy a rather different test in which design performance is compromised by production considerations. In other words, it is not sufficient that the prototype emanating from the R&D activities be highly refined and/or complex. To be commercially viable, the prototype will need to be adaptable to existing production capabilities in order that the final production be consistent with both operating performance and cost requirements.

Project Selection

Once a number of project ideas or proposals have been generated, project selection follows. Although peer review is frequently used to evaluate proposals, the actual selection of projects falls primarily under the jurisdiction of the agency staff. The following examples demonstrate the procedures being used by two agencies for conducting project selection.

At the National Institute of Health (NIH), a two part review mechanism is used. An initial review of proposals for research grants is delegated to approximately fifty study sections composed entirely of nongovernmental scientists. The recommendations of these study sections are then forwarded to the relevant divisions of the NIH. Each division of the NIH maintains an advisory council of nongovernmental scientists and informed laymen. The advisory council, by working its way down the project ranking as established by the study sections, decides how far the Institute's available funds can extend. In addition, the council may influence the priority of projects which appear to be most relevant to the Institute's program objectives. Without prior approval of their council, Institute officials cannot make research awards (Gustafson, 1975, p. 1060).

The project selection scheme being developed by ERDA's Office of Conservation (Division of Buildings Conservation and Division of Industry Conservation) is a three-stage process. Upon identification of a potential project, a project manager is assigned who oversees and administers the project during the selection process and, if acceptable, throughout the development process. Projects are first subjected to a preliminary review by the project manager; then a quantitative screening procedure is used to further weed out unacceptable projects; finally a "scoring" system is used to rank acceptable projects by priority.

The purpose of the preliminary review is to determine if the project conforms with overall agency objectives and falls within the sphere of responsibilities of Buildings and Industry Conservation. Additionally, in this initial, subjective stage of project screening, the project manager ascertains whether the project is oriented towards national or regional problems that relate to national energy goals.

During the screening stage, projects are eliminated if: (1) they should be financed by the private sector without public support; (2) their probability of success is so low that neither sector should support them; or (3) they do not provide sufficient benefits to justify their cost to the federal government. Most of this evaluation will be based on quantitative analysis of risk and return rates which assesses the incremental or marginal impact of the federally supported R&D on energy conservation.

Those projects which successfully pass through the screening stage are ranked under a system designed to incorporate the intuitive judgments used by ERDA personnel in project selection into a scoring methodology that enhances their abilities to choose among an increasing number of requests for project support. Projects are scored according to their value to ERDA and society, their potential for successful commercialization of the end product or technology, and the impact that federal funding will have on the project as opposed to no public support. There are a number of subelements to each of the three factors which are evaluated as a part of the process assigning values to them. The relative importance of the three major factors, as well as the subelements within the factors, is reflected in a weighting system incorporated in the scoring model. Each subelement is assessed qualitatively and assigned a numerical value, and the values given the factors and subelements, along with their impact assessment weights, are mathematically combined to give a single nondimensional index number. This number is termed the "expected value" of the project. This set of project-expected values provides a means of allocating resources among the competing projects.

Another division within ERDA utilizes a somewhat different procedure for project selection. In the appraisal methodology developed for ERDA's Conservation Research and Technology Division, a weighting and scoring systm is used to examine how the technical characteristics of a program relate to several different criteria: energy savings, technical risk, cost, commercial potential, uniqueness, resource availability, environmental impact, and social, legal, and institutional effects. These criteria, selected to satisfy national energy goals and ERDA priorities, are given weighting factors according to their relative importance in satisfying the division's mission objectives. For example, energy savings is an area of highest priority and is weighted twenty while the last two criteria (environmental and social and legal and institutional effects) are given low scores of eight. The total weighted scores add up to one hundred.

To evaluate a project by these criteria, a "criterion score" is compiled which is the sum of the scores assigned to individual subcomponents within each major criteria category. A "criterion rating" for each criterion is obtained by multiplying the criterion score by its weighting factor and dividing by a predetermined maximum possible score for that criterion. The sum of these criterion ratings is the "total score" for the project in question. Comparing the total scores for a group of projects, it is possible to establish a priority listing for the set of projects being appraised.

Clearly, there could be almost as many unique procedures for project selection as there are agencies and divisions within agencies. Despite this fact, there are observed similarities among the various procedures used. In general, it is found that the selection of research projects will include an evaluation, albeit subjective, based upon some or all of the following criteria:

- contribution of the project to overall programs
- question of whether the project proposes an interesting technical problem
- probability of successful completion of the project
- potential benefits of the project
- time to completion
- correct timing to obtain congressional and executive branch support for the project mission
- likelihood of meeting project specifications
- necessary staff resources to initiate and manage the required effort
- contribution to the project portfolio (i.e., maintain diversity and capitalize on agency assets)

Surveys on the use of quantitative decision techniques such as these used by the ERDA divisions have indicated that although theoretical interest in project-selection methods has been high and has led to a proliferation of various methods, R&D organizations have not significantly used these methods in making allocation decisions. Two studies, one in 1964 by Baker and Pound and the other in 1966 by Albert Rubenstein, indicated that there is very limited use of quantitative methods in program selection (Wirt, 1975, p. 616). The actual use for such mechanisms is to have the results to justify particular selections. It is safer to be able to present a systematic and therefore seemingly unbiased analysis to Congress, for example, as the basis for project selection, than to say that it was selected on the basis of professional expertise. In reality, schemes for project selection can do little more than formalize the professional judgments of the program managers.

Project Execution

Upon completion of the project-selection phase, project execution can commence. Integral to the activities associated with conducting R&D is the use of models or prototypes for testing the performance of the developed technology or concept. In addition, the project-management aspects of project execution, namely project monitoring and evaluation, are necessary components of an effective R&D management process.

The actual research and development activities may be carried out in-house or through contracts to external consulting firms, industry, universities, and profit and nonprofit research institutes. Table 4-2 indicates the distribution of R&D funds estimated for 1976.

When one measures performance by the amount of money received, private industry is the principal performer of federal R&D. Private industry receives over half of the total federal expenditures for R&D activities. Intramural research is second, with an estimated 27 percent, while universities and colleges receive an estimated 10 percent of the total federal R&D expenditures for 1976.

If research is not going to be conducted in-house, then the actual recepient of R&D funds is selected on the basis of several criteria, including: the submission of an acceptable proposal, the experience of the researcher, the research unit's demonstrated understanding of the problem, and the ability of the research to manufacture the end product. For exam-

TABLE 4-2

Estimate of 1976 Federal Expenditures for R&D by Performer

Industrial firms	52%
Federal intramural	27%
Universities and colleges	10%
FFRDC's Admin. by Universities	5%
Other nonprofit institutions	4%
Other	2%

Source: National Science Foundation, December 1975

ples, among Department of Defense (DOD) and National Aeronautics and Space Administration (NASA) allocations of R&D funds, contractor experience receives a high priority. Urban Mass Transportation Administration (UMTA) has followed the policy of contracting R&D to the potential manufacturers of the product (Milbergs, 1976).

While these effectively objective criteria are primary considerations in the awarding of contract funds, one cannot discount the extent to which subjective evaluations will influence the selection of a contractor. Often contracts are given to firms, or individuals within a firm, with which the project manager is personally familiar, or to firms which have a recognized reputation in the field of study to which the contract is oriented. These subjective assessments not only influence the choice of a contractor in a competitive proposal situation, but can also result in the letting of sole-source contract agreements.

There is a natural desire on the part of the project manager to want the contract performed by a group that can successfully conduct and develop the research. While this desire is really to maximize the output of a program within the amount of research funding available, the project manager is also concerned with the rewards associated with a successful project. Success not only can lead to recognition and additional resources for the program, but commonly brings recognition to the manager.

Having suggested why an agency chooses particular research groups, it is appropriate to turn to the question of why these groups choose to participate in federal R&D ventures. The reason we explore this is that understanding the motivation of different groups to participate in R&D activities will be useful to the development of revised implementation strategies. The incentives or motivations of researchers can be classified under the following categories.

- Financial remuneration
- Potential to enhance resource base and professional capability
- Potential for profitable commercialization
- Difficulty of challenge and interesting technical problem
- Synergistic effect on other company/agency projects
- Impact on the development of technology
- Opportunities to fraternize
- Potential beneficial impact on society

The motivations for participating in federal R&D are generally different from those of the private sector where the funds spent for R&D are from the company's own resources. The principal motivation driving private R&D is the development of new products that can be marketed for a profit; however, in the case of federal R&D, this is not necessarily true. Only two of the motivations listed above require end-user needs to be incorporated in project execution: potential for profitable commercialization and potential beneficial impact on society.

In both cases, an analysis of market sensitivity and an assessment of how the final products would be introduced

into the market are required. These, however, are not traditional concerns of federal R&D and, consequently, these two
motivations play only a tertiary role in influencing the
execution of federal R&D projects. Federally sponsored R&D
projects characteristically are conducted on a "proof of
concept" basis in which "success" requires only the demonstration of technical feasibility or the deployment of the
prototype technology. In the process, the original policy
mandate can be forgotten and demonstration can frequently
fall short of commercial adoption.

Discussions with researchers in the energy community
suggest that there may be a secondary motive behind the
recent surge in commercial interest and participation in
energy research. The availability of substantial amounts of
money to promote and support research activities in the
energy area has provided an opportunity for R&D to become
a profitable enterprise. In some instances, the R&D portions
of some companies have become profit centers whose objective function has shifted from product development to
performing research for a sponsor. This situation, to the
extent that it in fact exists, redirects the research in the
private sector energy area away from the commercialization
focus it had earlier to goals more commonly found in the
public sector (i.e., prototype development).

Having pursued the questions of who conducts federal
R&D programs and why, it is appropriate to turn to the
question of what project execution involves. As was indicated earlier, the construction and testing of a prototype represents an integral component in research project execution.
The function of a prototype during the execution phase of
an R&D program is to serve as a focal point for the project
analysis. This is distinct from the prototype construction
associated with a project demonstration to facilitate technology transfer. R&D involves a recursive process of analysis, testing, feedback, and revision. There is a point beyond
which theoretical construct and conceptual testing is not
sufficient. At this point, in order to advance the project,
empirical analysis becomes necessary. The use of a prototype
or model serves this need and becomes essential to the
identification and evaluation of the technical capabilities
and operation of the R&D product. If a technical problem
appears, then further research is conducted; whereas if the

testing indicates an acceptable level of performance, then the project-execution phase can be terminated and technology transfer activities initiated.

As a consequence of the fact that the vast majority of federally supported R&D is conducted outside the federal government, project monitoring is another essential component of project execution. Project monitoring is a task performed by the staff of the agency sponsoring the R&D project. The purpose of the monitoring function is to insure that specifications are followed, costs are met, and technical performance objectives achieved. Monitoring is usually conducted through (1) site visits, (2) technical assistance, and (3) requests for progress and cost reports. (Monitoring is also done by the organization conducting the R&D. The purpose and conduct of this internal review, commonly referred to as project management, is directly analogous to the process followed by the sponsoring agency.)

As federal expenditures on R&D have increased, a growing recognition of and concern about cost overruns, failures to meet specification, and failures to meet schedules arise. This concern has resulted in the proliferation of a large number and variety of management and engineering techniques (such as PERT, value engineering, and configuration management). Interestingly, studies of the effectiveness of these techniques suggest that the techniques have had no measurable effect on the performance of projects. Moreover, there is evidence to suggest that their application has contributed to the incidence of project cost, schedule, and performance difficulties (Gerloff, 1973, p. 6).

A final component of project execution to be introduced is that of project evaluation. It is during this aspect of project execution that an assessment is made with respect to how well the R&D product conforms to the established performance criteria. Performance evaluations have important implications with respect to the implementation of federally sponsored research. It is at this stage that projects that are not promising in terms of implementation can be altered or halted. The available literature on project evaluation is highly critical of the manner with which evaluations are generally executed. These criticisms revolve around the difficulty of halting a research project once it has gathered momentum and the lack of objectivity in staff-conducted evaluations. The establishment of periodic and rigorous procedures for project evaluation is a prerequisite to the formation of an effective R&D management process.

The Influence of External Forces on an Agency's Project Management Authority

The Congress, the executive branch, and individual actors who have influence over the R&D process rarely exert this influence at the project-management stage. As mentioned earlier, only when the public becomes sufficiently incensed by a federally sponsored project does Congress take action in response.

Congress has, however, taken an interest in the methods by which projects are managed in federal agencies. The most notable example is the controversy over the peer review system. Extensive debates over the desirability of the peer review to allocate R&D funds have been initiated by conservatives in Congress, among others. Representative R. E. Bauman of Maryland denounced the peer review system as one by which grants are "handed out in an unregulated and secretive manner. This system allows cronies to get together and finance their pet projects" (Gustafson, 1975, p. 1060).

Although there is likely some truth to these allegations, the peer review system is one of the only ways that research, particularly basic research, can be evaluated. What has to be done is to provide safeguards to insure that the worst abuses do not occur.

Investigations of research happen from time to time. Recently, for example, Senator Proxmire shook the research community by his investigation of R&D, especially at the National Science Foundation (NSF). This investigation seems to have had the unintended effect of moving the NSF's research away from basic R&D and toward applied research (which is more politically defensible).

In addition to this intervention by Congress, from time to time powerful constituents or supporters take an interest in a particular project that offers political payoffs. This intervention can take the form of halting, altering, and/or speeding up a project to enhance its potential as a showpiece. Larger and more innovative projects are more susceptible to these demands which often result in a less marketable prototype or demonstration. An example can be found in the Morgantown Personal Rapid Transit (P.R.T.) system, where the Nixon Administration became interested in the workability of the demonstration prior to the 1972 presidential election and ordered its hasty (and expensive) completion (see Chapter 6).

Stage 4: Technology Transfer

Once the prototype technology is tested and found to meet appropriate technical performance criteria, its potential for commercialization is assessed. If a market for the R&D product can be identified, the product is then considered for technology transfer.

Technology transfer (or research utilization) moves an R&D product to implementation. Using the broadest definition, it is the transformation from technology to product, including adoption and widespread utilization in the public or private sectors. Technology transfer may also mean the secondary application of research or technology developed for a particular mission that fills a need in another environment.

In practice, technology transfer as carried out by the federal government consists largely of efforts to disseminate information about the results of federal R&D. A recent study of twenty-five federal departments and agencies found that most agencies interpreted their mission in terms of documenting results and distributing information (Roessner, 1975).

A demonstration program is one highly specialized form of transfer mechanism which can be used to display a new technology. However, because of the high cost associated with conducting a demonstration program, its use is reserved for special, high-interest projects. Other mechanisms for technology transfer are more frequently used. These include seminars, field agents, newsletters, and personal contacts by the R&D performer.

Technology transfer programs as carried out by the federal government make three assumptions about the nature of the gap between building prototypes and their adoption by the private or public sectors.

- The private market did not develop the technology because it was too risky or they did not think of it
- Once the technology has been developed, it is suitable to the potential users as well as desirable
- The reason why intended users have not adopted the technology is that they did not know it existed

If these assumptions are correct, then the distribution of technical information is a correct and complete strategy. However, an examination of the factors influencing innovation and diffusion of production in the private market leads one to the conclusion that the adoption of new technologies is more complex than the rationale outlined above.

Table 4-3 summarizes a number of factors that are important considerations in a potential user's acceptance of a new technology. This list indicates the broad range of factors which intervene to influence decisions to adopt new technologies. It suggests the shortcomings of the present federal programs of technology transfer.

The factors influencing the addition of technologies have been categorized in Table 4-3 into four groups: (1) the characteristics of the transfer organization and agents; (2) the nature of the technology to be transferred; (3) the nature of the potential recipients; and (4) the nature of the system.

For most of the examples encountered in the course of conducting this analysis, the dissemination of technical information does not provide a sufficient basis for an implementing unit to reach a decision concerning feasibility of utilizing or adopting the new technology.

Information dissemination as a strategy for the transfer of technologies can, however, help eliminate a number of barriers to the utilization of new technologies. As seen in Table 4-3, information dissemination is more likely to work if the transfer organization (1) has the credibility, (2) has tailored the information to the needs of the recipients, (3) is selective about the technologies chosen for transfer, (4) has sufficient resources to reach large numbers of potential users, and (5) can achieve person-to-person contact. Also, as listed under the characteristics of the technology, the visibility of a technology can be improved through the dissemination of information or through the work of field agents; and, as implied under the characteristics of the user, the

TABLE 4-3

Factors Affecting the Transfer of Technologies

Characteristics of the Transfer Organization and Agents

1) The credibility of the transfer organization - if the transfer organization has built up credibility with potential users, then users will probably be more receptive to advice.

2) The selectivity of transfer organization - if the transfer organization is selective about which technologies are recommended to which users, then the technology transfer programs may be more effective and efficient.

3) The extent to which resources are tailored to the information needs of the recipients - if technology transfer activities provide the necessary information in the most appropriate form, then transfer is more likely to be successful.

4) The resources of the agency - if the agency staff is competent and motivated, then a higher proportion of technologies are likely to be adopted by users.

5) The use of person-to-person contact - person-to-person contact improves the likelihood that technology transfer activities will be successful.

The Nature of the Potential Recipients (Users)

1) The structure of the industry - the structure of the industry influences firms' receptivity to new technologies. This is discussed in additional detail in the private sector chapter.

2) The nature of the decision making unit - whether the management is risk adverse or innovative, growing or stagnant, regulated or unregulated; whether the state/local government or firm has access to capital markets - all are important considerations in accepting or rejecting new technologies.

3) The nature of the users market - whether the users market is dispersed or conglomerated; large or small; if low or high income are important considerations in adopting new technologies.

The Nature of the Technology to be Transferred

1) The quality of technological design - if a technology is well designed from an engineering standpoint, then it is more likely to be utilized.

2) The adequacy of testing - if a technology is well tested, then it is more likely to be adopted by users.

3) The extent to which the technology has been proven - if a technology has been proven (i.e., demonstration projects or operative prototypes), then it is easier for a firm or state/local government to evaluate it. They may be more likely to adopt it.

4) The suitability of the technology to the production process in the private sector.
   a) If the technology is an intermediate technology and it can be easily adapted to the existing process, then it is more likely to be utilized.
   b) If it is a final product, then the extent to which it requires major or minor capital investment is important to the technology's utilization.
   c) The existence of maintenance services are an important consideration to a potential recipient.
   d) The existence of qualified personnel to run the new technology is an important factor.

5) Is the technology affordable and cost effective? Whether the users are state/local governments or firms, the affordability and cost effectiveness are important considerations in the adoption of new technologies.

6) The visibility of the new technology - if the technology is visible, then it is more likely to be adopted and diffused.

7) The familiarity of the technology - if the technology is similar to known and existing technologies, then it is more likely it will be adopted than if the technology were unfamiliar.

The Nature of the System

1) The state of the economy - if the economy is good, then interest rates are likely to be low, and capital less expensive. Therefore, firms are likely to be more innovative.

2) The political climate - governmental support for various activities (e.g., mass transit, poverty programs, etc.) affect the kind of support that can be expected for various programs. This is likely to influence the adoption of new technologies. Another example is the present climate of improving energy efficiency which has led the automobile companies to be more receptive to new energy saving technologies.

information-gathering activity of the decision unit can be made easier and cheaper. In each of these activities, the distribution of information conducted in the above manner may facilitate the successful transfer of technologies. However, these cases are probably limited in number. The implication is that technology transfer programs either require a broader range of strategies or implementation concerns must be incorporated into the R&D management process before the construction of a prototype or the demonstration of a new technology.

From a Static to a Dynamic Model of the R&D Management Process

To this point in the chapter, the emphasis has been on developing and describing what might be termed a static model of the federal R&D management process. The model we have used implies an orderly progression of R&D activities conceived as a consequence of a policy mandate (which itself evolves as a response to a demand expressed in the political system) that develops a product or service which is meant to satisfy the initial demand. To imply this, however, would be misleading. Rarely does the R&D management process operate in such an organized and linear fashion.

In reality, the process of R&D management is buffeted by uncertainties, budget gamesmanship, political agendas, and a reluctance to abort projects even when they appear to be "going sour." In this setting, the social problem or political concern which generated a policy response can be drowned out by the "noise" of fire fighting, budget politics, interagency conflict, and personnel turnover. Even "the problem" to be solved can prove elusive as deeper investigation leads to successively more mature formulations of appropriate solutions.

Thus, the world of R&D management is the world of midcourse corrections. It is a volatile environment more frequently typified by reaction than anticipation, and by risk than certainty. More fundamentally, it is a world in which authoritative managerial control is beyond the power of the technologist. Unlike the space program, where implementation was a problem in systems management and procurement with a clearly delineated objective and equally clear lines of authority, the implementation of civilian R&D is frequently a problem in cooperation, negotiation, marketing, or regulation, requiring the skills not only of the technologist, but also of the marketeer and the interagency diplomat. It may, in addition, call for the powers of a economic or regulatory sanction. In a mixed economy of federally supported civilian R&D, technology adoption is a problem in politics and marketing as well as a problem in engineering and design.

This is because civilian R&D activities are imbedded in a larger economic and political environment where the actions of buyers, sellers, and policymakers as well as technological feasibility determine the probability of implementation. This is a setting in which the play of institutional, political, and economic forces can clearly bend and shape the process of technology planning and design.

While it is possible to generalize about the origin and character of these forces, it is more useful to specify the manner in which these factors influence the implementation of the R&D products. In turn, we find that these forces manifest themselves as perturbations to the flow of the R&D process itself and as barriers to the effective transfer of products from the prototype state to adoption and diffusion (i.e. implementation) in the marketplace.[1] The flow perturbations represent those factors which attack the R&D process directly and prevent and constrain the transformation of a policy into a prototype. Barriers, however, arise as the result of an incompatibility between the R&D product and the relevant operating environment. (Clearly these two phenomena are not independent. Barriers can arise as a consequence of flow perturbations.)

Both classes of implementation constraints will be expanded upon in the following subsections. A recognition and understanding of these constraints represent a requisite step toward the development of an effective implementation strategy.

Process Perturbations

As a consequence of the desires and influence of various

actors who participate in shaping the R&D management process, there are a series of organizational, institutional, and environmental factors which mold, constrain, and divert the flow of activities within the various stages of the process. These factors occur both within and outside the organizational boundaries of individual agencies and have a direct bearing on the extent to which the product of the R&D process is compatible with both its original policy thrust and the dictates of the marketplace. This, in turn, affects the implementability of the product. The factors most frequently encountered are discussed in the following paragraphs.

Organizational Factors

Organizational factors consist of a broad spectrum of conditions which occur at the agency and interagency level. These factors can be grouped into three general categories: agency orientation, fiscal concerns, and program execution.

Commonly, the specification of programs and projects which respond to the policy mandate is influenced by interagency conflicts arising when more than one agency becomes involved in a policy issue. In this situation, agencies become competitors for legislative, presidential, and interest group support (Rourke, 1969). The resolution of this conflict usually involves differentiation of products. Consequently, we find several different agencies pursuing a common objective, but from unique and typically narrow perspectives emerging from the strengths of each agency. In the case of pursuing a policy which strives to achieve energy conservation in transportation, we find DOT encouraging system modifications such as greater use of transit, Federal Energy Administration (FEA) touting regulatory programs such as gas rationing, and ERDA pursuing advanced engine technologies. While a broad-based approach can be desirable in maximizing the performance of their nondirectional approach, often other dimensions of the problem or policy are ignored, meaning that the various efforts may prove incompatible.

Fiscal constraints are another form of control which influence the nature of the projects undertaken by agencies. Fiscal constraints caused by adjustments in government priorities and spending policies can have the effect of eliminating projects or reducing their scale. For example, the shift in emphasis from the space programs to social and economic programs during the mid-sixties resulted in a 42 percent cutback in NASA space program funds.

Fiscal uncertainties can have the effect of hindering the process of searching out new program ideas and approaches, limiting the range of program alternatives proposed, and ultimately restraining the growth of existing programs. This in turn proffers incrementalism. The demands for producing a deliverable, given the uncertainty of funding support, discourages venturing far beyond the current state of theoretical or technical knowledge.

The remaining category of organizational constraints relates to the capabilities of the R&D staff and the management of the programs. In addition to the effects which fiscal uncertainties impose on program planning, the disciplinary biases and the sociotechnical capabilities of the planners and staff affect the range of ideas that are generated, the options that are deemed feasible, and the programs and projects that are ultimately selected. For example, engineers have been criticized for analyzing problem solutions in terms of technologies (as opposed to reorganization of existing capital) and for selecting projects based upon technical criteria alone without addressing issues concerning social, political, or economic impacts. An example of this will be found in the case study of the short take-off and landing (STOL) aircraft. The project generation, selection, and design reflected the technical orientation of the NASA engineers. This acted to limit project generation to certain technological solutions, while nonmechanical strategy alternatives were not considered.

Another manifestation of this internal conflict is in the assigning of priorities to programs and projects within programs. This is perhaps one of the most common forms of intraorganizational conflict which might delay the process and in turn jeopardize the viability of the project.

While agency staff maintains substantial freedom to manipulate and interpret the organizational mandate into an acceptable program agenda, actual or potential intervention by supporters or constituents constricts or limits options. In addition, institutional factors constrain and force adjustments in the program's fiscal objectives. Once this process of adjustment is resolved and an "acceptable" program agenda defined, the actual project management phase of R&D is undertaken.

Once again, the traditional conflicts between management and staff can compromise the R&D product. The manager who is concerned primarily with budgets and timetables is often at odds with the scientist who is concerned with seeking an optimum solution. While pursuing a course desired by the technologists can mean unnecessary delays and costs for only marginal improvements in performance, the imposition of artificial deadlines can result in a premature and more expensive prototype design and construction and the utilization of inappropriate technology.

Institutional Factors

Institutional factors influence the manner in which the R&D process operates. By making reference to those constraints which occur at the institutional level, we are encompassing the interrelationships between various actors within the federal government who have an involvement in the R&D process (e.g., legislatures and executive offices as well as the operating agencies). Often, these institutional factors arise as a consequence of defects in planning, activating, and evaluating policies and programs (Gross, 1966). In other instances, they occur as a consequence of the fact that R&D activities are but one functional responsibility of the government and that these activities must be pursued in a manner consistent with other unrelated policies and objectives.

One principal source for institutional problems is the original formulation and structuring of the policy mandate. Often a policy may not be implemented because of the manner in which the policy statement or legislation was drafted. The wording may be too vague to give a clear idea of how to go about carrying out the policy, or it may reflect conflicting goals, in which meeting one objective might mean the defeat of another. Similarly, while there may be a number of aspects to the problem, the policy itself might attack only one, making it impossible for the policy to solve the problem comprehensively (Anderson, 1975).

In addition, the wording of the legislation may make it susceptible to legal question, or may leave it no legal means of implementing the policy objectives. The latter case might occur with regulatory policies. While the objective of regulating a particular industry might be laudable there may be no vehicle for implementing this goal without it being challenged on constitutional grounds. Once a plan has been formulated and adopted, there is often a tendency to place too much emphasis on the formalized documents. In order to improve the marketability of the project, greater flexibility is required. Although some attention to preparing the formal document and its implementation is, of course, mandatory, it should be realized that the written plan, while useful for supplementing people's memories and enhancing communication, cannot by nature be up-to-date and reflect situations and trends that have occurred after the plan is formulated and formalized. Thus, both inflexibility in adhering to original plans and overemphasizing prepared documents can seriously impede implementation (Gross, 1966).

Although evaluation is critical to the implementation process in determining how the policy might be adjusted to facilitate implementation, over- and underevaluation are common barriers to policy application. Many programs suffer from underevaluation because it is difficult to obtain reliable data on the progress of the policy. Even if adequate data is collected and the tedious exercise of analyzing the data is done responsibly, the information may never get back to those who would be able to change the policy based on the findings of the data. Overevaluation, on the other hand, may stifle the implementation that it is supposed to assist by diverting too much time and energy into data collection and analysis. Moreover, data is often distorted, since it is easier to give positive feedback on a program than to reveal that it has no or negative results.

Institutional forces also affect the R&D management process through the constraints and implicit controls tied to allocating R&D funds. The equitable distribution of R&D funds among states and regions often is a crucial political prerequisite to the successful continuation of the R&D management process. Conflicts over this issue can eliminate projects or cause substantial delays. A case in point was the controversy over the location of a proton accelerator by the Atomic Energy Commission (AEC) (now part of ERDA). This conflict delayed the locational decisions while congressional committees, state and local governments, AEC, and special committees such as the National Academy of Sciences bargained over the site (Murphy, 1971, p. 291). The location of the new solar research facilities is another case in point.

This is an especially important conflict because it is common that R&D contracts are made on a regional equity basis when another site would prove to be better suited on efficiency criteria. In the accelerator case mentioned above, it was felt that it was the Midwest's turn for a major facility. To locate the accelerator on either coast would have created a great deal of political conflict.

The location of laboratory facilities for the NIH, EPA, DOD, and ERDA are also partly a function of geographical sharing, although a better correlation can be found between the location of these facilities and the home states of powerful members of Congress, especially appropriations committees.

A final institutional factor arises as a direct consequence of the way in which the R&D process is executed. At each stage of the federal R&D management process, programs, projects, and prototypes have been structured to accommodate and attract the interest of financial and political benefactors. At the project execution phase of the R&D management process, these established supporters become the source of organizational inflexibility. As such, these supporters create an environment where the reassessment and discontinuation of prototype development is nearly impossible. Personal prestige, financial remuneration, organizational commitments, reputation, and supporting constituency are at stake if prototypes (and thus projects) fail to reach a successful completion even if this means only a technological success. Therefore, even when prototypes exhibit low probabilities of commercial success, it is difficult to halt the financial flow that ensures the program's continued support.

Environmental Factors

Environmental factors pertain to those constraints and regulations arising out of the milieu of federal R&D efforts. These factors establish "rules of the game"; that is, they define the conditions under which the R&D activities are conducted. The consequence of imposing artificial or arbitrary controls is that the R&D process is forced to respond in predicted and contrived ways to stimuli from the project participants or the market. This in turn frustrates implementation.

One environmental factor which has far-reaching implications in terms of what type of market demands receive federal attention through R&D is the role the government plays in a private enterprise economy. Government philosophy restricts the federal R&D management process to programs which neither compete with nor replace the private sector. On the other hand, the private sector favors, and to an extent expects, government intervention in situations where the private sector would be benefited. An example of this debate over appropriate roles, or turf, can be found in comments by E. S. Storkman, a G. M. vice-president, in a recent congressional investigation. In discussing R&D requirements in the automotive industry, Mr. Storkman stated:

> We question the need for the government to develop prototypes of products for ultimate sale in a competitive market. Private industry is better equipped and sufficiently motivated to respond to that phase of the problem. Government research of a basic type, in areas which now represent critical bottlenecks in the industry's efforts on advanced power plants, would supplement rather than duplicate the efforts of industry and thus make real contributions to progress (Hearings before the Committee on Commerce, U.S. Senate, 94th Congress, 1975).

In short, G.M. feels that the appropriate role for the government is to conduct basic research in those areas of automotive technology involving high risks and uncertainty.

Perhaps more rudimentary are the problems associated with the government's policy on patent rights. Patent rights are a continual source of controversy between public policymakers and private industry. To clarify patent policies, President Kennedy set forth a criterion which was to be used to determine who has claim to the patent rights in situations where inventions were made by private contractors working under government contract. The agencies were charged with the responsibility for claiming the patent title if the inventions were related to the public's health and welfare. However, this policy statement did not eliminate the need for individual patent settlements. DOD, NASA, and ERDA have each found it necessary to develop individual patent policies with their contractors.

An example of the debate over who has the patent right in a given situation can be found in the area of auto engine development. Briefly, the DOT patent policy states that all information, whether

> ... patented or unpatented in the form of trade secrets, know-how, proprietary information, or otherwise—resulting in whole or part from federally assisted research shall be made available at the earliest possible date to the general public, including but not limited to nongovernmental United States interests capable of bringing about further development, utilization, and commercial applications of such results (U.S. Congress, Senate Hearings, Sec. 509-a-1, 1975).

Further, the Act states:

> Whenever a participant in an advanced automobile development project holds background patents, trade secrets, know-how, or proprietary information which will be employed in the proposed development project, the Secretary shall enter into an agreement which will provide equitable protection to the right of the public and the participant.

> The Secretary shall make a determination as to whether patent licenses shall be granted on a royalty-free basis or upon a basis of charges designed to recover part or all of the costs of the federal research. The Secretary shall make Government patent rights and technological and scientific know-how available on nonexclusive and nondiscriminatory terms to qualified applicants (U.S. Congress, Senate Hearings, Sec. 509-9-3, 1975).

This kind of debate is common because patents continue to be a source of conflict and an obstacle to the effective utilization of products of federal R&D.

Barriers to Implementation

Implementation barriers, as defined earlier, are those factors which frustrate the successful adoption and diffusion of the R&D product. There are many different ways in which the barriers to implementation can be categorized. For the purposes of this section, they will be discussed under technological, economic, institutional, and political/ideological headings. These categories are not meant to be all-inclusive or strictly defined. As a result, some of the barriers will overlap into more than one category.

Before beginning this discussion of the four specific types of barriers, some attention should be given to the separate class of barriers for which policymakers and implementors are at a loss to find solutions. For lack of a better term, these might be referred to as the "states of nature" around which officials have to work. The most obvious of these is the state of the economy; in times of recessions, the increased demands on government services to take up the slack left by an ailing private sector do not leave enough funds to implement expensive new projects. For energy planning and most other types of planning related to the maintenance of our high standard of living, a second state-of-nature constraint is encountered. The realization that traditionally relied-upon natural resources are limited means that new production techniques and/or consumption patterns must evolve.

Anderson (1975) poses two additional state-of-nature barriers that might make the implementation of a specific project appear a less than hopeful task. First, while policymakers are working on one problem (with the hopes of finally discovering workable solutions) another issue may come into focus that distracts policymakers from the original concern. Thus, energy has become the issue of the 1970s, diverting attention from and sometimes even negating the positive results of the environmental movement of the 1960s.

The most pessimistic proposition is that despite all efforts, some problems simply have no solution—or at least not a completely satisfactory one. For example, educators have come to the painful realization that there are some children who are just unable to respond to all their attempts to help them learn.

With this framework in mind, the analysis of specific barriers,becomes appropriate. In the case of the first state-of-nature barriers, one can only be aware of their existence and attempt to accommodate them when possible. The following set of barriers should be viewed with the idea that intervention strategies can be developed to relax their impact as constraints.

Technological Barriers

If the objective of a policy is the widespread adoption of some technology, then this goal will be attainable only after it has been proven that the new technology is superior to the one it is meant to replace, if it is a replacement technology, or that it can meet its designated performance criteria in the case of a new technology. The intended users will be reluctant to accept and adopt a new product without assurances of its improved and reliable performance.

Projects often fail because implementation is initiated before the technology has been fully developed and proven reliable. If a new technology is prematurely introduced as a demonstration program and fails to perform as planned and anticipated, then the chances of the project maintaining the support needed to further refine the technology (particularly after its failure has been publicized in the media) are reduced unless an influential politician or constituency becomes the project's champion.

Economic Barriers

Sometimes economic barriers are intertwined with technological barriers. It is not enough for something to be technologically practical; it also must be economically feasible if it is to be successfully implemented. A product will rarely be adopted on purely ideological or technological grounds. A product must also have some economic justification to be acceptable. Although Operation Breakthrough was able to demonstrate the possibilities of producing industrialized housing, for example, it was unable to achieve the original objective of producing low-income housing at a cost lower than by using traditional building methods. It became apparent that the original objective relating to the economic feasibility of this program was unattainable. To avoid having the project labeled a failure because of its economic infeasibility, this objective was dropped in order not to cloud the promise of the project's potential technological gains.

The major economic restraint in any kind of policy or technology implementation is the fact that fiscal resources are limited and subjected to more demands than they can satisfy. In a developed country such as the United States, capital is usually the constraining resource. Since many innovations in technology and policy require heavy capital investment, they must compete with other areas in the private and public sectors for funding. In addition, adopting a new innovation or policy is often a replacement process, negating a large part of the time and capital investment expended on the old innovation. Besides justifying a project economically by demonstrating that society would be better served by allocating resources to it rather than to another project, it must also be shown that it is worth what could amount to abandoning a substantial prior investment and capital infrastructure.

Frequently, the implementation of a federal project requires the cooperation and support of state and local government. At this point, several economic barriers may arise. First, the state and local governments may not have available the matching funds necessary to initiate the program. Second, because of chronic fiscal problems, these jurisdictions traditionally have not all been able to attract and maintain a staff that can keep up with the changing administrative and technical knowledge necessary to implement and operate new programs. Finally, once the federal funding support terminates, if the jurisdiction can provide the required funds to initiate a program, then the local governments often find themselves in a situation where they can no longer afford to maintain and operate the program at its intended level. These conditions each work to thwart the implementation and diffusion of programs both at the initial site and at other locations. Examples of this occur in areas of water treatment systems and public transit systems.

Related to these issues, another kind of economic barrier arises when a policy is passed and allowed to proceed toward implementation without providing for sufficient federal funding to facilitate adoption. The war on poverty and public housing programs are examples of how a policy will fail if the money is held back.

Institutional Barriers

Institutional barriers arise as a consequence of the setting in which the program is to be implemented. These barriers reflect the interactions, influence, and motivations of those interests which play a role in supporting the adoption and diffusion of new programs.

Perhaps one of the most visible institutional barriers is the quagmire of bureaucratic red tape which state and local jurisdictions must wade through in soliciting federal support in implementing programs. In addition to the unending copies and documentation which must accompany grant applications, jurisdictions also must satisfy a variety of additional federal requirements such as clearing house reviews, affirmative action plans, and environmental impact statements. The level of staff commitment and time required to obtain federal assistance often precludes following this course; and, without this assistance, the program cannot and will not be undertaken.

The fragmentation of local agencies and organizations also acts to hinder the implementation of programs which have broad-ranging impacts. It is up to the primary implementing agency to maintain control over other organizations and individuals which might be affected by and thereby involved in the local implementation of the program. Hierarchical and jurisdictional relationships are difficult to set up when trying to coordinate these varied institutions. In these situations, conflicts among organizations and individuals are almost inevitable. These conflicts often lead to delays and sometimes impasses.

At the agency level, institutional barriers to implementation are evident in two areas (Anderson, 1975). First, the agency responsible for implementing a policy is affected in its abilities to function by its relationship to its constituency. Some agencies are treated with more deference than others. Those agencies whose expertise is based on science usually draw more respect than those in social welfare. Thus, although both agencies have the health of the population as a primary goal, the National Institute of Health—comprised of members from the scientific community—can more easily garnish support for its programs than the Department of Health, Education and Welfare.

Second, the power and influence an agency can exert varies over time depending on public priorities and the status of its mission. The deference given to the Environmental Protection Agency (EPA) in the 1960s has waned, and ERDA's has grown, with the switch in emphasis from the environment to energy. With the advent of this shift in interest the enthusiasm and zeal exhibited by EPA in its early years have given way to bureaucratic routine. The ability to overcome implementation barriers, reluctance, and resistance is directly related to the status level and influence of the supporting agency. As these forces lose their momentum, so do their programs.

We have often suggested the importance of political support to the initiation and execution of R&D programs. This support is crucial to the implementation process as well. However, implementation often is of less importance to political supporters than the act of promoting R&D activities. Elected policymakers have a relatively short time frame under which they work within the term of their office. In order to be reelected, they need to show their constituents during their present tenure that they have taken positive action on problems of concern. Given this circumstance, the act of formalizing a policy to solve a particular problem is often viewed as having actually solved it. Whether or not the policy is ever successfully implemented is immaterial to the policymaker's political record. Implementation failure can be presumed to be a technological or administrative problem. This type of goal displacement is one reason why implementation is often treated as a separate part of policy information. Because it is handled this way, the policy is often doomed to failure.

Political/Ideological Barriers

The strongest impediment to implementing a new policy or technology often has an ideological or political origin. Innovation means change, and change implies uncertainty. The present might not be without its problems, but at least they are problems people have come to know and have generally learned to live with.

The idea of altering our institutions and changing our present ways of doing things in order to try out a new innovation or policy (without any guarantee of success) is bound to meet with resistance on political and/or ideological grounds. The idea of change poses a threat to individuals or organizations who have a vested interest in the status quo. Whether this threat is real or imagined is not as important as the fact that it must be recognized by policymakers and implementors. Caution must be taken to ensure that it does not engender a movement that could successfully block implementation.

Resistance can come from a variety of sources. Probably the strongest resistance stems from a sensed conflict of interest. People will oppose a policy that they feel will impose additional costs or burdens on them without providing equivalent rewards or benefits in exchange. A second kind of resistance might come from those through which the innovation is to be implemented. In the case of a new technology, resistance may be experienced from persons who might feel their jobs or status would be threatened by the introduction of the innovation.

Public apathy provides yet another form of resistance to implementation. Apathy can be interpreted as a general satisfaction with existing things, so officials might be reluctant to provoke their constituency at the expense of reelection. If the public cannot see how a situation has a direct, adverse impact on the quality of their lives, then as far as they are concerned there is no problem and, consequently, no need for intervention.

If the opponents to a policy fail in blocking its formation and legitimization, they still have a number of paths open to them to delay or even block its implementation. The enabling legislation might be challenged on legal grounds; even if the attempt to block it through the court fails, lengthy legal proceedings can often delay a project until it is no longer feasible. Many regulatory policies have succumbed to such a fate. Convincing the relevant appropriations committees in Congress not to fund the project adequately is another way of impeding implementation. In addition, if officials in the implementing agencies are opposed to a policy, they can assign it a low priority or find out ways to impede its progress.

Since policy opponents and others who might be convinced to resist its implementation have ample opportunities for impeding its progress, those responsible for policy formulation have to be careful not to antagonize opponents and to give them a minimum basis on which to organize the opposition. This brings us full circle in describing one of the main barriers to policy implementation. In order to reduce resistance, the policy must reflect a diverse group of interests and objectives; because this often results in a vaguely worded policy, there is usually lacking a well-defined mechanism for carrying it out; or so much is left to the agency's discretion that the implementors, either of their own volition or in response to outside influence, may administer the policy in a particular way to reduce its impact.

Even if the policy objectives are clear, the implementation process is straightforward, and those responsible for carrying it out do not offer resistance, it does not necessarily mean that the policy clientele will not be able to circumvent its intent. Seat belt warning buzzers and affirmative action programs are only two of a countless number of examples where programs have come up against and been diluted through passive resistance to their implementation.

Nonprocess Conflicts

Up until this point in the chapter, the orientation of the discussion has been to identify and describe how implementation of federal R&D is frustrated as a consequence of the R&D management *process*. In addition to these interferences, there exists a related, but separate class of constraints, forces, and conditions which are at work and which can be construed to represent barriers to implementation. This new set of factors pertains directly to the nature or dimension of the project itself, or its parent program. This section briefly introduces the concepts related to a project's scope and scale, and indicates the manner in which these dimensions act to influence the implementation outcome. This dimensioning has five components: project goals; project time frame; project size; size of change proposed; and final user.

Before proceeding with this discussion it is relevant to make the point, perhaps at the risk of being redundant, that these barriers do not operate in a manner which is exclusive of the process perturbations and the barriers to implementation presented earlier in this chapter. In reality, these various implementation factors are interrelated and operate collectively and simultaneously in a manner which often defies prescription or labeling. The stratification we propose here has its foundation in the fact that it facilitates the organization and discussion of the myriad of factors which influence product implementation.

Project Goals

There is a cartoon that circulates throughout the federal bureaucracy every so often, and the caption reads: "When you are up to your hips in alligators, it is difficult to remember that the original objective was to drain the swamp." The cartoon reminds the bureaucrat that his career is a constant attempt to interpret and make true the goals and hopes of both the Congress and other policymakers in the White House or at the top of his agency. Unfortunately, although many of these goal statements sound desirable, they prove to be too ambitious and unrealistic. Project Independence, racial integration, and the early versions of the clean air and water legislation are a few recent examples. Other goals are inherently unrealizable or unclear as to meaning, such as "improving the quality of life" or "peace in our time." In these two cases, the concept of implementation is made very difficult because it is unclear what the specific projects are being carried out for: if you don't know where you are going, it is difficult to rationally discuss whether you are getting there efficiently or not.

In short, the very first requirement for a workable implementation strategy is that a clear, attainable goal be articulated. Moreover, no research should be undertaken unless it is specifically tied to a previously agreed upon goal. This means that projects should be undertaken to save or produce energy, not build reactors or auto engines; to clean up or reduce pollution, not build catalytic convertors or sewer treatment plants, and so forth. Such respecification is not a mere exercise in semantics. It means that the agencies and those responsible for research programs will have to justify their programs in terms of ends, not means. If an agency begins to think in these dimensions, the concepts of end users and implementation become more appropriate and relevant.

Project Time Frame

There appears to exist an inverse relationship between the amount of time and the cost to complete and implement a project. In dealing with this notion, the project manager may need to consider the amount of resources it would take to develop a new technology on a crash program basis versus a more leisurely paced development. The former would likely require considerable duplication as redundancy is built-in to help ensure success. The much referred to Manhattan Project, for example, built three separate prototypes of the atomic bomb, each so different that the individual explosions were all experiments. Had there been more time, such redundancy might not have been necessary and the cost could have been reduced considerably. On the other hand, opting for the "leisurely paced development" would likely have been an unacceptable option—one which did not conform with the specific needs of the problem. In this case, the implementation requirements prescribed the time and cost dimensions of the project. An alternative time and cost combination (specifically a lower-cost path) could have culminated in a product which was untimely, and thereby not implementable.

A second consideration is the amount of intervention, above and beyond resources for building a prototype, that social institutions are willing to endure. Change, particularly dramatic change, is difficult to introduce into an ongoing system. Consequently, as the odds are high that a rapid introduction of a new idea is apt to represent significant change, to facilitate the adoption and diffusion of the idea it will be necessary to provide for government intervention plans and policies. Given this probability, research programs that are designed to ensure the production of a technological prototype but do not include a specification of the steps required to implement the technology seem more likely to fail.

Project Size

The size of the project, in terms such as manpower or financial resources per unit of time required to do the job, seems likely to affect the probability of implementation. In general, in the case of a relatively small project where the end user is clearly identifiable, there seems to be a greater probability that the project will result in implementation. In this situation, close cooperation with a firm or firms is possible so that once a prototype is developed, the marketing and manufacturing sections of the firm(s) can take over the production responsibilities. Careful choice of the partnership between the government and the firm(s) might assure that there is capacity available to carry out the production and sales. In this case, the government merely provides the development capital to entice a part of the private sector to produce a product either before the firm would otherwise or to make the product relatively more attractive in terms of rate of return than other competing uses of the funds.

At the other extreme are the very large projects that require large sums of money and other resources. Large projects pose two challenges. First, generally, as a consequence of their size, large projects become separated, both in terms of time and activity, from the end user and the point in time or place where implementation is to occur. This protraction acts to increase risk and uncertainty and, consequently, the chances of implementing the product in its developed form.

Research projects often become large as a consequence of their complexity. Therefore, a second aspect of project size has to do with the extent to which the research involves the development of new processes and/or delivery systems.

Because of the state-of-the-art nature of the product or technology, prior production and marketing experience may be limited. In these cases, the public sector may be the only market segment which has the capability and interest to develop the facilities to produce the required product or service. Building large and complex projects most likely will require the involvement of several contractors and federal agencies. In the absence of a clear mandate and authority to amass and coordinate these functionaries, the agency sponsoring the project will most likely find itself in a situation where it cannot proceed and the project itself will fail to materialize in its present form. A recent example of this is the involvement of ERDA in the promotion of synfuels.

Size of Change Proposed

A related concern is with the amount of change that the new technology to be developed by the project represents to the existing state of the art. Small incremental changes are likely to assure a greater measure of success in terms of market acceptance, as the culture is used to seeing improvements to existing products as part of normal marketing. If an agency strategy is set up so that the incremental approach is stressed, although it will be easier to implement in the society, it will likely place greater reliance on the planning function at the public level. The reason for this is that the type of changes required by the public sector are characteristically broad in scope and complexity. Consequently, an incremental approach would have to be staged so that the acceptance of one stage would trigger off the one that followed.

At the other extreme, the requirement for revolutionary change in a technology will probably mean that the supporting infrastructure for the technology will have to be prepared and the present structure modified.

Finally, there is a question of whether there is any difference between implementing something in the state and local or private sectors. In general, it would likely be held that there is. Certainly, there is a greater possibility of direct intervention in the government areas. On the other hand, there are fifty state and hundreds upon hundreds of local units. Even policing regulation is difficult. Cooperation, the other extreme, is apt to be quite expensive. Further, there is no assurance that the subsidies offered to encourage a certain action will be sufficient because of the large number of competing pressures from various agencies that are attempting to elicit certain actions by offering matching funds to subsidize activities they want the localities to pursue. In the end, there is no guarantee that the programs promoted will be carried on beyond the subsidy period, even if the project is wholly agreed to.

Perturbations and Barriers: A Closing Thought

One should not, however, lose the proper perspective when assessing the extent to which there exist obstacles and barriers to the R&D management and implementation processes. While with most policies or technologies there will appear to exist a number of obstacles and barriers which frustrate implementation efforts, a closer examination of the problems will often reveal a domino type situation where, if one particular problem area could be resolved, then the other problems and conflicts would fall as well. Conversely, if there are problems that cannot be overcome, solving a myriad of other problems will not be sufficient to get the program implemented. Obviously, as noted earlier, the amount of intervention that the public sector will have to do to insure implementation in this case would tend to get the agency into policy areas that are outside its charter. Considerable coordination with other agencies would be necessary.

Final User

In devising a strategy for implementation, it is necessary that attention be focused on the identification of the ultimate client of a technology or of the service the technology produces. Even if the segmenting is as crude as federal government, state and local government, industry, and consumer, the implementation strategy would be different. In the case of federal government research that is being done for a federal agency, for example, the Department of Defense or NASA, the implementation problem is more straightforward. However, in the case where the business community is the ultimate client or end user, the implementation strategy chosen would depend upon factors such as the project's scope, cost, and timing.

In certain instances where it is deemed in the public's interest that the government become a direct seller of products, the consumer can become the ultimate client of federal R&D. Even if the private sector is used, it may be that the federal government can influence the success of implementation by helping to overcome some form of institutional resistance or inertia: for example, launching an education campaign or regulating a change.

Synopsis

The formalized R&D management process has been represented as comprising a structured and sequential series of activities whereby broad mandates, initiated at the policy level in response to politically mediated demands, are transformed into programs, projects, and eventually prototypes. We have also shown how this process exists within an environment where decisions relating to the conduct and scope of the R&D activities are constrained and influenced by politics and ideology, and turf and domain. Throughout the R&D management process, various actors (including constituents and supporters) make demands or provide resources in a manner which must be strategically balanced by those responsible for managing R&D programs and projects. The result is a bending and shaping of programs and projects such that the final product of the R&D process (the prototype) may no longer respond to the initial demand or problem which gave impetus to the program. This is a setting in which it becomes easier and safer for technologists to view the demonstration of engineering feasibility as the payoff of applied R&D, rather than the more difficult objectives of user acceptance or problem resolution.

The same forces which bend and shape the flow of the R&D management process are also encountered at the technology transfer stage where they manifest themselves as barriers to the adoption and diffusion of R&D products. While not unrelated to the issue of the mismatch between prototype performance and market requirement, a significant number of implementation barriers seem to arise as the result of the difficulty of coordinating and managing the decision-making processes of the competing agencies, levels of government, and two sectors which are found in a mixed economy.

Thus, some implementation barriers seem to arise because various governmental and private sectors often pursue exclusive objectives. They also seem to arise when program managers take the position, "implementation is none of my business."

Consequently, we find that what appeared to be a static process of R&D management is, in reality, a dynamic one wherein strategic adjustments, concessions, and compromises are significant components of the process which generates an R&D project.

In understanding how the R&D process and its attendant environment evolved, it was necessary to make a retrospective assessment of the government's involvement in R&D activities. What we gleaned from this perspective is that the current R&D process was created and matured during a period when the principal orientation of federal R&D activities was national defense and space exploration. The federal R&D management process was not intended to support "product research" which is an essential requisite for commercialization. Moreover, the lack of product research experience has left the government ill-prepared to respond to the increasing emphasis on civilian needs for R&D.

Many critics of federally sponsored R&D have noted the infrequency of prototype adoptions. They maintain the technologies which emerge as responses to problems identified and defined by federal agencies are not the solution that end users want and need. We can say this another way. The push of federal policy does not seem to produce technologies that match the pull of market demand. If policy push and market pull are out of alignment, it is not surprising that technology transfer does not occur. And this appears to be what is at work when prototypes are developed and perhaps demonstrated but not adopted.

The central question in the case of implementation failure is, then, why are policy push and market pull "out of synch?" This is the subject we turn to next.

Notes

1. Throughout this discussion, the term "market" is used to mean "end user." The end user may be a group of consumers

or an intermediary such as a state or local government or a private enterprise. As before, a market requirement comes about as a result of several factors, including the failure of the private enterprise system to provide products and services desired by consumers or their failure to internalize externalities associated with their actions (see page 110). In other words, government itself is a market, albeit a nonprofitable market, for products and services to which the private enterprise/consumer economic model does not adequately respond.

Bibliography

Anderson, James E. *Public Policy Making*. New York: Praeger Publishers, 1975.

Anderson, William and John Gous. *Research in Public Administration*. Chicago: Public Administration Service, 1945.

Barber, Richard J. *The Politics of Research*. Washington, D.C.: Public Affairs Press, 1966.

Bartlett, Joseph W. and Douglas L. Jones. "Managing a Cabinet Agency: Problems of Performance at Commerce." *Public Administration Review*, Vol. 34, No. 1 (January/February 1974), pp. 62-70.

Beyk, Thad and George Lathrop, ed. *Planning and Politics, Uneasy Partners*. New York: Western Publishing Co., 1970.

Breslin, Jimmy. *How the Good Group Finally Won*. New York: Viking Press, 1975.

Chen, Kan, ed. *Technology and Social Institutions*. Proceedings of a 1973 Engineering Foundation Conference, sponsored by IEEE, 1964.

Cleaveland, Frederic N. *Science and Stale Government*. Chapel Hill: The University of North Carolina Press, 1959.

Doctors, Samuel I. *The Role of Federal Agencies in Technology Transfer*. Cambridge, Mass.: M.I.T. Press, 1969.

Douds, Charles F. "The State of the Art in the Study of Technology Transfer—A Brief Survey." *R&D Management*, Vol. 3 (1971).

Drucker, Peter F. *Technology, Management and Society*.

New York: Harper and Row, 1967.

Edel, Matthew. *The Economics and the Environment.* Englewood Cliffs, N.J.: Prentice-Hall, 1973.

Freeman, Leiper. *The Political Process.* New York: Random house, 1965.

Furash, Edward E. "The Problem of Technology Transfer." From *The Study of Policy Formation.* Edited by Bauer and Gergen. New York: Free Press, 1971.

Gerloff, Edwin A. "Performance Control in Government R&D Projects: The Measureable Effects of Performing Required Management and Engineering Techniques." *IEEE Transactions on Engineering Management,* Vol. EM-20, No. 1 (February 1973), pp. 6-14.

Gross, Bertram M. "Activating National Plans." In Lawrence, J.R., ed., *Operational Research and the Social Sciences.* New York: Tavistock Publications, 1966.

Gustafson, Thane. "The Controversy over Peer Review." *Science,* Vol. 190 (12 December 1975), pp. 1060-1066.

Havelock, Ronald and David Lingwood. *R&D Utilization Strategies and Functions: An Analytical Comparison of Four Systems.* Ann Arbor: Institute for Social Research, The University of Michigan, 1973.

Hoos, Ida. *Systems Analysis in Public Policy: A Critique.* Berkeley: University of California Press, 1972.

Jones, Charles O. *An Introduction to the Study of Public Policy.* Belmont, Calif.: Wadsworth Publishing Co., 1970.

Kaysen, Carl. "Governmental and Scientific Research—Some Unanswered Questions." *The Public Interest,* No. 24 (Summer 1971), pp. 80-85.

Lakoff, Sanford A. "Congress and National Science Policy." *Political Science Quarterly,* Vol. 89, No. 3 (Fall 1974), pp. 589-610.

Lewis, Frank L. and Frank G. Zarb. "Federal Program Evaluation from the OMB Perspective." *Public Administration Review,* Vol. 34, No. 4 (July/August 1974), pp. 308-317.

Little, Arthur P. *Federal Funding of Civilian Research and Development, Volume I: Summary.* Prepared for E.T.I.P., U.S. Department of Commerce. Washington, D.C., February 1976.

Milbergs, Egils and Robert E. Quick, Jr. "Experimental

Technology Incentives Program, Management of Federal Civilian R&D Programs." Draft Copy. Stanford Research Institute, April 1976.

Miller, Jim. "NASA Aeronautical Research and Development Priorities." Unpublished in-house paper. Institute of Transportation Studies, University of California, Berkeley, August 1975.

Moynihan, Daniel P. *Coping, On the Practice of Government.* New York: Random House, 1973.

Murphy, Thomas P. *Science, Geopolitics, and Federal Spending.* Lexington, Mass.: D.R. Heath & Co., 1971. (University of Maryland).

Musgrove, Richard and Peggy B. Musgrove. *Public Finance in Theory and Practice.* New York: McGraw-Hill Book Co., 1973.

National Science Foundation. *An Analysis of Federal R&D Funding by Function, 1969–76.* Surveys of Science Resources Series, NSF 75-330, Washington, D.C.: Government Printing Office, 1975.

National Science Foundation. *Federal Funds for Research, Development, and Other Scientific Activities.* Washington, D.C.: Government Printing Office, December 1975.

National Science Foundation. *National Patterns of R&D Resources, 1953–1974.* Washington, D.C.: GPO, 1974.

National Science Foundation. *Research and Development in Industry.* Surveys of Science Resources Series, NSF 75-315. Washington, D.C.: GPO, 1973.

Phelps, Edmund S., ed. *Private Want and Public Needs.* New York: W.W. Norton & Co., 1962.

Reagan, Michael D. *Science and the Federal Patron.* New York: Oxford University Press, 1969.

Roessner, J.D. *Federal Technology Transfer: Results of a Survey of Formal Programs.* The American Society of Mechanical Engineers, 30 July 1975.

Roessner, J.D. *The Structure of Federal Technology Transfer Activities: Implications of Current Research.* National Science Foundation. Washington, D.C.: GPO, 1976.

Rosenthal, Albert H., ed. *Public Policy and Administration.* Albuquerque: University of New Mexico Press, 1973.

Rourke, Francis. *Bureaucracy, Politics, and Public Policy.* Boston: Little, Brown and Co., 1969.

Schultze, Charles O. *The Politics and Economics of Public Spending*. Washington, D.C.: The Brookings Institute, 1968.

Steelman, John R. *Administration for Research*. Volume Three of *Science and Public Policy*. Washington, D.C.: GPO, 1947.

Souel, Terry M. *Technology Transfer—A Selected Bibliography*. Prepared for NASA. Denver: Denver University, June 1969.

Sundquist, James L. *Politics and Policy*. Washington, D.C.: The Brookings Institute, 1968.

The Struggle to Bring Technology to Cities. Washington, D.C.: The Urban Institute, 1971.

Thompson, J.K.L. "Barriers to Information Transfer and Technological Change." *Accelerating Innovation*. Papers given at a symposium held at the University of Nottingham (March 1969).

U.S. Congress. Senate. *Automobile Fuel Economy and Research and Development*. Hearings before the Committee on Commerce. 94th Cong., 12 and 13 March 1975.

U.S. Department of Transportation and National Aeronautics and Space Administration. *Civil Aviation Research and Development Policy Study Report*. Washington, D.C.: GPO, March 1971.

U.S. Department of Transportation. *Analysis of Fiscal Year 1976 DOT R&D Management Objectives—1974–1976*. Washington, D.C.: GPO, 1976.

U.S. Department of Housing and Urban Development. *Tomorrow's Transportation*. Office of Metropolitan Development, Urban Transportation Administration. Washington, D.C.: GPO, 1968.

U.S. Congress. Joint Economic Committee. *Priorities and Efficiency in Federal Research and Development*. 94th Cong., 2nd sess., 29 October 1976.

U.S. Congress. House. *Hearings before the Subcommittee on Science, Research, and Development of the Committee on Science and Astronautics*. 92nd Cong., 1st sess., 22, 23, 24 June; 13, 14, 15 July; 5 and 6 August 1971.

U.S. Congress. House. Select Committee on Government Research. *Documentation and Dissemination of Research and Development Results*. 88th Cong., 2nd sess., 20 November 1964.

U.S. Department of Transportation. *Innovation in Public Transportation.* Washington, D.C.: GPO, 1975.

U.S. Department of Transportation and NASA. *Civil Aviation R&D Policy (CARD) Implementation Plan.* Washington, D.C.: GPO, March 1973.

U.S. Department of Transportation. *The Role of Government in Transportation R&D and Their Implementation.* Report of the 4th workshop on National Transportation Problems, 5–6 May 1975. Washington, D.C.: GPO, 1975.

Waldo, Dwight, ed. *Ideas and Issues in Public Administration.* New York: McGraw-Hill Book Co., 1953.

Webber, Melvin. "Dilemmas in a General Theory of Planning." Institute of Urban and Regional Development, University of California. Working paper no. 194, November 1972.

White, Michael J. *Management in Federal Agencies.* Lexington, Mass.: D.C. Heath & Co., 1975.

White, Michael, Michael Radnor, and David Tansik. *Management and Policy Science in American Government.* Lexington, Mass.: D.C. Heath & Co., 1975.

Whitlock, Charles Henry III. "A By-Product of NASA: Transfer of New Technology to Various Sectors of the Economy." Master's Thesis, College of William and Mary, 1970.

Wirt, John G., Arnold J. Lieberman, and Roger E. Levien. *R&D Management.* Toronto: Lexington Books, 1975.

5

Public Sector-Private Sector Comparisons

The previous two chapters have focused on analyzing the R&D processes in the public and private sectors. In this chapter, we turn to a comparison of R&D activities in these two sectors for the purpose of identifying factors which may affect the low rate of adoption and diffusion of technologies developed with public funds.

The intent of this chapter is *not* to suggest that the commercialization of government-sponsored technologies would be assured "if only government behaved more like a private industry" (although such an hypothesis was clearly tested). This chapter serves as an analytical staging ground for the development of hypotheses and propositions that explain why the commercialization of public sector R&D findings and prototype technologies is infrequent and difficult. In turn, the explanatory propositions developed at the end of this chapter will be evaluated in a series of case studies and then used to generate strategies for facilitating the implementation of publicly sponsored R&D.

Critical Differences Between Public and Private Sector R&D Activities

When one reviews the public and private R&D processes in terms of the differences in sectoral orientation, setting, and behavior, it is possible to identify four generic areas wherein conditions and extraneous influences interact with the R&D activities to frustrate the commercialization of government sponsored R&D. These areas are (1) role and motivation, (2) project selection and termination criteria, (3) client relationships, and (4) conduct of R&D activities. Each of these areas will be discussed in turn and related to the implementation problem.

Role and Motivation

The most fundamental difference between public and private technology R&D activities is the difference in role and motivation. Private R&D is a business activity which pursues profitmaking opportunities by responding to market demands. Most authors characterize the process as market-responsive or market-disciplined. They qualify this appraisal in the case of regulated industries and oligopoly-controlled sectors where "concentration" prevails.

In contrast, many government-sponsored R&D activities are policy-responsive. Where private companies are market-focused, governmental agencies tend to be mission-oriented. For example, ERDA's mission is the implementation of federal energy policy. The birth of mission-oriented agencies is often a response to the failure of private sector initiatives or the perceived inadequacy of market or enterprise solutions. Risk aversion of private capital is one form of market failure which explains the growth of public investment in high-risk R&D. The inability of traditional markets and pricing mechanisms to resolve problems of air and noise pollution and other externalities offers another explanation for the creation of mission-oriented agencies. The supply of public goods, merit goods, and income redistribution objectives also explains the growing role of mission-oriented agencies.

The growth of mission-oriented agencies has evolved as a result of the failure of traditional enterprise solutions, and the policy-responsiveness of these agencies sharply distinguishes their role from the market-responsive, profit-seeking mode of private industries. As a consequence of this orientation, the goals of the public sector are not always clear, nor are measures of effectiveness commonly agreed upon. Interestingly, one finds that technical standards prevail in this vacuum.

In some instances, mission-oriented agencies and market-oriented firms take on an adversary relationship. This is true of EPA and the auto industry. In other cases, mission-oriented agencies have positioned themselves to serve an industrial clientele. In the latter case, governmental agencies such as NASA and the Department of Transportation have undertaken R&D of a long-range character at the boundary of the state of the art. Research that must advance the state of the art or orchestrate the design of large-scale, complex systems often entails higher risks than private capital is willing to assume.

The preemption of much of the short-range R&D by private industry and the private sector's general opposition to government intervention in product development both contribute to the location of government R&D far "upstream" in the implementation process where early commercialization is less feasible, market response more difficult to forecast, and end users more difficult to identify. One reason firms oppose governmental intervention in downstream short-range R&D activities is found in the structure of U.S. patent laws. Federally funded research and development is typically nonproprietary and not protectable under patent rights. In areas where commercialization feasibility appears imminent, the private sector prefers to establish proprietary rights and patent protection and to avoid public involvement that would dilute their ability to "corner the market" on a product or process. This has built-in negative implications for the early adoption of federally sponsored R&D and has caused special patent arrangements to be sought and made by agencies in certain cases.

These differences in role, motivation, and location in the R&D process have implications for project selection.

Project Selection and Termination Criteria

Policy-responsiveness and mission orientation lead government agencies to organize technology R&D programs around "the proof of concepts." The often-perceived objective is to establish the feasibility of a technology which advances the state of the art within a specific mission area such as pollution control, energy conservation, transportation, or manned space flight. Once the feasibility of the technology is demonstrated, the R&D is considered complete, and the project is terminated.

In contrast, private sector R&D programs have a different success standard based on "the proof of sales." The perceived objective is to develop a product that can be marketed profitably. Marketability requires that the technology perform on multiple dimensions—dimensions broader than the mandate of a mission-oriented agency. Thus, the marketability criterion imposes simultaneous tests of performance, price-competitiveness, imageability, and manufacturability.

It should not be surprising if a technology satisfying a feasibility test within the context of a policy mission falls short of the multidimensions of the marketability test.

These differences in project and product selection criteria are exaggerated by differences in the client relationships of government agencies and the private sectors.

Client Relationships

It is an accepted wisdom of business practice to "lead from strength." This means that businesses shape their R&D programs to service markets where they have already established reputations, expertise, and sales networks. By "leading from strength," businesses avoid or reduce the risks and uncertainties that are associated with new clients, new markets, and radically new products. The production and sales activities of the firm can be scheduled and made efficiently routine because the consumer or client has relatively well-known and predictable wants and needs. R&D focused on incremental improvements in product design supports this continuity of clientele and marketing strategy. (In contrast, federal R&D is often sufficiently advanced or basic that it is difficult to identify end users.)

Public sector agencies must typically serve and satisfy a more diverse clientele, which places conflicting demands on the agency's staff and budget. Federal agencies must frequently position themselves to simultaneously satisfy congressional policy and appropriations committees, Office of Management and Budget budgeteers, cabinet-level coordinating committees (such as the Domestic Council), industrial clients, and implementing agencies at the state and local level. Budget competition and turf conflicts between agencies also constrain an agency's discretion in a manner analogous to sales competition between private firms.

The cross-pressures of conflicting demands influence the mix of R&D projects and can bend the outcome of particular research and design activities. Critical to the issue of implementation failure is the fact that signals from potential users or manufacturers of a technology are diluted by demands from the political process and the exigencies of interagency politics. To be adopted, prototypes must satisfy the political requirements and the evaluation by the private sector and the local implementing agencies. In responding to the political demands (which are more eminent in that they are most closely related to project support and budget appropriation), the resulting prototype is often incompatible with the user's demands.

The demands of competing constituencies are amplified by the fragmentation of authority in the public sector. In Congress, responsibility for technology oversight and policy development is dispersed among literally dozens of committees with competing territorial prerogatives. The responsibility for technology development is also chaotically distributed throughout the executive branch. Private industry also evidences specialization and division of responsibility; but in the private sector, command responsibility and the ability to orchestrate functional units is available at the top of the corporate hierarchy. Dysfunctional conflicts between divisions—marketing, R&D, finance, manufacturing, and sales—can occur; but they can also be resolved by the exercise of higher authority. In the public sector, the balance of powers and traditions of independence mean that policy conflicts must frequently be resolved through negotiations and compromises not disciplined by a command structure.

The absence of a viable command structure means that the natural entropy of mission-oriented R&D agencies works against the formulation of a coherent technology development strategy. As a result, technology initiatives in the area of energy conservation can easily conflict with technology initiatives in the area of air quality and travel safety. Interagency conflicts—whether rooted in competing objectives or organizational rivalries—serve to diminish the ability of the private sector to adopt technologies (witness the automobile industry) and to frustrate the development of cooperative relationships between government and the private sector.

Conduct of R&D

There is substantial exchange of personnel between government, private industry, consulting firms, and universities. This tends to dilute differences in the conduct of technology R&D. Research and design techniques are similar in the two sectors. Nevertheless, differences can be found.

Probably the most critical is the multidisciplinarity of R&D activities in the private sector, compared to the stronger disciplinary biases of in-house public agency R&D.

Federal R&D activities display what might be considered a significant engineering bias while private sector R&D is shaped by orchestrated interaction between design technicians, marketing specialists, financial analysts, cost-control engineers, and practitioners from sales and production. Engineering optima and cost-conscious design are substantially different. (Public implementing agencies—typically state or local agencies—display biases comparable to federal R&D agencies. Local agencies tend toward capital-intensive, engineered, or "built" solutions that can be programmed as projects. Routinization and a limited array of solution strategies—a limited product line—is a trademark of local implementing agencies as it is with federal R&D agencies.)

Even where public agencies contract with private firms for R&D, it appears that agencies do not usually take advantage of the full range of available corporate services. Contract R&D seems to display the same engineering bias as in-house R&D because contracts do not typically involve the financial analysis, market analysis, and sales engineering divisions of the companies engaged to develop or test prototypes.

While federal R&D efforts commonly reflect a narrow disciplinary scope and an engineering bias, the same process can also be characterized by management discontinuities and volatile, crisis-responsive changes in policy objective. In part, this is due to quadrennial changes in partisan control; but it also appears to be due to the high "burn-out" rate of managers in policy-sensitive positions. In comparison, private industry evidences relatively stable objectives (profits and growth) and maintains a relatively high degree of management continuity.

The continuity of objectives and management in the private sector means that firms have been able to develop relatively routine procedures for new product development and that corporate planning can be used to control as well as predict exigencies. As projects move from concept to product, they accrue executive sponsorship and career identification. This gives them an "extra push" toward implementation that even the best-planned federal extramural projects and prototypes are unable to match.

Despite sponsorship, the technical, financial, competitive, regulatory, and organizational barriers can readily confound the process of private sector technology development and implementation. If the barriers cannot be overcome, the project will be terminated. However, the termination of an R&D effort typically does not threaten the viability of a firm or one of its divisions. In contrast, government agencies are vulnerable to political embarrassment and budget cutbacks if a project sours. This provides an incentive to prolong R&D activities past the stage at which a private firm would write off the project and its losses. Project termination is also difficult given the plenitude of policy objectives that can be advanced to justify continuing public R&D efforts.

A final, and perhaps the most basic, difference between the private and public sectors in their conduct of R&D is the extent to which implementation and marketability concerns are integral components of the two sectors' processes. In the private sector, marketing management has a major role in the decision making throughout all stages of the R&D process. In the public sector, however, implementation and marketing are generally not considered until the final stages of the R&D process (e.g., the technology transfer stage at which time the supporting agency finds itself in a position of having to "hawk" the prototype to an uncertain market).

A Recapitulation of Sectoral Differences

The critical differences between the public and private sector R&D processes and their effect upon project implementation can be demonstrated by two alternative approaches. This is accomplished by Table 5-1 and Figure 5-1. The information presented in these two exhibits supplements the preceding discussion of the critical differences between public and private sectors' R&D activities. Taken together, this discussion, along with Table 5-1 and Figure 5-1, provides a comprehensive assessment of those factors

TABLE 5-1

Summary of Literature on Differences Between Public
and Private Organizations: Main Points of Consensus

Topic	Proposition
Environmental Factors	
Degree of market exposure (reliance on appropriations)	Less market exposure results in less incentive to cost reduction, operating efficiency, effective performance.
	Less market exposure results in lower allocational efficiency (reflection of consumer preferences, proportioning supply to demand, etc.).
	Less market exposure means lower availability of market indicators and information (prices, profits, etc.).
Legal, formal constraints (courts, legislature, hierarchy)	More contraints on procedures, spheres of operations (less autonomy of managers in making such choices).
	Greater tendency to proliferation of formal specifications and controls.
	More external sources of formal influence and greater fragmentation of those sources.
Political influences	Greater diversity and intensity of external informal influences on decisions (bargaining, public opinion, interest group reactions).
	Greater need for support of "constituencies" -- client groups, sympathetic formal authorities, etc.
Organization-Environment Transactions	
Coerciveness ("coercive," "monopolistic," unavoidable nature of many government activities).	More likely that participation in consumption and financing of services will be unavoidable or mandatory. (Government has unique sanctions and coercive powers.)
Breadth of impact	Broader impact, greater symbolic significance of actions of public administrators. (Wider scope of concern, such as "public interest.")
Public scrutiny	Greater public scrutiny of public officials and their actions.
Unique public expectations	Greater public expectations that public officials act with more fairness, responsiveness, accountability, and honesty.

contributing to and facilitating the failure of the public sector to generate and execute R&D programs which are commercially relevant and implementable.

Table 5-1 consists of a summary of the principal differences between the sectors as described by Rainey et al. in their paper "Comparing Public and Private Organizations" (1976). The differences have been organized into three categories: environmental factors, organization-environment transactions, and internal structures and processes.

Figure 5-1 is a schematic representation of the R&D process operating in both the public and private sectors. This figure serves as yet another technique for illustrating some of the principal differences in sector orientation and

TABLE 5-1
(continued)

Topic	Proposition
Internal Structures and Processes	
Complexity of objectives, evaluation and decision criteria	Greater multiplicity and diversity of objectives and criteria.
	Greater vagueness and intangibility of objectives and criteria.
	Greater tendency of goals to be conflicting (more "trade-offs").
Authority relations and the role of the administrator	Less decision making autonomy and flexibility on the part of public administrators.
	Weaker, more fragmented authority over subordinates and lower levels. (1. Subordinates can bypass, appeal to alternative authorities. 2. Merit system constraints.)
	Greater reluctance to delegate, more levels of review, and greater use of formal regulations. (Due to difficulties in supervision and delegation).
	More political, expository role for top managers.
Organizational performance	Greater cautiousness, rigidity. Less innovativeness.
	More frequent turnover of top leaders due to elections and political appointments results in greater disruption of implementation of plans.
Incentives and incentive structures	Greater difficulty in devising incentives for effective and efficient performance.
	Lower valuation of pecuniary incentives by employees.
Personal characteristics of employees	Variations in personality traits and needs, such as higher dominance and flexibility, higher need for achievement on part of government managers.
	Lower work satisfaction and lower organizational commitment.

Source: Rainey, et al., 1976.

priority. Project origin, project organization and evaluation, and implementation/end-user orientation are among the differences characterized. This figure also distinguishes between a "minimal survival path" which is followed by the federal R&D agency, and the "full implementation path" which is essentially within the domain of the private sector or local implementation agency directly orienting their products and services to the end user.

From Critical Differences to Explanatory Hypotheses

Although no systematic accounting has occurred, it is generally believed by R&D practitioners and congressional

FIGURE 5-1. R&D Process in the Public and Private Sectors

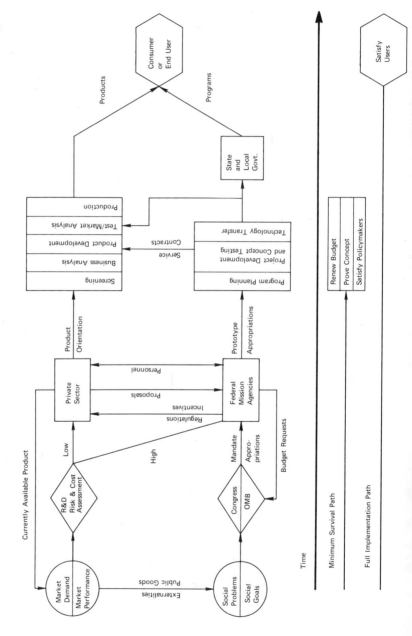

oversight committees that the products of federally sponsored R&D are underutilized. When the test of deployment is used to assess the performance of R&D programs, it seems that technology development is proceeding apace; when the more demanding implementation test—that of adoption and diffusion—is considered, it appears federally sponsored R&D efforts are less than successful. This is not an observation based on systematic survey evidence, but a conjecture based on a reasonable number of empirical observations, professional experiences, and secondary reports.

If the conjecture is reasonable, and we believe it is, then we must be concerned with "why": why are the products of federally sponsored R&D failing to achieve greater acceptance in the commercial marketplace and the arena of state and local government?

The previous section which compared the differences in role, behavior, motivation, and clientele of the public and private sectors begins to offer some critical insights and clues. It may be that the principal cause of implementation failure is the mismatch of policy push and market pull. It may be that mission agencies in the federal government are not producing technologies that perform the way consumers want them to. It may be that the enterprise system is not performing in a way that matches the public interest as defined by legislation and presidential policy.

We can state these explanations of implementation failure more formally. Implementation failure may be a function of "market incompatibility"—the dissonance between a candidate technology and the wants and requisites of the firms manufacturing products and the consumers using them. Or implementation failure may be a function of "market failure"—the dissonance between private wants and social needs.

In the first case, market incompatibility, implementation failure would occur because the technology was out of synchronization with consumer desires or with the structure of incentives guiding product-policy decisions of the firms which make up the technology delivery system.

In the second case, market failure, implementation failure could occur because the technology delivery system is not motivated to achieve policy-defined notions of social welfare, but to serve the private interests of producers and those consumers whose incomes are sufficient in the aggregate to constitute a market.

For an instance of dissonance between policy push and market pull, consider the comments of Thomas A. Murphy, Chairman of the Board of General Motors Corporation.

> All we can do is make the cars that people are interested in buying . . . (They are) interested in the utility of the vehicle under all categories of use . . . I don't think that anybody is going to pay more for an automobile because it pollutes less than the one next to it. So unless you have some standards, unless the Government establishes them and unless the Government administers them, it probably isn't going to happen.

> To some degree this is true with some safety features. But I think that in setting mileage standards the Government has invaded the marketplace when it didn't need to. The marketplace will straighten that one out because we will all try to improve our fuel economy and we will all try to get the best in fuel efficiency that we possibly can, because then we can demonstrate its value to the customer (*U.S. News and World Report*, January 10, 1977, p. 45).

Murphy makes an interesting case: gasoline prices will encourage consumers to demand more fuel-efficient automobiles; and responding to the signals of the marketplace, General Motors will manufacture them. But Murphy's case can be seen as flawed and partial: the price of gasoline is controlled and, thus, does not reflect the "true scarcity cost" of petroleum-based fuels; nor does the cost of gasoline reflect the value we as a nation place on "energy independence" and the associated freedom in the pursuit of American foreign policy. The price of gasoline also does not reflect balance of payment problems raised by the cartel price of crude oil.

In combination, these factors can be used to argue that the price of gasoline may not adequately reflect the public interest in the conservation of petroleum and the development of more fuel-efficient vehicles and driving habits.

This, in cameo form, is one example of the mismatch between policy push and market pull. Another, perhaps more common, case of dissonance between policy push and market pull may arise because mission agencies fail to anticipate differences in the role and motives of the federal government and the technology user, forgetting or mistaking consumer preferences in the process.

Thus, we postulate the general hypothesis that implementation failure and adoption lag are a function of the mismatch between policy push and market pull and that this dissonance can involve situations which reflect a failure in technology conception and design or a failure in market performance.

If the general hypothesis is to offer a credible explanation for implementation failure, then it must be explicable as empirical hypotheses that offer evidentiary tests based on empirical findings. The explication of empirical hypotheses follows:

Empirical Hypothesis #1

Marketing and market research tend to be an afterthought in the public sector. Marketing techniques are used in disseminating research findings and information about prototypes, but play only a limited role in shaping the R&D agenda and the process of technology design. The engineering bias of public sector R&D means that engineering optima influence technology development while market analysis (evaluations of the consumer's price tolerances and total performance expectations) is generally conducted late, if at all. It is probable that the over-engineered products and technologies which result will be ill-suited to compete on grounds of cost or manufacturability.

Empirical Hypothesis #2

Public sector R&D managers feel pressure to stay off the private sector's turf and to avoid downstream research and development activities preempted by profit-seeking capital. The sometimes adversary, sometimes collaborative relationship between mission-oriented agencies and private firms serve to confine government R&D efforts to high-risk, complex system research having a higher probability for implementation failure. The same ideological and political pressures limit technology transfer programs to information dissemination. In many instances, information dissemination alone is insufficient to motivate adoption, particularly where a technology is developed to serve a social welfare objective defined in terms of a policy mission rather than a target market.

Empirical Hypothesis #3

Policymaking and public expenditures typically occur in a bureaucratic setting of Byzantine complexity. For our purposes, the most important consequence of this multiagency, multi-interested environment is the incongruity of clients and consumers. Agency outputs must satisfy a large number of constituencies—only two of which are composed of producers and end-point consumers. To the extent that agency outputs are bent by political or institutional demands, they may be unsuited to satisfy the requirements of manufacturability, profitability, and consumer acceptance.

Empirical Hypothesis #4

Most agencies do not have explicit objectives or explicit rules for making trade-offs between objectives. Best judgment and rules of thumb prevail. In part, this is a consequence of the multiple demands placed on them (as discussed above) and in part a consequence of a *modus operandi* which emphasizes the pursuit of narrow, mission-oriented goals. Most agencies operate without a measure of failure or success that takes implementation into account. Most have a "sense" of sufficiency, but no rigorous or quantifiable measure of effectiveness. Quite clearly, there is no "profitability" criterion which guides public decision making, nor is there typically a useful measure of "effectiveness" to be used in cost-effectiveness analysis. The absence of measures of effectiveness for determining the feasibility of programs or technologies evolving from public R&D efforts gives rise to two process aspects. First, professional standards tend to be used as a yardstick for agency performance. Second, peer standing tends to replace implementation, commercialization, or marketability as measures of management performance.

Empirical Hypothesis #5

Competition is looked upon with favor in the private sector where it is associated with product and price differentiation and economic efficiency. In the public sector, competition tends to be expressed in terms of rivalries over turf and domain. The resolution of domain conflicts tends to divert agency attention from its functional mission and seems to produce illogically compromised technical outcomes.

Empirical Hypothesis #6

Failure to implement (or less than effectively implement) may be a consequence of the same economic forces which required public intervention. Where public intervention was precipitated by externalities, income inequalities, risk aversion of oligopoly capital, or other forms of market failure, it is reasonable to look for the causes of unsuccessful implementation in the structure of the economy rather than in the shortcomings of a particular R&D agency. Thus, the problem may be one of insufficient power or authority rather than inefficiency or ineffectiveness. In this instance, implementation would flounder due to lack of penalties or incentives rather than to failure of technique or technology.

In cases where public intervention followed market failure, implementation may be frustrated by the continuing hegemony of the private market, absent strong incentives, or penalties. Where this is the case, we would expect to find that public agency priorities are dictated by a public-goods evaluation methodology, whereas marketable technologies must satisfy profit criteria. Thus, the availability of a new technology would not result in private adoption unless the technology could be produced profitably as well as be socially desirable.

The investment decisions required for the supply of public goods and the relief of externalities involve larger tests of efficacy than the "profitability" test of the private sector. These tests may be a better measure of the public interest than "marketability." In the case of providing public goods, the failure of commercial adoption may be a function of not imposing adequate incentives and penalties in the private sector.

Empirical Hypothesis #7

Federal R&D has historically and traditionally been conducted for public clients: the military, the space program, and implementation agencies at the state and local level. Commercial and industrial firms are a relatively new client group for federally sponsored R&D. It appears that R&D screening criteria have not been modified to incorporate the requirements of private implementation.

Summary

The assessment of the differences between the private and public sectors' R&D processes has indicated the presence of numerous institutional, technical, and financial problems that act to frustrate the implementation of public R&D products. Some of these problems are exacerbated by the structure of the public sector, its mission, and the view it has of its R&D mandate. Others are complicated by the private sector's resistance to public intervention in downstream marketing and development activities. Although it is possible to get a feeling of helplessness because of the large number of barriers that can intervene to stop successful implementation, it is not our purpose to create this impression. A study of all of the potentially dangerous bacteria, viruses, as well as potential physical accidents and mental and physical traumas that could happen to a person would hardly encourage one to get out of bed. It would also be frustrating for medical scientists to study disease in depth unless they could see clear causal links between individual sickness and a vector. Without stretching this analogy too much further, it is this search for causality that is behind the case studies that follow. The preceding analysis has yielded a general hypothesis and an attendant set of empirical hypotheses which can be used to explain the implementation failure of public R&D products. The following chapter will present a series of case studies undertaken to evaluate and assess the validity and completeness of these hypotheses.

Bibliography

Rainey, Hal G., Robert W. Backoff, and Charles H. Levine. "Comparing Public and Private Organizations." *Public Administration Review*, Vol. 36, No. 2 (March/April 1976), pp. 233-244.

"Sizes . . . Prices . . . Engines . . . Mileage Ahead for Auto Buyers." *U.S. News and World Report*, 10 January 1977, pp. 45-48.

6

Integrating Theory and Experience

Introduction

The previous chapters have been woven around a common proposition: products of federally sponsored R&D are likely to fail the test of implementation where the "push" of federal policy is dissonant or mismatched with the "pull" of user needs. These earlier chapters identified two special cases of mismatch between policy push and market pull. In the first case, the one we called the "market compatibility problem," technologies fail the test of adoption and diffusion because they have been conceived and designed without regard for their compatibility with the needs of the individuals and firms that would manufacture, market, and use the technology. In this case, commercialization fails or lags because the technology is not readily manufacturable, because it is not cost-competitive with close substitutes, or because there is little or no "need" for the technology in terms of consumer wants and preferences.

The second case of mismatch is the one we called the "market failure problem." Here, the delivery system rather than the technology is flawed. In this case, public policy goals and social objectives cannot be accomplished without sacrificing profit margins or taking risks that private capital views as unacceptable. Or, adopting a technology may require a budget that is beyond the short-range capability of a local government's tax base. Here the issue is not the screening and design of technologies to match the market, but the motivation of the delivery system to achieve policy goals by using the incentives and penalties available to the federal government. Subsidies, loans, grants, tax deductions, and regulatory standards all constitute measures to change the structure of incentives in the technology delivery system and, therefore, alter the pattern of its outputs.

A large amount of federal R&D is carried out to promote innovation in failing industries (such as mass transit and railroads) or to accomplish policy objectives that are not valued by markets (such as pollution control and energy independence). It is precisely because accomplishment of these goals has been frustrated by enterprise economics that political commitment and public action are necessary to achieve them. This in turn engages the R&D process in a conflict over the control of decisions that were once the preserve of commerce and industry. It can also engage federal authorities in conflicts over standards and compliance with local communities as well as with the private sector. Thus, it should not be surprising to see the push and pull of these conflicts lead to a fairly high fatality rate for federally sponsored R&D.

In referring to "market compatibility" and "market failure," we are using the word "market" to refer to the linkages that connect the consumers and producers of technologies.[1] We might also describe these linkages more laboriously, but definitively, as "the technology delivery and utilization system." This formal language is a reminder that technology "markets" include governments as well as the relationships in the private sector between the buyers and sellers of commercial products. In fact, previous chapters identified five markets for federally sponsored research, development, and demonstration (R,D&D).

1. Local and state government infrastructure programs such as roads, mass transit, and sewage treatment
2. Governmental programs instituted to provide a minimum standard of some necessity such as education, health care, or housing
3. The military, space programs, and Army Corps of Engineers
4. The private sector motivated by the traditional incentive of return on investment
5. The private sector motivated by governmental regulations, tax incentives, subsidies, and fines

In each of these "markets" or "technology delivery and

utilization systems," slightly different rules of acceptance, adoption, and diffusion prevail. While the fine points of implementation strategy may differ from market to market, we are still proposing that the technology transfer problem can be capsulized as the problem of bringing policy "push" and market "pull" into better alignment by either rigging the market through incentives or better matching of technologies and their delivery systems at the time of project selection and screening as well as throughout the process of design.

In order to understand the nuances of the implementation problem in each market and to assess the merit of the hypotheses advanced in Chapter 5, a case study approach was used. This chapter reports the logic of case selection and the results of case analysis.

The Need for Case Studies

Case studies offer a crude means for testing our general hypothesis about the cause of implementation failure and also provide an opportunity to add nuance to the content of the hypotheses advanced in Chapter 5.

Case analysis is insufficient to validate research hypotheses; but it is an appropriate method for sophisticating and amending them and for identifying explanatory variables that have escaped attention in previous research. This is the spirit in which the cases were selected and the analysis conducted. At the heart of the case analysis was the intent to assess (1) the extent to which market research enters federal R&D screening; (2) the extent to which barriers to implementation were anticipated and the R&D path adjusted accordingly; (3) the extent to which implementation and diffusion serve as agency objectives and are internalized as measures of R&D effectiveness; and (4) the extent to which R&D strategy is coordinated with economic and regulatory policy in order to motivate innovation and adoption. If such concerns are not evidenced in R&D management and execution, it is reasonable to conclude that the match between policy push and market pull is a matter of happenstance and that market adoption will become a matter of chance.

Case studies provide a reasonable method for refining our

model of implementation failure; but case studies should not be mistaken for a survey of federal R&D activity that will produce estimates of the frequency of failure. Estimation is beyond the capability of case methods. This is due to the purposive sampling procedure used in selecting cases and the limited but strategic role they are intended to play in this study. With this caveat about the purpose of the cases and the ability to make generalizations on case findings, we can turn to the logic of case selection.

Assumptions

There were a few general requirements placed on the selection of the case studies that could potentially have biased the outcome of this phase of the research. For example, we required that the research project be largely or completely finished so that there was a potential for evaluation. Further, because it was not possible to do a large amount of primary research, weight was given to the existence of other case studies on the project; and finally, preference was given to projects where there was a high probability of locating a public official who was no longer professionally involved with the project and who might be able to speak more candidly about the effort.

Because of these decision criteria, the study tends to focus on projects conceived during the Great Society era, although several more recent cases are also included. Specifically, the criterion for completed projects that had people available for interviews meant that many of them were performed during the last decade when R&D efforts were still imbued with the optimism bred by "the conquest of space." The confidence of the New Frontiersmen and antipoverty warriors led to projects with a tendency to become "bigger than life." Further, there were a fair number of systems analysts and engineers from the space field who actually participated in or influenced the projects. Finally, the requirement for other sources of case studies tended to result in an emphasis on large, high-risk projects.

A number of less ambitious projects were included among the cases selected to avoid results that can be generalized only to large-scale projects with associated high risks. The richness and variety of the findings suggest that this effort was at least reasonably successful.

Case Selection

Technology R&D serves multiple markets in the public and private sectors. Therefore, cases of both technology and policy implementation were selected to illuminate the process of market adoption or rejection in each of four R&D markets. The following matrix shows the "sampling frame" which was used in case selection and shorthand description for the cases studied.

Market	Cases
State or local government infrastructure programs (public goods)	Urban Information Systems Transportation System Management Personal Rapid Transit
Social Welfare Programs motivated by minimum standards of well-being (merit goods)	Housing Rehabilitation ("Instant Rehab") Newtowns
The military and space program	Nul
The private sector motivated by the traditional incentive of return on investment	STOL: commuter aircraft Poultry Waste Processing
The private sector motivated by governmental incentives, penalties, or regulations	Jet engine retrofit and noise suppression Stack gas desulphurization Seat belts and air bags Transbus

In all, eleven case studies were conducted—three focusing on a technology program designed for a local government client; two projects with a social welfare context; two projects with a private sector client; and four projects with a private client motivated by regulations or subsidies. No studies were undertaken in the case of the military and space program. While this category accounts for the majority of federal R&D activity, it was judged to be a special problem in procurement that involves fundamentally different issues from the problems of technology adoption in civilian markets.

Case Study Execution

The case studies were conducted to test the general hypothesis that failure of technology adoption and diffusion is most likely to occur where the push of policy and the pull of markets are dissonant or mismatched.

In order to explore the merit of this hypothesis, the case studies focused on four questions concerning R&D planning and execution.

1. Was market demand considered in the screening and selection of candidate R&D projects? Did market analysis inform the process of research execution and prototype design? If so, how?
2. Were technical, political, financial, and institutional barriers to prototype adoption anticipated? Was the technology development path adjusted to match the dynamics of the delivery system?
3. Was market adoption considered a measure of project success? Was "proof of concept" or "proof of sales" the intended end point of the research, development, and demonstration process?
4. Was overt supplier or consumer resistance a primary cause of implementation failure, indicating the need for "market-making" strategies such as tax subsidies or surtaxes or more forceful political commitment to the enforcement of standards?

The case studies were conducted through a review of project documents, articles that could be found in the trade and technical journals, and interviews with project managers and technical personnel. Most interviews were conducted in person. Interviewees were selected to provide a range of policy level and technical viewpoints. Emphasis was placed on market adoption and diffusion as a primary measure of project "success." We now turn to the case-by-case findings.

In reporting the case study findings which follow, we will be taking a critical view of program effectiveness, focusing on the extent of adoption and diffusion of the products of federal research, development, and demonstration efforts. In taking this critical view, we have the comfort of hindsight. Hindsight invariably obscures the atmosphere of risk and uncertainty in which research and demonstration projects are undertaken. Thus, we warn the reader that these after-the-fact analyses will appear to render harsh judgments, and that compensating respect for the difficulties associated with advanced planning in a setting of uncertainty should be kept in mind while reading them.

Two other caveats are in order here. The first is that demonstration efforts have an experimental function. Demonstrations offer a way of making small-scale mistakes as part of a learning experience and a means of avoiding large-scale and irretrievable commitments in situations of uncertainty. This function of the research and demonstration process is an important benefit of demonstration failures, providing R,D&D projects are planned with attention to experimental design. The case studies understate these benefits.

The second caveat is that R&D can produce spin-off benefits even when the adoption of an innovation-as-a-whole is limited or stymied. These payoffs include the adoption of technology subcomponents, process innovations, and the lowering of expectations. These benefits are also understated in the cases which follow.

We raise these caveats and qualifications about the case findings to remind the reader that the technology and program planners of the 1960s did not set out to fail—and that our test of "success" is an exceedingly demanding one: the adoption and diffusion of the technology prototype. In many cases, "the best and the brightest" of America's planners and technologists set ambitious targets and fell far short. Our intent in critically evaluating these endeavors is not to reach we-could-have-told-you-so conclusions. Rather, we hope to use the shortcomings of this era of ambitious social planning and technology demonstration as a laboratory which yields strategies for anticipating barriers and bottlenecks that will confound future implementation efforts. Thus, the analysis is expressly critical for the purpose of starkly illuminating classes of barriers and bottlenecks in a fashion that uses past projects as a learning experience to inform future planning. The case analyses should not be construed as damning a whole generation of R&D programs. We, after all, have had the opportunity, metaphorically speaking, to review the game films and study the instant replays. The R&D managers of the period, like umpires and referees, did not have that luxury. They had to "call them the way they saw them" in the middle of the fray.

Thus, the cases, while framed as critical analyses, should be read with their constructive, future-looking intent in mind.

Case Study Findings

Personal Rapid Transit

Personal Rapid Transit (PRT) is one member of a family of automated guideway transit systems intended to make travel by transit more attractive.

PRT—otherwise known as "Advanced Group Rapid Transit" or "People Movers"—involves the application of advanced computer systems in the control of small four-to-twelve passenger vehicles operating on exclusive transit guideways. The PRT research and development program is sponsored by the Urban Mass Transportation Administration (UMTA) of the U.S. Department of Transportation. The course and direction of PRT research has changed several times during the past decade and has been variously described as a response to:

1. The higher labor costs associated with conventional bus transportation[2]
2. The transit needs of suburban areas where the scatter of origins and destinations requires flexible routing and scheduling competitive with that of the private automobile
3. The high volume people-moving requirements of airports and central business districts
4. The limitations of conventional rail rapid transit in terms of the time penalties associated with transfers at origin and destination
5. The time penalty associated with the operation of buses in mixed traffic

While these objectives have at one time or another framed PRT design activities, the real impetus for PRT development seems to have stemmed from the availability of electronic guidance and control technology and the hopeful expectation that it could make a significant contribution in the civilian transport arena. As research has proceeded on PRT concepts, it has been learned that extremely high passenger volumes are necessary to justify the capital costs of the system and that it is unlikely that a fully automated, driverless operation can be realized on any extensive basis, given the labor-protective provisions of federal transit legislation. This has turned the program to an emphasis on very high-volume markets where split second computer control can increase the line-haul capacity of this small vehicle system to 14,000 passengers per lane, per hour.

The ability of PRT to attract the immense passenger volumes necessary to justify its front-end cost remains to be tested, although many independent observers concerned with the cost of building and operating the system view it as conceptually and economically untenable. The opportunity to test the market penetration that could be achieved by current generation PRTs with relatively crude guidance and control systems was lost due to the selection of a relatively small university town (Morgantown, West Virginia) as PRT's first demonstration site and the subsequent miscarriage of that demonstration project.

In its initial conception, PRT was advanced as a competitor to the private automobile—a new transit technology with the ability to function as a close substitute for the comfort, privacy, and door-to-door serviceability of the automobile. In its latest conception, it appears that PRT is no longer being conceived as a head-on competitor to the auto in a situation of mode choice and market competition. Rather, PRT is being seen as a system which operates in auto-restricted zones where traffic bound for downtown areas has been intercepted by "park'n ride" lots. If auto free zones of any substantial magnitude prove politically infeasible, then the economics of PRT will depend on its ability to generate passenger volumes to match a design capacity equivalent to that of a four-lane highway. Most observers agree that it is unlikely these passenger volumes can be achieved in head-on competition with the automobile unless PRT is heavily subsidized and the auto severely regulated. This means that PRT would have to return immense benefits in urban redevelopment and central business district (CBD) revitalization to justify the cost of deployment. The likelihood of capturing such benefits is speculative at best.

The Morgantown PRT Demonstration

With hindsight about PRT's costs, it is obvious that the choice of Morgantown as a PRT demonstration site was misguided. Morgantown PRT users were to be college students, not work-bound commuters or downtown shoppers; the traffic volumes in Morgantown do not approach the design capacity of even first-generation PRTs; an elephant train in the mode of the Disneyland parking lot shuttle would have sufficed to satisfy student demand at a far lower cost; and, the traffic volumes in Morgantown are insufficient to justify any experiment in guidance and control technology because a dedicated right-of-way alone would have been sufficient to meet local need.

The investigator who looks into the selection of the Morgantown site finds that Morgantown appears to have been selected as the result of a political commitment in the Nixon presidential campaign and that UMTA (more interested in testing and deploying PRT technology than in obtaining a meaningful assessment of its consumer acceptance in an appropriate test market) yielded to pressure. In short, the Morgantown demonstration was motivated by presidential politics and by the failure of UMTA to recognize that hardware deployment is not the same as a test of the ability of PRT to attract urban patrons or compete with the auto. As such a test, the Morgantown demonstration was largely irrelevant.

Even the costing, testing, and deployment of PRT as a hardware system was not completed successfully. The implementation schedule of the Morgantown system specified by UMTA professionals was overridden by the White House, and the prototype demonstration date was scheduled to conform to the schedule of the 1972 presidential campaign.

This scheduling required the simultaneous design of vehicles, guideways, and control system and their after-the-fact integration. As a result, design engineering and construction costs far exceeded estimates and forced the project's engineers to truncate the planned guideway and reduce the number of planned stations.

The demonstration project failed to produce virtually any of its intended deliverables: reasonable estimates of PRT construction and operating costs; field testing of advanced vehicle control technology; a realistic assessment of user acceptance in an operational setting; a cost-effective transportation system to connect two campuses of the University of West Virginia. In failing on each of these dimensions, the Morgantown venture has proved far more costly than just a demonstration that falls short of establishing the marketability or effectiveness of a new technology. Because Morgantown has not produced reliable estimates of passenger acceptance or investment costs, PRT research and development continues despite virtually no evidence that the technology is cost-effective when compared with less exotic transit or auto alternatives. Morgantown might have supplied the evidence; political intervention seems to have prevented even that learning experience from being realized.

Having discussed the seriousness of Morgantown's shortcomings as a demonstration project, it is appropriate to identify the reasons for these conspicuous failures. Two are most critically obvious.

1. The distortion of the site-selection process by an uncommon degree of politicization
2. The scheduling of the project timetable to fit political exigencies

But other factors also need to be mentioned. The UMTA PRT program in general seems to have had the character of technology promotion rather than assessment. To date, PRT transit appears to be a solution in search of a problem and a technology in search of a mission. As a case in point, it can be noted that UMTA is currently pursuing PRT "Urban Deployability" studies. If UMTA were pursuing these studies in the *modus operandi* of technology assessment, "deployability" would be concerned with assessing the relative cost-effectiveness and urban compatibility of PRT compared with other transportation options. However, in the spirit of technology advocacy, "deployability" has been construed to involve "the definition of service policies, development of routing and scheduling algorithms, and failure management." R&D as technology advocacy rather than R&D as technology assessment seems to have permeated the PRT program. While this approach may prevent PRT's early demise as a research effort, it also means that PRT continues to claim research dollars that might be used for more cost-effective transportation alternatives.

Transbus

The Urban Mass Transportation Administration finances 80 percent of the capital cost of most buses acquired by transit properties in the United States. This has positioned UMTA to develop performance specifications for buses in a fashion that aggregates the market for buses and assures coach manufacturers that investments in tooling and parts inventories will be recouped due to a sufficient number of orders to insure payback.

Present bus designs were introduced in 1959, a time when most bus transit operations were failing enterprises supported by local but not federal assistance programs. Without assurance that there would be a replacement market for buses, innovation in motor coach technology was extremely limited. The "Transbus" program is a response to this problem—a UMTA R&D program intended to stimulate innovation in the design of a standard-sized, 40-foot urban bus. The big three manufacturers—General Motors (GM), AM General, and Flxible—were engaged in a $29 million research, development, and demonstration program with many of the characteristics of a competitive procurement process.

An engineering contracter—Booz, Allen and Hamilton—developed specifications for passenger safety, ride quality, low-cost maintenance, and accessibility to the elderly and handicapped. In response, the bus manufacturers developed and produced prototype vehicles for proving-ground testing and special production vehicles for operator testing. The resulting test data is currently "being evaluated to develop recommendations on production design and configurations."

Before UMTA was able to issue performance specifications for a next-generation bus, General Motors unveiled its new Rapid Transit Series (RTS) bus—a 40-foot design embodying many but not all the features of Transbus. The Flxible Co. followed GM's lead, readying its own transbus derivative for production. AM General has sued UMTA, seeking to enjoin the federal agency from approving the use of federal funds in the purchase of the GM RTS or Flxible 870.

AM General's attorneys have argued that UMTA's legislative charter mandates competitive bidding on a lowest-cost basis and prohibits "procurement utilizing exclusionary or discriminatory specifications." AM General has urged UMTA to hold out for specification of the full transbus option (allowing the big three to "start even"), while a number of transit properties have pressed for the flexibility to purchase the models currently available from GM and Flxible although they do not embody all Transbus features.

Several standard features are missing from GM's Transbus derivative that would make the buses more accessible to the elderly and handicapped, but also more costly to purchase and operate. The transit industry has not been particularly enthusiastic about the social-serving features of Transbus, including wheelchair lifts, a reduced height step, and a wide door—this despite the fact that the industry now receives an average of more than 50 percent of its operating revenues from tax sources and is heavily colored with the attributes of a "merit good."

The outcome of the Transbus/intermediate bus controversy remains uncertain at this time, with the issue embroiled in litigation and the manufacturers threatening to shut down all domestic bus production.

While the Transbus/intermediate bus controversy has not been resolved, the case is nevertheless an instructive one.

It is clear that federal participation in the renewal of transit fleets and the capitalization of new bus operations has revived the urban bus market in the United States. UMTA's capital grant program has aggregated a market for coach manufacturers; but UMTA has been less than able to dictate the rules of the market. On the one hand, urban bus operators have insisted on independence in the specification of bus design requirements. On the other hand, the manufacturers have resisted incorporating features to serve the elderly and handicapped as standard equipment, arguing that these would complicate operations and increase costs; at the same time, spokemen for the elderly and handicapped have pressed for these standard features as a right or entitlement.

This issue pits two elements of UMTA's political constituency against each other—transit operators and transit-dependent social groups—while dividing the vehicle manufacturers who make up UMTA's third constituency. Each of these constituencies has different expectations about bus design criteria. For manufacturers, the critical issue is the volume of sales and consequent return on investment, a net which can be diminished by a model which must be consequently abandoned or by a vehicle which involves "excessive" warranty payments. For transit-dependent social groups, the issue is bus accessibility and, more fundamentally, the social mobility it entails.

In this setting, UMTA's fundamental dilemma is to balance the demands of these constituencies in a fashion that creates *certainty* in the market aggregated by its capital grant program. To date, a certainty-insuring solution has been illusive. UMTA has been unable to promulgate bus standards that the transit industry is confident will be realistic in operation, and as a consequence, the manufacturers have been unwilling to risk the tooling necessary to commit themselves to the Transbus design. Instead, two of the manufacturers have produced designs that incorporate the user cost-saving features of Transbus, but have not incorporated as standard features those elements of Transbus design that would serve the special needs of the elderly and handicapped.

Since the urban bus market is now effectively secured by a long-term commitment to federal capital assistance, it is instructive to examine why public monies were necessary to stimulate bus technology innovation in the first place. That is, why were public rather than manufacturer funds necessary to develop a next-generation bus?

Two explanations appear reasonable. The first is that a high degree of concentration has discouraged competition in the bus manufacturing industry; and the second is that the legislation governing UMTA grants has discouraged the manufacturers from developing innovations to improve the quality or reliability of bus technology (low-bid requirements constrain UMTA to resolve quality/cost trade-offs in favor of economy).

Seen in this context, the public investment in Transbus was designed to: (1) preserve at least the current competition in the bus-manufacturing industry and (2) establish standards that allowed the industry to move to higher quality at higher cost without disrupting the competitive relationships of the industry. This effort to produce simultaneous standard setting and technology innovation ran counter to the accustomed autonomy of the individual manufacturers and transit properties.

Thus, this case shows the dilemmas of technology procurement and setting of standards in a mixed economy where both private investment and social welfare objectives are being pursued.

Transportation System Management: A Process Innovation

In the 1960s public transportation (highways and mass transit) commanded tax revenues that constituted a major share of federal, state, and local budgets. In fact, transportation agencies were "rich" by public investment standards. But in the seventies, revenues have not kept pace with rapidly escalating costs, and in 1977 the dominant feature of the transportation landscape is an unparalleled fiscal shortfall.

Highway programs are caught in a cost-revenue squeeze because the primary source of road funds, the gasoline tax, is not indexed to keep pace with inflation. At the same time, actual fuel consumption has declined due to the improved fuel efficiency of new automobiles. In the case of mass transit, operating deficits are the commanding fiscal constraint. Those deficits have risen due to a conscious public policy of fare stabilization intended to increase transit patronage.

The ability of highway and transit agencies to expand services and construct facilities has declined during the same period due to the impacts of inflation on construction costs, the rising cost burden of maintenance, the increasing share of the budget required for rehabilitation and replacement of aging facilities, and litigation associated with environmental impacts.

The cost-revenue squeeze in combination with the new priority attached to energy conservation and air quality have led transportation policymakers to place greater emphasis on the efficient management of the existing transportation system rather than the construction of new facilities. Both highway and transit agencies are trying to squeeze more capacity out of existing road space and make more efficient use of the facilities already in place.

Transit and highway agencies have adjusted to the cost-revenue squeeze by conflating project plans and focusing on short-term remedial strategies not involving large-scale capital investment. Facility plans scaled to twenty-year traffic projections are being abandoned, and priority is being placed on "filling gaps in the existing system" rather than extending roads and transit routes.

The result is a new vocabulary in transportation planning with less emphasis on "building" and more on "managing." This change in vocabulary symbolizes and exemplifies a more significant change—a change in the understanding of the character of the "transportation problem." For decades the transportation problem was conceptualized as the problem of engineering and constructing the capacity necessary to accommodate forecast traffic volumes. The cost-revenue squeeze has given credibility to a new set of solution strategies that define the transportation problem in a different fashion. Low-capital strategies such as ramp-metering, the dedication of freeway lanes to high-occupancy vehicles, staggered work hours, the promotion of carpooling and vanpooling—all of these "traffic management" strategies begin with the presumption that it is possible to manage the *demand* for transportation as well as the supply of facilities.

This emerging understanding of the transportation problem was given formal recognition by the simple exigency of *naming* it. The Federal Register for 17 September 1975 refers to "Transportation System Management" (ISM) and mandates the inclusion of a Transportation System Management Element in regional transportation plans.

The so-called "TSM Regs," issued jointly by the federal highway and transit administrations, mandate the consideration of low-capital alternatives in the transportation planning process and encourages metropolitan areas to explore techniques such as:

- freeway ramp-metering

- preferential treatment of high-occupancy vehicles
- staggered work hours and flextime
- parking taxes and congestion tolls
- carpool and vanpool promotion programs
- pedestrian malls and bicycle paths

While none of these measures is particularly "new," their bundling together and "naming" is new. In this sense, TSM is an advertising coup rather than a technical innovation.

But the regs did more than name TSM. They also required the adoption of a TSM plan by regional transportation planning agencies. In effect, the regs place a federal imprimatur on a new role for *regional* agencies (a short-range, operational planning activity that has traditionally been the reserved turf of implementing agencies such as state highway departments, local public works departments, and transit properties). In proposing that *regional* planning agencies should begin to occupy this planning role, the regs place a new emphasis on the coordination of transit and highway planning and the engagement of private employers in the planning process (through vanpooling, staggered work hours, and preferential parking spaces for carpoolers). In this sense, the regs embody a process innovation and a desired change in institutional roles.[3]

Casting regional planning agencies in this role has inevitably led to conflict over turf and authority with state highway commissions, local public works departments, and transit operators who resent the intrusion of regional planners in their traditionally independent programming and short-range planning activities.

This conflict has subverted the intent of the regulations in that most of the nation's metropolitan areas have produced TSM plans which are not the result of regional planning or decision making, but rather are the rubber-stamped compilation of projects proposed independently by highway and transit agencies.

TSM planning is occurring; but it is being pursued by state and local *implementing* agencies rather than regional *planning* agencies as the regs intended. The co-option of TSM by the implementing agencies and their continuing independence in project programming are measures of the relative power of planning and implementing agencies.

Those fundamental power relationships have not proved amenable to change through federal policy and procedure memoranda.

Even with implementing agencies in charge of TSM planning, implementation will not be readily accomplished. Highway construction and transit development are supported by a powerful constituency with a stake in jobs and the growth of metropolitan areas. But TSM has no comparable constituency because it, unlike capital investment, is not the instrument of economic growth and urban development. It will be particularly difficult to implement those TSM measures involving auto-use disincentives. Measures such as parking taxes and reserved bus lanes are both controversial and without constituency.

Where TSM measures have been implemented, they have been conceived on a far smaller scale than the federal regulations imply. Implementation of TSM measures has occurred where:

1. Projects have been limited in scale, scoped to a manageable political environment; they have often been initiated with the assistance and support of general-purpose government
2. They have generally involved the pursuit of limited operational goals such as ameliorating specific design deficiencies or achieving savings in travel time
3. Project implementation has improved the quality of service available without substantially disadvantaging any class of users or political jurisdiction
4. Project managers have approached implementation with a demonstration philosophy and a readiness to abort or adjust design strategies as problems arise
5. Project design has been negotiated with affected jurisdictions and interests, which is a time-consuming process involving intensive liaison and marketing efforts
6. Project motivation has frequently been provided by the ability to capture federal funds in excess of formula entitlements
7. The project's team has controlled resources which allowed it to make side payments that off-set adverse impacts (these side payments have typically been of the

> log-rolling variety: tree planting and beautification
> have been used to convince merchants to accept bus
> lanes on commercial streets; states have financed the
> cost of resetting signals on local streets where ramp
> metering has been introduced)

Thus, TSM measures have been implemented on a piece-meal, negotiated basis that reflects the diffusion of political power within metropolitan areas (Jones, 1976).

The success of TSM measures of a limited scale and negotiated character does not insure acceptance of TSM measures conceived at a systemwide scale. In fact, it appears unlikely that TSM will be able to assemble the kind of powerful constituency that permitted the construction of freeways and rapid transit lines despite community disruption and localized opposition.

In summarizing this case, it is important to note that transportation system management *is* occurring, but not in the comprehensive fashion or in the institutional setting contemplated by the federal regulations. The mismatch between the original federal intent and metropolitan political relationships has been recognized at the federal level, and federal expectations seem to be changing accordingly. The critical conclusion to be drawn here is that federal process and procedure requirements are weak instruments for the creation of political power and policymaking authority. Regional planning agencies are the creatures of federal planning requirements, but are not, in most instances, the embodiment of local power relationships. They are not in this sense authentic political entities. Because most of them lack power and a political base, they also lack the ability to influence implementation.

STOL Aircraft

In 1967, Congress and particularly the Senate took an activist role in establishing a policy framework for civil aviation R&D and urged the newly established Department of Transporation to develop a plan for the nation's airways.

Congressional interest was spurred by a number of factors.

- Federal Aviation Administration warnings that air traffic congestion was overburdening traffic control sys-

tems
- Hostile reaction from residential communities located near airports to jet aircraft noise and soot
- A slowdown in the pace of private investment in aviation R&D and increasing governmental investment in R&D by Britain, France, and the Soviet Union

A Senate committee report urged that NASA should be encouraged to develop quiet jet engines and air traffic control hardware as well as to keep pace with developments in international aeronautics in a cooperative effort with the Department of Transportation (DOT) and its Federal Aviation Administration (FAA).

The report stimulated the formation of a joint DOT-NASA task force charged with developing a Civil Aviation Research and Development (CARD) Policy. The so-called CARD study developed projections of future air traffic volumes based on trend extrapolation, and concluded that hub airports were on their way to becoming intolerably congested—to the point of becoming a safety hazard in the air in addition to a congestion and delay problem on the ground. For the short-haul air traveler, ground congestion would soon mean spending more time in city traffic than in the air.

The CARD study recommended relieving ground and air traffic congestion simultaneously by developing satellite or reliever airports located close to population concentrations such as central business districts (CBD). Commuter-style, short-haul trips would be accommodated at these reliever airports, theoretically reducing portal-to-portal travel time through the proximity of airport location to CBD destination. The same strategy was expected to distribute the demand on airspace in a fashion that would relieve the approaches to metropolitan airports.

The lynchpin of the satellite airport concept was the development of short take-off and landing (STOL) aircraft—a technological derivative of work underway at NASA for the military. NASA's military R&D program included research on jet fighter aircraft capable of rapid maneuver and steep angles of attack. Advances in wing and engine technology, NASA argued, could be incorporated in quiet civilian STOLcraft suited to operation from CBD-located STOLports.

With the space effort winding down and the DOD-financed research on STOL components nearly complete, NASA found itself in search of a mission. Similarly, its STOL technology was a capability in search of a civilian problem to solve. The joint NASA-DOT policy study provided the opportunity to assert NASA's role in short-haul aviation technology and to link STOL with what was perceived as the increasingly serious national problem of air traffic congestion.

What does not seem to have been fully considered at this point was the logistics of STOL implementation or the cost penalty associated with an aircraft designed to the precision performance requirements of using 2,000-3,000-foot runways near densely populated areas.

The CARD study concluded that STOL operation and STOLport development are "both technically and economically feasible," but conceded that "the establishment of a comprehensive metroflight service will not be free of difficulty since its chief components—suitable aircraft, landing sites, and navigation technology—are not yet fully developed."

What better challenge for NASA, the wonder-workers who had put a man on the moon, than to put all the pieces and players together in a comprehensive systems design? The challenge, the CARD study emphasized, was both technological and institutional.

> Institutional fragmentation has blocked any substantive achievements toward (implementation). The development of an operational STOL system must involve the integrated efforts of a large number of private organizations and government agencies at the federal, state and local level. Two major components of a STOL system are the responsibility of the government—the air traffic control system and the airport, or STOL ports. The customers must look to the government (CAB) to delineate the circumstances under which they could operate STOL aircraft, while the manufacturer must look to the FAA for certification of the airframe and engines. Finally, both the private sector and the Federal Government must look to state and local government for the approval and development of STOL ports. A STOL system has not been instituted because no single participant in the process needed to create

the entire system has the ability to proceed independently of
all the others.

CARD proposed that NASA, FAA, and the Civil Aeronautics Board should each get a piece of the STOL action
and that they should develop, by late 1973, a coordinated
national plan for the development and implementation of
an improved short-haul air transport service in high-density
corridors. The plan would include technological advances
in quiet-engine technology, avionics, wing design, and
validation of STOL in relation to air traffic control and
noise control requirements. *"Soft R&D" would be conducted to determine passenger demand, manufacturing cost, and
operating cost.* This basic cost information was *not* available
in 1971 despite the fact that STOL had been pronounced
economically and technologically feasible in 1970. CARD's
confidence in STOL's economic viability seems to have been
grounded in optimism rather than rigorous economic analysis that compared STOL with more conventional forms of
commuter air transportation.

The "cycle of inaction" which the CARD policy committee saw as the predominant barrier to STOL implementation
continues today, but not primarily because of the "jurisdictional fragmentation" cited in the CARD report. Rather,
STOL has not been implemented because of its own serious
conceptual and economic flaws.

1. The STOL concept was based on jet aircraft using CBD
   airports and sharing suburban general aviation airports. While STOLcraft are quieter than today's jets,
   they would inflict noise on new areas and new popula-
   tions. This appears to be politically unacceptable to
   local governments.
2. STOL has not been able to establish that it is realistically cost-competitive with conventional aircraft operated
   from hub ports even when the value of traveler time
   spent in airport access is considered.
3. Many short-haul trips are so-called linked trips that
   follow a transfer from a cross-continent route. When
   these trips are "subtracted" from the short-haul corri-
   dor market, travel volumes appear to be too small to
   support a reliever system operated from separate

STOLports.

The economic and conceptual shortcomings of STOL should not be terribly surprising. STOL/METROFLIGHT was conceived as a technological system in the space flight mode without sufficient regard to the behavioral dynamics of the social environment where the agency would have to gain community acceptance and overcome aircraft manufacturer and airline reluctance based on costliness.

Equally important is another conceptual flaw—the notion that social systems can be organized and optimized in the same comprehensive fashion as hardware components. Staged and incremental adjustments are the norm in socio-political systems; plans requiring the simultaneous implementation of vehicles, infrastructure, and traffic-control systems require a degree of managerial control that is realistic in outer space, but rarely in American cities in peacetime.

Operation Breakthrough

In 1966 and again in 1967, two blue-ribbon commissions evaluated the state of the nation's housing stock and the rate of new housing production and found them wanting.

The Kaiser Committee (chaired by industrialist Edgar Kaiser) and the Douglas Commission (chaired by Senator Paul Douglas) both concluded that the nation's housing industry is producing housing units at a pace insufficient to meet a basic standard of decency in housing and that low-income persons, in particular, were ill-housed and would remain so in the absence of public intervention.

The Douglas Commission estimated the nation's ten-year housing needs at 20 to 23 million units for the decade ending in 1976, with 5 million of these units needed by low-income Americans. The Kaiser Committee recommended a ten-year goal of 17 million new housing units and 9 million rehabilitated housing units, including at least 6 million subsidized units for low-income families.

Two other factors gave housing problems impetus on the federal agenda. One was the creation of the Department of Housing and Urban Development and the appointment of a department Secretary with cabinet-level status. The second was the state of emergency felt in Washington in the wake of the ghetto rioting in Watts.

This was the setting in which President Lyndon Johnson declared war on poverty, inviting the same commitment to solving the problems of hunger and shelter that the nation had dedicated to the conquest of space. It was also the setting in which aerospace industries began exploring opportunities for engineering applications in the civilian arena. If there was to be a "war on poverty," then there were the makings of a "socioindustrial complex" that offered new contract opportunities to replace those of the gradually diminishing effort in space.

The confluence of these events—the report of a commission chaired by one of the Senate's leading liberals, the formation of HUD, the optimism of the antipoverty warriors, the urgency created by ghetto unrest, and the confidence of systems engineers in the wake of the space program—shaped the federal response to housing problems in the late sixties.

One of the Douglas Commission's eight recommendations to reduce the cost of housing available for moderate and low-income families was to conduct a limited experiment with industrialized housing to assess its quality and costs. Congressional authority to construct 25,000 units of mass production housing was included in the 1968 Housing Act. The Douglas Commission report recommended in 1968 that HUD should use part of this authority to test modular and component housing construction systems at the rate of 1,000 units per year for five years. The Commission emphasized that the approach to industrialized housing should be *experimental* and that "the primary objective of this program is to stimulate technological innovation."

> Contracts would be awarded on the basis of proposals that aim to achieve economies through mass production without sacrificing the goal of well-designed, quality housing. The choice of areas for such projects would be based upon the readiness of communities and community groups to waive restrictive building regulations and current work rules in those instances where the proposed technological innovations would otherwise be inhibited. A necessary part of this

experimental approach would be to provide for a committee of impartial appraisers to make design and cost comparisons between the various experiments and conventional construction (National Commission on Urban Problems, 1968, p. 482).

The Commission's prudent emphasis on cost-consciousness and experimentation was incorporated in the early design of the HUD project that came to be called "Operation Breakthrough," but these were among the first ingredients to be jettisoned as Breakthrough gained momentum.

At the center of Operation Breakthrough (OBT) were large industries with little prior experience in construction management at the small scale of residential housing. Among twenty-two "housing system producers" who were to supply housing components, modules, and assembly systems were Alcoa, Republic Steel, TRW, General Electric, and other lesser-known aerospace and defense-related firms.

With the engagement of these firms and the design of the program by a former NASA space flight engineer, Operation Breakthrough began to take on some of the "can-do" confidence and enthusiasm of the space program. The mood is captured in a symposia paper by John Rubel, who is a veteran of GE, Lockheed Aircraft, the Department of Defense, and the President's Task Force for the War on Poverty. In 1967, Rubel wrote about the creation of new housing through the application of the aerospace project approach to the building of new communities.

It should be obvious that if it is possible to send a satellite to land softly on the surface of the moon and send back pictures that can be viewed by millions of Americans in the comfort of their homes, there is no merely technical or technological problem affecting everyday life that is not readily solvable in planning for and creating new cities. . . .

The barriers to innovation are not technical. The important barriers are institutional—cumbersome and overlapping political and administrative jurisdictions; the codification of conventional techniques that forbid innovation; the fragmentation of markets for urban betterment that foreclose it. . . .

The answer, it seems to me, is to start handling the creation of new cities or new towns the way we handle the creation of new, never-before-attempted projects in space. This means: making ad hoc projects out of the development, creation and administration of new cities. It means creating a marketplace, a wholly new marketplace, one that does not now exist and never has, where private industry can come and sell the development, creation and administration of new cities. That is how we built our bombers. That is how we created the Atlas, the Titan, the Polaris and a host of incredibly complex, wholly new, never-before-attempted missile systems. . . .

In short, not only do the projects themselves establish a marketplace for the evolution of the methods and the technologies needed to get them done, the very existence of a continuing series of projects creates a market for the corresponding continuing evolution of the technologies that are likely to be needed to support them and to permit the creation of new and as yet impossible projects (Rubel, 1965, p. 856 ff.).

While the Douglas Commission had contemplated a small-scale and experimental approach to industrialized housing systems, Project Manager Harold Finger led OBT in the direction proposed above by Rubel. Finger saw OBT as a lever to revolutionize the housing industry and saw industrialized housing operating at a *new community* rather than multiunit scale.

Thus, Finger saw the aggregation of a market for industrialized housing being accomplished by cost reductions achievable through the combination of scale economies in the construction of prefabricated housing elements, scale economies in transportation and scale economies in the dedication of land. In contrast, it appears that the Douglas Commission expected industrialized housing to compete predominantly on the grounds of construction and materials cost and that market aggregation would be assisted through the Department of Housing and Urban Development's (HUD) housing assistance programs for low-income groups.

Finger's approach was clearly more ambitious: the demonstration of whole mixed-income community development, rather than single or multiunit components that would be supplied to the small-scale housing contractors who make up the bulk of the nation's residential construction industry.

For authority to pursue his more ambitious experiment, Finger reached back to the 1966 HUD Act, rather than the 1968 Act, which embodied the Douglas Commission Recommendations. Under Finger's management, OBT shifted from an experimental program designed to assess costs to the first phase of a program intended to aggregate large-scale markets for industrialized housing on the model of Rubel's "aerospace project approach." The program was no longer motivated by cautious experimentalism, but by the confidence that OBT could:

1. Capitalize on the full resources of private industry to help provide the 26 million homes needed in the next ten years
2. Help form housing markets large enough to make volume production possible
3. Work with state and local leaders to find sponsors, developers, and local authorities to undertake large-scale housing programs
4. Locate available land for innovative housing use and for construction of prototype demonstration units

In the process of this shift in program design, OBT was being scaled in terms of the resource endowments of very large-scale manufacturing firms rather than the small-scale, often family-owned firms which make up America's conventional housing industry.

In order to accomplish this effort in market aggregation, OBT worked with states and localities to develop common construction trade work rules and housing inspection standards and to relax zoning codes.

It also worked with HUD's mortgage insurance arm to provide Federal Housing Administration (FHA) loans for the purchases of OBT demonstration housing. HUD subsidies for low-income housing were also provided in OBT communities.

Thus, Operation Breakthrough evolved into a broadly

based attack on the entire mechanism for producing housing services. Although such an integrated systems approach to increased efficiency in residential construction was probably overly ambitious, it is difficult to determine, *ex poste*, precisely how far OBT fell short of its objectives. The Urban Institute reported, for example, that:

> Because of the program's design, it will be impossible, in practice, even to tell anything definitive about its effects on the nation's housing production, on the characteristics of the housing production and related industries, or on the institutional and attitudinal constraints to the use of industrialized housing production methods (Weidman, p. 2).[4]

Furthermore, any evaluation of Breakthrough must contend with the fact that the U.S. housing industry has been severely depressed since 1973 due to the cost of credit available for housing and the increase in its housing prices. This broad-based slowdown in construction activity makes it extremely difficult to determine the near-term impact of Operation Breakthrough on the housing industry.

Some OBT objectives *were* attained:

1. Houses were built, sold, and occupied in Phases II and III of the program. Twenty-nine hundred units were built in the prototype demonstration Phase II; and approximately 25,000 units will be completed in Phase III. The total cost of Phases I and II (design, development, and prototype construction) was $147.6 million and can be disaggregated as follows: net federal government cost, $72.2 million; financing by private and state lenders, $65.4 million; rents and sales, $8.1 million.
2. The houses were displayed within communities which were integrated racially and economically. In addition, these community developments embodied the planned unit development design concept in which a variety of housing types are used on a single site.
3. The Phase II housing units and developments exhibited a high degree of consumer acceptance. A 1974 survey of the residents in eight of the prototype sites indicated that 90 percent of the respondents were satisfied with

the dwelling units (60 percent were very satisfied), 92 percent were satisfied with the site features (56 percent were very satisfied), and 80 percent were satisfied with the site management (42 percent were very satisfied) (Huth, pp. 1416).

4. A comprehensive set of performance-based evaluation and testing procedures has been created. Some aspects have been incorporated into FHA's minimum property standards, although they have not been adopted by local regulatory agencies. Some changes have also been made in testing procedures and standards for evaluating testing laboratories.

5. A majority of states have adopted state-wide building codes, and a number of reciprocative agreements among the states have been made. The evidence that this can be attributed directly to Breakthrough is, however, circumstantial.

6. Several major companies became active in housing production for the first time, and some remain active. Of the fourteen housing system producers that built in Phase III, ten are still marketing domestically (four are also marketing abroad), and one is marketing solely abroad. The relationship between Housing System Producers participation in Operation Breakthrough and success in the post-Breakthrough factory-produced housing market is difficult to determine, largely because of the non-Breakthrough related recession in residential construction activity since early 1973. According to some observers, the most successful of the manufacturers, primarily firms whose systems were being produced and sold before the program's inception in 1969, would have been successful without Operation Breakthrough. However, Breakthrough did contribute to an increased sophistication in the technology of these firms' housing systems and did provide them with an introduction to the low-income (i.e., subsidized) portion of the housing market.

7. A large number of cooperative labor agreements were signed during Phases II and III.

8. Transportation charges (point-to-point tariffs) for completed housing modules were reduced.

9. A few local developers were given experience with new

approaches to housing. And some minority group
subcontractors and workers were provided with new
opportunities in the housing field.

10. State housing finance agencies have begun to engage in
    significant housing market aggregation activity in the
    subsidized, multifamily portion of the market. In order
    to lend, many of these agencies (especially in Massa-
    chusetts and Michigan) have had to induce the reorgan-
    ization of demand and supply of all of the participants
    in the housing industry. Approximately 10,000 of the
    25,500 units in Phase III were financed through these
    state-level agencies.

However, OBT's central program objectives were *not* accomplished, at least in the short term.

1. Operation Breakthrough did not directly stimulate
   significant innovation in housing production technology.
2. The quality of the Operation Breakthrough housing
   was not as high as expected, and the production costs of
   the Breakthrough systems were not appreciably lower
   than those for conventional housing of comparable
   quality. (On the other hand, the program did demonstrate the economic superiority of panelized or component systems *relative* to housing modules under pre-
   vailing transportation tariffs.)

A significant issue posed by Operation Breakthrough is
the appropriateness of governmental action in aggregating
housing markets in a fashion that matches them to the scale
economies of large industrial firms, but that makes them
inaccessible to the small firms making up the conventional
housing industry in America. At issue is whether the "small
entrepreneur" should be valued when the scale of small
business operation conflicts with the social objective of
efficient housing production. This is clearly a value question and not an economic issue to the extent that public
powers or public monies are used to aggregate the market for
industrialized housing projects (while profits accrue to the
housing manufacturer).

With hindsight, it appears that the critical decision point

in OBT was, indeed, the change in course which emphasized community-scale development rather than efforts to experiment with sites sized to the scale of the conventional housing industry. In taking this course, OBT framed the housing problem as an issue in industrial organization and structure as well as an issue in the adoption of new materials and processes. Experimentation with the more readily manageable problem of how to get new materials and processes adopted by the *conventional industry* would have been a more appropriate first step than the demonstration of new materials and processes and a simultaneous effort to create a new social-industrial complex at a wholly new scale of economic aggregation. Instead, Operation Breakthrough sought to create a new technology with consumer acceptance and to construct a radically new housing delivery system at the same time. One can argue that the task was too ambitious.

Municipal Information Systems

By the late 1960s, computers had found application in many of the bookkeeping functions of municipal government; but their role in the diagnosis of municipal service problems and the analysis of local policy was limited.

Eyeing the state of the art in municipal information processing, information scientists saw an opportunity to:

- make the collection, storage, and retrieval of local government data more efficient
- coordinate the data collection and storage activities of individual city departments
- enhance the ability of city managers and planners to monitor and coordinate the activities of operating departments, and thereby
- rationalize municipal decision making

The application of computerized information storage and retrieval methods in the development of Integrated Municipal Information Systems was part and parcel of the federal emphasis on comprehensive planning, program coordination, and the application of "scientific management" techniques such as PPBS and Program Evaluation Review

Technique (PERT). These methods, championed by the Office of Management and Budgets (OMB) and the Department of Housing and Urban Development (HUD), implied the development of management information systems and large-scale data bases to permit comprehensiveness in decision assessment.

To encourage coordinated, comprehensive, and continuing planning at the local and regional level—so-called "3C planning"—HUD formed the Urban Information Systems Interagency Committee (USAC). USAC was intended to promote management information systems. HUD's intent was to bring together other cabinet-level federal agencies (the departments of Transportation, Commerce, HEW, and Justice and the antipoverty agencies) in the financing and demonstration of computer-based information systems. At the same time, HUD expected the project to integrate the data-management activities of municipal government, resulting in the coordination of data systems of the public finance, public safety, physical development, and social welfare branches of local government.

The result of HUD's initiative was an $8 million, six-city demonstration of computer-based information storage and retrieval systems. Four of the demonstration cities were to develop information system modules specialized by function: financial management; police and fire services; physical and economic development; and human resources development. These modules were also developed as an Integrated Municipal Information System (IMIS) in two other cities.

The demonstration project was intended to produce a working prototype suited to the "field conditions" found at the community level. The prototype IMIS was to:

- function in support of operational activities
- increase staff productivity
- permit assessment of community change
- assist problem analysis and program development
- facilitate the coordinated management of different operating divisions

The project was less than successful on virtually every measure of effectiveness: the prototype information systems have not been fully adopted by other communities; they seem to have had little impact on governmental decision making in the demonstration cities except for the Long Beach Public Safety System; the prototype systems involved far less integration and coordination than has been posted as the rationale for the projects; the demonstrations fell far behind schedule.

Various evaluation efforts have attempted to explain the shortcomings of the IMIS demonstration. These evaluations focused on:

- overly ambitious objectives
- lack of executive-level support in local government
- difficulties in coordinating the multitude of agencies and contractors involved in each demonstration
- excessive reporting and monitoring
- lack of program continuity due to personnel turnover in HUD

While these factors offer the most obvious explanation for the USAC demonstration's shortcomings, they may be only the proximate cause of the project's shortcomings. In fact, it can be argued that perfect execution of the same project would have produced comparably disappointing results. This is because of the incongruity between the actual processes of muncipal governance and the project's notion that governance is the same as "rational planning." Public decision making tends to be remedial, incremental, sequential, and frequently reactive. The USAC demonstration started with the assumption that public decision making *ought* to be—and *is*—rational, comprehensive, anticipatory, and intentional.

Thus, it seems likely that the project had little impact because it was not matched to the real decision environment of local government. It did not begin with the decision environment as it is, but as its sponsors thought it should be. The resulting mismatch with the information needs of municipal executives was virtually inevitable. In specific, routine municipal operations require very little *integration* of information. Rather, routine operating decisions usually only require the experienced reaction of a line manager for problem solving and program adjustment.

On the other hand, the nonroutine, policy-level decisions

of local government are fundamentally political decisions which require, rather than the marshalling of data, the assessment of alternative courses of action, and the development of political consensus. These nonroutine decisions require the action of policy elites and recommendations based on policy analysis. IMIS are ill-suited for both policy and analytic roles—due to time constraints and the critical prior need for theory and causal models.

IMIS, as conceived by USAC, provided information relevant to a class of long-range planning activities typically distant from the sources of power in local governments. These long-range planning activities have rarely commanded the attention of municipal executives in line agencies, nor have they commanded the political support of elected leadership. Therefore, it is not surprising that the USAC project was unable to develop this relationship or offer guidance to inform the working decisions of local government.

Thus, the demonstration project's failure is rooted in the deeper failure of the project team to identify the purposes to which the data management capabilities would be put and purposefully design *analytic* tools as well as collection, storage, and retrieval capabilities. In the absence of an effective effort to match system design to *decision* needs, it was almost inevitable that the IMIS contribution would be limited to efficiencies in the handling and management of data rather than the expected improvements in governmental performance.

HUD Newtowns

The New Communities Program of the U.S. Department of Housing and Urban Development (HUD) started as an ambitious experiment in community development and urban design. The program limps on today with HUD serving as the trustee for $85 million in federal loan guarantee obligations on which private housing developers have defaulted.

The HUD New Communities Program, better known as the Newtowns Program, was intended to promote the development of planned communities—communities that would incorporate the newest in urban design concepts; provide housing for a mix of income groups; offer job training and job opportunities for the underskilled; provide residences, services, and industrial job opportunities in a mix appropriate to a nearly self-contained community; and contribute to the construction of the housing stock necessary to meet the "needs" estimated by groups such as Senator Douglas' National Commission on Urban Problems.

The HUD Newtowns Program was initiated at the confluence point of two pressures: (1) city planners and urban architects sought a test of urban design principles that traced their lineage to the "Garden Cities of Tomorrow" promoted by Ebenezer Howard, the influential English architect; (2) HUD sought to develop a program with the ability to provide incentives for private investment in new housing while incorporating a wide range of social services and environmental amenities that were not available in public housing ventures. Center-city interests opposed the program in its initial form, then supported it after provisions for the so-called Newtowns-in-Town were incorporated. Significantly, developers also did not support the program until it provided them access to community development grants, social program funding, and cheaper access to venture capital markets.

The HUD program, particularly as viewed by its staff and its constituency of urban design professionals, was to differ from traditional housing tracts and subdivision development by incorporating social services and subsidized housing financed by HUD and other federal agencies (such as HEW). Newtowns would also be distinguished from townhouse-style "Planned Communities" financed by venture capital in that industry would be located on-site and job training programs and day-care services would be provided. The program also emphasized experimentation with new forms of housing design and innovations in construction techniques.

In order to attract developers and venture capital, Congress enabled HUD to guarantee loans; provide planning assistance through community planning grants; subsidize housing for low-income persons; and cooperate with other agencies of the federal government in obtaining grants for day-care, job training, industrial development, and community health services. HUD staff activities were to include the screening of development proposals, liaison with other federal grant-giving departments both within HUD and beyond, and program monitoring and evaluation activities. The value of these "carrots" as an incentive for developer participation in the social welfare element of the program was never tested in practice because of the Nixon administration's impoundment of low-income housing funds and the introduction of "revenue sharing" as a replacement for categorical grants.

Without these incentives, it is not surprising that the Newtowns program fell short of achieving its social welfare objectives and is now trying to salvage a few economically viable residential developments.

Four communities out of fourteen have filed for bankruptcy and have been acquired by HUD. The prospects for a fifth community are dim, and negotiations to determine its future are now in progress.

Among the remaining nine communities, all have had financial difficulties. HUD has assumed interest payments for all of them at some stage since their conception.

Presently, these nine communities are either meeting operating costs or believed to have the capability to meet costs in the future. In all cases, development plans have been drastically scaled down, and all are behind schedule. In the words of one HUD official, "All projects were optimistic; none were realized."

None of the communities will provide, in the foreseeable future, the composite of social services including low-income housing which provided the original justification for federal intervention.

Just how short the program is falling is shown in the following comparison of goals and achievements for those new communities which are considered "most successful."

HUD planned to construct 262,504 housing units in 9 communities in a 20-year period.	Only 10,817 units have been completed.
These communities were planned for a population of 509,190 in 20 years.	To date, they have attracted only 18,546 residents.

Nine communities plan to construct a total of 181,286 housing units over a 20 year period.

They have constructed a total of 5,728 units to date.

All communities planned to construct "a reasonable amount of low-income housing."

None of the communities is producing low-income houses at the current time. St. Charles developers are building moderate-income housing and most of the others have selected to focus on higher-profit housing until their financial picture improves.

All of the communities planned to provide child-care, job-training, and health care.

These plans have been shelved in every case.

The Newtown was to offer a balance of jobs and population, services and tax base.

They have attracted approximately 9,500 job-holding people, but have provided only 3,500 jobs.

In short, the HUD Newtowns program appears— although not all the returns are in—to have been as large a failure as it was an ambitious undertaking.

A large number of factors seem to have contributed to the program's collapse, first as an experiment in social design and then as a housing development effort. The following seem to be most important:

1. The Nixon administration sought and won changes in the way funds for low-income housing and social services are delivered to localities. Categorical grants for specific designated programs were replaced by formula block grants for Community Development in general. HEW categorical grants were replaced by federal Revenue Sharing grants delivered by formula. These changes in intergovernmental finance diluted HUD's role in providing financing for nonmarket services and low-income housing.
2. HUD's analysis of the financial viability of developer proposals seems to have been inadequate. HUD policymakers do not seem to have understood the economic dynamics of the real estate market, and where prudent economics would have argued for downscoping, HUD

seems to have pushed for larger and more ambitious projects.

3. The Newtowns demonstration occurred during a period of recession and simultaneous inflation. Inflation in the construction industry was particularly virulent, pricing many of the communities out of their local housing markets. The impacts of inflation were complicated by the delays and red tape associated with HUD review and approval of development plans.

4. The nature of the "contract" between HUD and Newtown Developers was sufficiently uncertain and contingent that a cooperative working relationship was never developed. The continually changing circumstances of the program's financial structure prevented the development of a confident working relationship between the public and private sectors, and in fact, the HUD-developer relationship was the relationship of adversaries.

5. Localities appear to have been less than enthusiastic and less than cooperative in pursuing the social welfare objectives of the program.

6. The program seems to have been ill-conceived in terms of the economics of industrial location.

7. It also seems to have presupposed on a high and unlikely degree of intergovernmental cooperation— among federal agencies and between federal and local government.

Of these factors, two stand out as particularly important and can be restated at another level of abstraction which gives them more general import. First, program incentives— loans, subsidies, and grants—must be of sufficient magnitude to have economic weight and must also be of sufficient longevity to insure the program the continuity necessary to attract reputable investors. Continuity is necessary for both staff learning and for assuming reasonable risk taking in the commitment of venture capital. Second, in the absence of weighty incentives and program continuity, a cooperative relationship between the public and private sectors will be difficult to forge, given the different objectives of private and public managers. If public managers expect to achieve social welfare objectives which cannot be priced as value added, they should carefully assess whether they command sufficient powers and incentives to motivate the private sector as intended. In the absence of such powers, it may be preferable to abort a program rather than to assume the relationship of a contentious adversary—a situation in which welfare objectives are likely to be pursued in only a token manner.

Instant Rehab

The deterioration of the urban housing stock in so-called "slum" areas was placed on the agenda as a national issue and federal concern in the mid-sixties. As a consequence, HUD was chartered with financial authority to rehabilitate tenement housing and foster urban renewal.

One of the dilemmas of urban redevelopment that HUD encountered is the problem of renewing neighborhoods without removing their inhabitants. Early HUD renewal and redevelopment programs redeveloped large blocks of urban land, but displaced the original residents in the process, earning for urban renewal the sobriquet "Negro removal."

Responding to these criticisms, HUD sought methods of renewal that would permit the occupants of apartment structures to vacate a dilapidated tenement and return to a rehabilitated dwelling in a period of forty-eight hours. The ambitious vacate-rehabilitate-return timetable earned this HUD project the title "Instant Rehab."

Instant Rehab was intended to prevent dislocation and relocation problems during the renewal process while reducing the cost of refurbishing tenement housing stock. At the basis of the solution strategy was the concept of modularization and prefabricated modular components—kitchens and bathrooms that could be manufactured and assembled off-site and installed on-site. Tenement residents would be displaced only during installation and not during the time usually required for standard construction.

This dimension of the rehabilitation problem was the result of systems analysis methods borrowed from the space program applied to the war on poverty.

The Instant Rehab demonstration included two components: (1) the development and manufacture of modularized housing components and (2) the demonstration of their installation in a New York City common law tenement. The demonstration objective was to achieve the rehabilitation of a three-story building in forty-eight hours or less.

At the project's initiation, it was believed that off-site manufacturing of housing modules and the reduction of relocation costs would more than compensate for cost increases due to the accelerated installation and construction schedule. This did not prove to be the case; costs far exceeded both early HUD estimates and the cost of alternative rehabilitation methods. In part, this seems to have been the result of a reluctance to relax the forty-eight-hour goal even when major cost penalties were encountered.

The demonstration poses an interesting question: whether the ability to return residents to their homes in a very short time period is worth the incremental cost of instant rehabilitation. The answer provided by the demonstration project appears to be "no." The renewed housing provided by Instant Rehab deterioriated rapidly and the rehab process involved only *housing* rehabilitation, not the *neighborhood* regeneration that HUD planners have come to understand is essential for a meaningful improvement in the quality of residential life.

The Instant Rehab project was never replicated by HUD. No further efforts were made to trade off cost against time, and no private sector developers have imitated the process. The industrial production of modular housing components has been imitated abroad, but to a limited degree.

Despite a systematic effort to dimension the rehabilitation problem before pursuing a specific solution, Instant Rehab was not a success.

This case illustrates the momentum of the political commitments which accumulate in the process of conducting a demonstration project. Commitments to the City of New York and to the contractor were honored by HUD despite the fact that it seems apparent, on the basis of final bids and estimates, that the demonstration would establish that Instant Rehab was *not* cost-effective.

This dilemma—the momentum of political commitments—is by no means unique to Instant Rehab and illustrates a problem inherent to the demonstration process in general. Two factors seem certain to invite this problem: cost-plus contract arrangements and a penny-wise, pound-foolish reluctance to spend agency funds to obtain detailed cost estimates and contract specifications. In all too many instances (Instant Rehab being one) the demonstration process has been viewed as a means of obtaining reliable cost estimates rather than a means of validating them. More attention to cost estimation appears to be in order *before* the political momentum of the demonstration process makes project cancellation infeasible.

The same emphasis on the earliest feasible cost estimation is appropriate to avoid a second component of the momentum of the demonstration process—the identification of the sponsoring agency's reputation with the project and a consequent reluctance to "cancel out" for fear of "losing face."

Seat Belts and Air Bags

By the mid-1960s, highway accidents were causing 4 million injuries per year—50,000 of them fatal and 100,000 more resulting in permanent injuries.

Through most of the 1950s, public debate over traffic fatalities focused on highway design, law enforcement, and "the problem driver," particularly the drunk driver. At the close of the fifties, the debate over accidents began to shift, based on the recognition that most traffic deaths and injuries are the result of the motorist's crushing collision with his or her own vehicle—the "second collision" which follows the collision of two vehicles. This understanding reshaped the debate over traffic safety, and greater attention was given to injury prevention as well as the traditional objective of accident prevention.

The emphasis on injury prevention focused the traffic safety debate on the crash-worthiness of the automobile and the restraint of the driver and passengers in the event of collision. With the introduction of these concerns, the responsibility for corrective action was placed with the automobile-manufacturing industry, as well as with the highway engineer and highway patrol.

Identification of the problem did not result in industry action. Perhaps this should not be surprising. It has been estimated that as much as 20 percent of the total volume of auto industry production is required to repair or replace damaged vehicles. The hundreds of models of domestic cars are strategically market-positioned to fit a price/performance niche in the market; the additional cost of some safety features may be sufficient to upset the industry's price structure achieved through the careful, competitive positioning of economy, family, and luxury models. As Moynihan argued in 1966, "it can no longer be doubted that within the higher executive levels of the industry there has been a conviction that an excessive concern with safety is bad for business" (Moynihan, 1975, p. 86).

Industry inaction prompted an increasingly acrimonious debate over the morals and merits of federal regulation. The industry insisted that regulation would invade consumer sovereignty and that safety features such as seat belts and air bags should be made available as optional rather than standard equipment. Industry critics responded that consumer sovereignty arguments were a "red herring" and that the issue was one of standards—both moral standards and performance standards. They argued that "grounding" should apply as forcefully to unsafe automobiles as to airplanes and that comparable safety systems should be mandatory as a supplier rather than user responsibility. Before sale, industry critics argued, industry engineers should be willing to give a "warranty" that their product was collision-safe.

But how safe and at what cost? These were the issues that dragged on unresolved during the first half of the sixties. Moynihan explains federal inaction in two ways.

1. The problem of traffic safety (had not) associated itself with a professional group that would apply to it standards of evidence, evaluation and self-criticism that the solution of problems of this kind requires.
2. The power of the automobile industry and the ambivalence of the public have combined to prevent effective governmental action. We . . . opted for an arrangement which is, I suspect, not unusual in such circumstances: working at the problem in ways fairly certain not to succeed. One of the most effective ways in which a government cannot do something is to assign the task to the kinds of people who never get anything done (Moynihan, 1975, p. 89).

In 1966, Congress enacted the National Traffic and Motor Vehicle Safety Act which established the National Traffic Safety Agency with standard-setting regulatory powers. The agency acted in 1967 to mandate lap and shoulder belts as standard equipment in all passenger cars except convertibles.

Due to the low utilization of seat and shoulder belts—the public's failure to "buckle up"—the Traffic Safety Agency— now called the National Highway Traffic Safety Administration (NHTSA) of the Department of Transportation— began to explore so called "passive" restraints protecting the occupant without any action on his or her part. Later when efforts to mandate passive restraints failed, NHTSA imposed a requirement for ignition interlock systems that forced drivers to "buckle up" before starting their cars.

The first notice of intent to mandate passive restraints such as air bags was issued in 1969, and a succession of target dates for implementation have been waived since.

In 1971, with passive restraint regulations postponed, the NHTSA issued its now-infamous interlock regulation requiring this most obtrusive of all active restraint systems to be manufactured as standard equipment. Public reaction was so hostile that Congress voided the interlock standard in the safety act of 1974. Interlock had been proposed by the manufacturers as an alternative to the more costly air bag restraint system being promoted by the safety agency.

With the collapse of the interlock option, passive restraint systems were restored to their position as the critical item on the safety administration agenda—but in a new political environment complicated by the public furor over interlock. In this setting, it was judged that precipitous introduction of air bags could produce a comparable political backlash and that a large-scale demonstration was a more prudent way to achieve gradual introduction. As a consequence, the Secretary of Transportation decided in December, 1976 to make air bags available as *optional* equipment on some 1980 models. Five manufacturers have agreed to demonstrate the technology and promote their adoption using standard advertising techniques. This compromise decision— reached by the Secretary of Transportation in the eleventh hour of the Ford Presidency—rejected the mandatory standard equipment approach urged by the NHTSA and, in the process, obtained a "good faith" commitment from the auto manufacturers to undertake the tooling and production changeovers necessary to accomplish the demonstration. Some describe it as an eleventh-hour coup—others a last-minute cop out.

The delay will probably permit introduction of air bags on a schedule consistent with the model-change cycle of the industry, allowing them to conduct further tests and to escape the costs associated with interrupting their standard design, tooling, and production cycle.

Seat belts (a tack-on feature) did not threaten the industry's styling and engineering cycle and therefore apparently were not resisted with the same vehemence.

Again, we turn to Moynihan for an industry critic's perspective on the history of federal traffic safety efforts. Writing in 1966, Moynihan noted the dynamics of the regulatory process.

> The industry has now announced that it will not only accept but actually request government regulation. This is a normal, predictable outcome. For its own protection the industry has to get itself regulated by the Federal Government. What only a decade ago was unthinkable has now become all but inevitable. The companies must get their products formally certified as safe in order to protect themselves from massive litigation. If everything continues according to form, the next step will be for the industry to seek to dominate the government agency charged with regulating it, and so we commence another chapter of exposure leading to legislation imposing regulation that ends up more like collusion than anything else (Moynihan, 1975, p. 97).

In one significant way, Moynihan's prediction has not been realized: NHTSA has not been co-opted by the industry and remains a vigilant watch dog agency.

This has left the Secretary of Transportation in the role of arbiter between a reluctant industry and aggressive regulator, facing the trade-off decision of "how safe and at what cost?"

The dilemma with any regulatory approach, of course, is that there is no "right" answer to such a trade-off question. To understand the impact of decision alternatives is not sufficient to determine the "right" course of action. The "right course of action" is fundamentally a value judgment requiring a personal assessment of the economic consequences of higher-cost automobiles resulting in reduced sales volumes *versus* the life-saving results of a technology that has not been tested in the context of a full-scale production regime.

The value dimension of any such decision is obvious, as is its susceptibility to recision. It is precisely these characteristics, the subjectivity and mutability of regulatory standards, that make technology development in a setting of regulatory rather than economic incentives so perilous—and so arguably arbitrary. It may well be that the ability to claim tort damages from the manufacturer of an automobile that is sold with less than the "state of the art in survivability engineering" would be a far more forceful incentive for innovation than federal regulations and performance standards. At any rate, it seems evident that mutable and debatable standards are a less-than-effective means of motivating the auto industry or resolving the evident conflict between policy push and market pull.

Poultry-Waste Processing

In 1969, the Federal Water Pollution Control Administration, now a part of the Environmental Protection Agency (EPA), approved a demonstration grant to test various water conservation and waste removal practices in a broiler chicken processing plant. The demonstration was conducted in cooperation with the Gold-Kist Poultry Company and the University of North Carolina.

The demonstration involved the application of techniques for monitoring water use, recycling waste water, and retrofitting various plant equipment with on-the-shelf components designed to conserve water and reduce the waste concentration of the plant's effluent discharge. In short, this demonstration advanced the state of the art in water conservation *practice,* but not the state of the art of water conservation or waste treatment *technology.*

The demonstration project occurred in the larger context of the EPA's water quality control program. This broader program's activities include: the establishment of federal water quality standards, the grant financing of municipal sewage treatment facilities, and the approval of capital grants conditional on municipal action to charge industrial plants the full marginal cost of treating industrial wastes. EPA financing of sewage plants is conditional upon municipal adoption of sewage surcharges that reflect the volume, contents, and concentration of industrial sewage. The EPA requirement departs from the traditional municipal practice of charging a flat hook-up fee and monthly charge based on the volume of discharges. By charging on the basis of contaminant content and concentrations, the municipal surtax offers an *economic* incentive for firms to seek the most cost-effective means for reducing contaminant volume and concentration. In some cases this means companies will pay the municipality to treat the sewage at full marginal cost; but in other cases, companies have undertaken in-plant processing of wastes, including efforts to recycle water and recover commercial quantities of processing by-products from the waste water.

Waste treatment surcharges had been adopted in Durham, North Carolina, where the Gold-Kist poultry plant is located and were in effect at the time of demonstration. The cost of the waste treatment charge and steadily escalating water bills provided a significant incentive for Gold-Kist to seek cost-effective methods of conserving water, screening chicken fats and feathers from its discharge, and introducing valves that permit the intermittent rather than continuous use of water in the cleaning of broiler chickens. The demonstration program allowed the company to share the costs of experimenting with various cost saving, water-conserving processing techniques. Gold-Kist contributed $85,000 to the project while the federal contribution was $198,000.

In exchange for what amounted to public financing of plant modernization, Gold-Kist provided a "real world laboratory" that allowed University of North Carolina researchers to experiment with conservation techniques, assess their costs, and evaluate their utility in an operational environment. The results of these assessments were disseminated widely in the poultry and other food-processing industries.

The process innovations that proved effective in reducing the company's water and sewage treatment costs have been permanently incorporated in the company's operating procedures, and Gold-Kist has realized a substantial savings in monthly operating costs. Many of the techniques have also become standard operating procedure in the poultry industry at large and have spread to other food-processing industries requiring intensive use of water.

This project is of particular interest because of the *potential* conflict between the objectives of the poultry company and the Water Pollution Control Administration (WPCA). The WPCA's objective was to control effluent discharge and, in particular, to control the discharge of nutrient matter that prompts algae buildup in rivers and streams. In contrast, the poultry company's objective was to reduce the cost of water and sewer bills. This is a situation in which the company's purposes might have been served by reducing water use and the volume of effluent discharge without concern for the *concentration* of organic wastes; this would have achieved the company's cost-cutting objectives without resolving the pollution problem caused by rich concentrations of nutrients in its sewage. This conflict over objectives did not occur because, as we have noted, the demonstration program took place in the context of an EPA-mandated effluent charge keyed to both the volume *and concentration* of industrial sewage.

These effluent charges, in combination with rising water prices, provided an incentive for the company to pursue cost-cutting strategies that proved thoroughly consistent with the water conservation and pollution control objectives of the WPCA. It is unlikely the company and agency's objectives would have been consonant without the incentive of effluent charges based on effluent content and concentration.

While "poultry waste processing" may sound like a mundane backwater activity, this case offers a rich learning experience for those concerned with implementation success. Among explanations for project success, the following seem to be the most critical.

1. The adopting industry was motivated by a policy embodied in a tax or charge that had to be treated as part of the usual costs of doing business. Technology adoption became a problem in good business judgment requiring a relatively straightforward assessment of

how to reduce costs most effectively.
2. The technology was readily available and thoroughly tested, requiring only special-case adaptation and application.
3. The process innovations and technology applications were proposed after a thorough analysis of plant operations, costs, and managerial practices. The technology was specified in light of a clear understanding of the particular problem it was to solve.
4. The charge scheme placed the burden of technology innovation on the actor with the greatest first-hand knowledge of production costs and technologies in the poultry industry—namely Gold-Kist and the other poultry companies that adopted techniques first implemented at Gold-Kist.
5. Gold-Kist management was committed to the project and was an active partner in components of the project requiring cooperation from plant supervisors and workers. This management commitment, however, was based on "good business judgment" rather than the social concern for water quality, as evidenced by the rapid adoption of these techniques by other poultry industry managers.

Project Refan

Aircraft noise became a public issue in the early sixties with the introduction of jet aircraft and the mounting number of complaints from airport "neighbors."

Public protests produced action on four fronts: congressional legislation authorizing the Federal Aviation Administration (FAA) to establish noise standards; congressional appropriation of funds to support NASA research on quiet engines and noise suppression technology; private manufacturer effort to design quieter engines for the next generation of aircraft; and local efforts to control urban development near airports and prevent incompatible land uses.

These actions stemmed the escalation of aircraft noise while fleet replacement began to slowly reduce the noise insult at hub airports. These initiatives did not, however, substantially mitigate the problem of noise from the existing fleet of jet aircraft. Noise abatement became, then, an issue in retrofitting aircraft already in the service of airlines rather than simply replacing them with quieter craft as their service life ended.

This issue emerged as a simultaneous problem in regulatory strategy, technology design, and air travel economics.

Part of the federal response to noise mitigation was embodied in Project Refan, a joint NASA-FAA project to design, test, and assess methods of retrofitting jet engines to reduce their noise impacts. The $45 million project was managed by NASA and involved contracts for development and testing with Pratt & Whitney, Boeing, McDonnell-Douglas, and two domestic airlines. The project involved modification of a JT3D engine by replacing the two small fans on the turbine shaft with a single larger fan thereby reducing the whine associated with jet engine acceleration and deceleration.

The NASA technology effort was intended to supply the FAA with information on the potential noise reduction characteristics of refanned engines—information the FAA could use in promulgating a retrofit ruling using its aircraft certification powers.

At the same time, the FAA was exploring the merit of muffling jet engines through the use of sound-absorbing materials called SAM. Comparative cost-effectiveness studies of the SAM and refan approaches to noise abatement indicated that:

- SAM could be introduced immediately, with retrofit completed three or four years before refanning could be accomplished
- Refanning would be four times as costly as SAM insulation
- Refanning would be three to four times more effective than insulation

The FAA resolved this cost/impact trade-off in favor of SAM, noting the precarious economic condition of the domestic airline industry. In the wake of the FAA decision, refanning has languished, and its implementation is dependent upon an unlikely turnaround in FAA's posture or in congressional action to finance retrofitting from the public purse.

This case illustrates one of the principal dilemmas of technology implementation in a regulatory context. Regulations can be contested, challenged, and resisted on legal, technical, and economic grounds. They place the public and private sectors in an adversary situation which provides an incentive for private companies to *bargain* or *resist* rather than an economic incentive to comply with politically defined social welfare objectives where these objectives conflict with return on investment.

The case of refan—with its dilemmas of interagency cooperation and its instances of conflict between cost and effectiveness—is particularly revealing in contrast to our study of poultry waste processing. In the case of poultry waste processing, emission taxes or so-called pollution taxes provided an *economic* incentive for an industry to behave in a manner that was simultaneously cost-conscious and public serving. In the case of refan, regulation provided no *economic* incentive for public-serving behavior on the part of the airline industry so long as the airlines were confident that the FAA would view noise-suppression costs as excessive. This confident resistance to expenditures that would not produce any return on investment appears to have been justified, given the FAA's disposition of the refan alternative. The case does not seem to illustrate lethargy or negligence on the part of the FAA, as its critics have maintained, but rather illustrates the shortcomings of regulatory solutions and the difficulty of successful technological innovation in a setting that involves sanctions rather than economic incentives.

Flue Gas Desulphurization

Fossil fuel burning power plants are a major source of air pollution emissions, including sulphur dioxide (SO_2).

In late 1971, the Environmental Protection Agency (EPA) promulgated emission standards specifying an upper limit on the permissible emissions of SO_2 per million BTUs of coal or fuel oil that could be released from fossil-fuel power plants built or enlarged after August, 1971. Given available flue-gas desulphurization technologies, the regulations had the effect of forcing power companies to build steam-generating units equipped with so-called stack gas scrubbers. Utility company alternatives include obtaining low-sulphur fuel or desulphurizing their fuel after delivery. Others have chosen to challenge the EPA regulation.

Power plants built before the EPA regs were promulgated are regulated by state and local air pollution control districts. These districts have issued a variety of regulations aimed at reducing SO_2 emissions. At least four regulatory strategies have been adopted by local air pollution authorities: (1) specifying the sulphur content of the fuel that may be burned; (2) setting standards for the contaminant concentration of stack gases; (3) setting standards for the ambient air quality that must be maintained at the power plant property line; and (4) requiring utilities to install the "best available control technology" or adopt the "best modern practices." Depending on the local control strategy, power plants can meet the standards by changing fuels, desulphurizing the fuel before combustion, installing stack gas scrubbers, or (in some cases) ceasing boiler operation during pollution episodes or increasing the height of the gas stack to dilute ground-level contaminant concentrations. In many regions, the sulphur content of the least costly fuel is such that local regulations serve in effect to mandate the installation of scrubbers.

It should be noted that none of the control standards—EPA's or those used by local authorities—is directly related to the ambient air quality of an urban region. So-called "source standards" are designed to reduce emissions and prevent air quality degradation; their stringency is unrelated to the severity of local air pollution problems or the cost of obtaining low-sulphur fuels. Utility companies have been particularly reluctant to comply with source regulations where air pollution is only a legal problem and not a health concern.

Utility reluctance is based on two factors: the cost of installing and operating scrubbers and the unreliability of scrubbers installed in the retrofit mode.

Some of the experience with scrubbers is the result of the R&D efforts pursued by Combustion Engineering. Until 1970, Combustion Engineering's scrubber research was conducted in the laboratory and was self-financed. After 1970, Combustion Engineering cooperated with EPA to demonstrate a lime/limestone wet scrubbing process—one of some ten methods of flue gas desulphurization.

The earliest field demonstrations of wet limestone scrubbers were not federally financed, but involved locally regulated utilities working with traditional trade partners like Combustion Engineering. The regulations served to aggregate a market for scrubbers and the four major vendors of power plant equipment have competed vigorously for their share. Some of this vendor R&D has been federally financed, with the equipment suppliers waiving patent rights on the theory that learning experience was paramount in a regulatory environment characterized by the potential of abatement authorities to insist on "the best available technology" rather than the least costly.

Combustion Engineering's early demonstration of wet limestone scrubbing was less than satisfactory. Scaling, corrosion, and plugging problems—problems in the chemistry rather than mechanics of desulphurization—resulted in two major overhauls in the system between 1968 and 1970. The utility company, Kansas Power and Light, was still not satisfied with the reliability of Combustion Engineering's system when the EPA regulations were issued in 1971, and rebuilding and modification were still continuing in 1972. By 1973, the Combustion Engineering/Kansas Power and Light system was operational; but its useful life ended in 1976. Corrosion had consumed the scrubber.

Other retrofit scrubbers have encountered similar corrosion and plugging problems that have increased the cost and diminished the reliability of power generation.

There are two predominant explanations for the problems encountered in this pollution-abatement process.

One is that utilities and their vendors are accustomed to dealing with problems in combustion engineering. The chemical engineering dilemmas of scrubber technologies caught them off guard.

The second is that emission standards were promulgated anticipating that technology barriers would fall more quickly than they have. EPA's regulations were issued in 1971 when desulphurization technology was unproved and when the most significant operating system was faltering. Without question, the regulations were promulgated without full information on the useful lifespan of scrubbing technology and, therefore, its cost.

In this context, it is not surprising that utility companies in regions with low levels of air pollution have vehemently resisted the EPA standards. In some of these cases, it appears that scrubbing involves very real costs, but offers benefits that are little more than a legal fiction.

The Case Findings in Overview

In this section, we report the causes of implementation failure that cut across two or more case studies—that is, factors that seem to have accounted for the failure of technology adoption and diffusion in more than one program area.

Five factors cropped up repeatedly as the proximate cause of implementation failure.

1. Inadequate attention to problem definition, "needs" assessment, and market analysis
2. Lack of program continuity
3. Excessively costly technology
4. Conflict between "the public interest" and the behavior of the technology delivery system
5. Insufficient foresight to anticipate the barriers that would be encountered during implementation

We will discuss each of these in turn.

Inadequate Attention to Problem Definition and "Needs" Assessment

In several cases of implementation failure—STOL, PRT, USAC, and Instant Rehab—a candidate technology was allowed to define the problem it was to solve. In each of these cases, the problem (air traffic congestion, deteriorated housing, etc.) was defined in terms of the capabilities of the proposed technology rather than in terms of a multidisciplinary assessment of consumer preferences or social needs. As a consequence, the implementation problem was viewed as a problem in technology design and testing rather than in design and introduction of a component of a sociotechnical system.

In using the abstract language "component of a socio-technical system," we are trying to denote a "solution package" that does not yet have a specific technological form. This function can, most probably, be performed by several technologies or by various mixes of technological, managerial, and organizational resources applied at various leverage points in the relevant sociotechnical system.

Conceptualizing "the problem" without specifying a candidate solution is an intellectually difficult task. But it appears to be necessary to avoid too hasty a focus on the engineering of technology components. One method for conceptualizing problems without leaping to the endorsement of a particular mode of technological resolution is to view the problem as a deficiency and the resolution as a search among multiple alternatives. This particular abstraction of the problem focuses on "need" rather than "product," and promotes a multidisciplinary approach to problem assessment and implementation strategy before undertaking technology design and assessment.[5] In projects in which implementation failure occurred, this problem-focused phase of the R&D planning process was either omitted or foreshortened.

In emphasizing the technology rather than its role in a sociotechnical system, these projects avoided the issue of whether the technology matched consumer wants and needs. Similarly, these programs spent little time considering alternative solution options and their fit with the technology delivery systems. As a result, the technology assumed a center-stage position in these projects, and the prototypes went to demonstration without anyone having a clear sense of the need they were to fill, the demand they were to satisfy, or the acceptance they would receive.

Where inadequate attention was paid to problem definition and "needs" analysis, it also appears that project management was characterized by technology "boosterism" and salesmanship rather than critical assessment of market potential. These projects seem to have survived the R&D screening process without being put through "needs" analysis in time to influence technology design. In these cases, the question of implementation feasibility was given short shrift, postponing consideration of the following.

- Whether the technology component of the project was consistent with the managerial, organizational, and financial capabilities of the delivery system
- What products this technology would replace or compete with
- The size of the market for the closest available substitutes currently available
- In what sense the currently available products or technology were inadequate
- Whether improvements in the closest available substitute could be implemented at a lower cost than the new technology
- Whether the benefits of a new technology could be priced by manufacturers and realized by consumers or whether they would accrue to the public at large

It appears that STOL, PRT, USAC, Newtowns and Instant Rehabs were pursued without systematically asking these fundamental questions about cost, need, and marketability. Thus, it is not surprising that the resulting technologies were, in effect, solutions in search of a problem.

Lack of Program Continuity

Lack of program continuity appears to have been a crippling factor in two of the projects reviewed in the case analyses—Newtowns and USAC.

Program continuity and certainty are critical dimensions of the learning process necessary to refine a program and develop a mature technology delivery system. The importance of program continuity has been argued by Brooks.

> It takes a very long time to establish the linkages between the R&D process and the ultimate "market" which it is designed to serve. . . . It really took the trauma of World War II and 25 years of the Cold War to establish the complex of linkages between technology and the military which sometimes goes under the pejorative sobriquet of the military industrial complex, but which, for good or ill, connect the whole world of science and technology to its military market and assure the rapid exploitation of technical opportunities wherever and whenever they appear. . . . It is these linkages which are

missing in relation to many of the societal problems which are being talked about as the new subjects of technical effort (Brooks, 1971, p. 23ff.).

For these linkages to develop, a number of critical ingredients are necessary—or at least so the Newtowns and USAC cases indicate. One necessary ingredient is policy continuity—even if management continuity cannot be achieved. The second is fiscal continuity; rapid changes in appropriations or restructuring of funding streams are unlikely to build the confidence necessary for local governments and private industries to make financial commitments with a tolerable level of risk.

Rapid changes in personnel, in appropriations levels, or in agency priorities serve to discourage the development of the constituent components of technology delivery systems that are able to plan on planning and count on a reasonable degree of program continuity and financial certainty. Operation Breakthrough's approach, while overambitious, is instructive here.

The previous chapters appear to be on target in identifying the quadrennial exodus and entry of executive branch personnel as disruptive to program continuity. Even more disruptive are cases in which federal aid funds are restructured or redirected as they were in the case of Newtowns.

Excessively Costly Technologies

The mission orientation of federal R&D agencies—"save energy," "reduce pollution," "house the poor"—focuses their evaluation of technologies on a relatively small number of performance attributes. By comparison, the manufacturers of products are concerned with a wide range of technology attributes which determine manufacturability and user acceptance. Manufacturers and consumers are, it should be said, most often unconcerned about questions of broader social welfare when they decide to buy or sell a product.

In some cases where implementation failed or demonstrations have not led to diffusion, it appears that agency professionals expected producers to share their objectives. Some also seem to have assumed that improvements in mission-related technology performance would be wanted and valued by the potential user. Where agencies, vendors, and users have different wants, implementation failure has resulted. This appears to have occurred in the case of Newtowns and, to date, in the case of Transbus. These are cases in which the critical variable is the willingness of political leaders to use an incomes policy to rig market outcomes in a manner that achieves social objectives. Where political action to rig the market is lacking, designing a technology to be compatible with the dictates of enterprise economics may offer the only feasible path for technology implementation—a path that may well require sacrificing larger social welfare objectives. This appears to be the situation in the cases of Newtowns, air bags, and Transbus.

Thus, the case findings are consistent with the expectation of economists: implementation failure is highly likely when the benefits attributed to a project cannot be priced by a manufacturer or realized by the individual consumer. This rule of thumb, an application of the economic theory of market externalities, suggests that project managers should make the earliest possible assessment of four technology attributes before proceeding to prototype development or demonstration: (1) Is the production cost of the new technology likely to be more or less than for currently available products? (2) Are user costs likely to be higher or lower than for currently available products? (3) On what dimensions of performance is the new technology likely to be superior to currently available products, and on which inferior? (4) Are the dimensions of superiority ones which accrue as benefits to the user or to the society at large?

Where production or operating cost is increased and a substantial number of technology benefits accrue for the public at large, implementation failure is likely unless forceful incentives for adoption and use are imposed—incentives such as tax advantages, subsidies, grants, or regulations that increase the cost of competing products.

By comparison, market adoption is most likely where a new technology can be produced or operated at a lower cost than available products without a loss of product quality. In between is a "grey area" in which both cost and performance increase. Here, the R&D manager needs better knowledge of demand elasticities. If costs increase and the performance increment accrues to the society at large rather than to the user, then marketability is improbable without extraordinary incentives or penalties.

Conflict between the Public Interest and the Behavior of Markets

In the previous paragraphs, we have presented part of the story of conflict between policy push and market pull, those case studies in which implementation failure seems to have resulted because research, development, and demonstration were conducted with little attention to a technology's comparative cost, its compatibility with the production and price requirements of the delivery system, or its fit with user requirements. We noted that in these cases, federal R&D managers often viewed technology development as a "pure engineering" problem rather than a problem in "matching" which requires engineering a technology so that it fits into a preexisting deployment and delivery system. We noted, for example, that Operation Breakthrough and STOL/ METROFLIGHT both involve a simultaneous effort to change a technology and the technology delivery system.

There is another dimension of the dissonance between policy push and market pull that is evidenced in at least four of the case studies—poultry waste processing, seat belts/air bags, Newtowns, and stack gas desulphurization. Here we find fundamental conflict between the goals and motives of the political system and those of the private enterprise system. These studies demonstrate that markets often do not price at levels consistent with the public interest as expressed by legislative policy—and that markets must be rigged in order to coerce producers into compliance and coax consumers into acceptance. Economists call this situation "market failure," referring to the inadequacy of product information, the costliness of using up common resources such as clean air or water, or the market power of very large companies in concentrated industries. These are settings in which policy implementation requires the use of penalties and incentives to motivate the technology delivery system to behave in the public interest.

The success story presented in one of the case studies, the demonstration of poultry waste processing techniques in the context of effluent charges, suggests the merit of "pollution charges" or "policy taxes" as strategies for bringing market performance and policy push into better alignment.

In contrast, the contests over seat belts, air bags, and stack gas desulphurization points up the political hazards raised by the inevitable arbitrariness of regulatory strategies that rely on the specification of standards or prototype technologies. This lesson seems particularly significant for energy R&D where a scarce fuels surtax would provide a meaningful incentive for conservation and technological conversion without political and legal contest between regulators and regulatees.

This argues that the incentives for technology adoption should be as critical a concern of energy program managers as the availability of the requisite technology. In short, policy implementation and technology adoption may require extraordinary efforts to motivate the technology delivery system in the absence of market pull. The poultry waste processing case indicates the efficiency of a surcharge or "policy tax" as a pricing instrument and incentive for technological innovation of a cost-effective character.

Insufficient Foresight to Anticipate Barriers in the Technology Delivery System

If project managers could have had the foresight of hindsight, many of the projects reviewed in the case studies would probably not have been undertaken or would have been undertaken in drastically modified form. This raises the interesting question of whether the impediments to effective implementation could have been anticipated.

The answer appears to be, "not if technology implementation is treated as a problem in pure engineering." But if the implementation problem is viewed as the merger of engineering expertise and the requisites of the delivery system (i.e., the demands and requirements of producers and consumers), then it appears that foresight could permit improvements in both program and technology design.

If implementation had been viewed as a matching problem rather than a design problem, then it appears that there would have been a higher probability of anticipating which technologies would fail and which might have succeeded if they had been fine-tuned for compatibility with the technology delivery system and the needs of users.

If the implementation problem were pursued as an incremental process involving the matching of programs to needs and the engineering of technologies to accommodate the warrants of the delivery system, the case studies indicate that some implementation failures could probably be anticipated and reduced. In some cases, this would involve eliminating the candidate technology at the screening stage; in other cases, it would involve the forceful use of incentives such as subsidies or the postponement of demonstrations until intervention authority was sufficient to ensure a higher probability of success; in other cases, it would involve trade-offs between performance and cost in technology design; and, in still other cases, it would mean downscoping unrealistic program objectives or time schedules such as those for Operation Breakthrough. In any case, the critical concern here is the anticipation of a mismatch between policy goals, the technology, and the technology delivery system at the earliest point that credible cost and performance estimates become available.

This matching of technology, markets, and delivery systems did not occur in the case of STOL, PRT, and Instant Rehab. In the case of STOL—but more dramatically in the case of PRT—research, development, and testing seem to have been pursued past the point where, prudent, conservative judgment would suggest that the technology is too costly to achieve implementation success.

The hypotheses about organizational enhancement and political sponsorship advanced in Chapter 5 seem to partially account for the failure to anticipate barriers and costs and to change course accordingly. The case studies indicate that another dynamic may also be at work. Many of the projects reviewed in the case studies were managed by veteran systems analysts with roots in the space program or military R&D such as STOL, OBT, and Instant Rehab. It appears that the learning experience of these projects led this generation of federal managers to view technology as a "hardware system" rather than the hardware component of a politicized sociotechnical system. As a result, the boundaries of the relevant system were drawn narrowly, ensuring a manageable research problem, but insulating the process of technology design from implementation concerns. In another case, that of STOL, "the system" was defined broadly; but its susceptibility to management, optimization, and malleability was greatly overestimated. The pitfalls and failures encountered seem to have provided a valuable learning experience, and it appears that many of these same managers are paying far greater attention to the political and economic attributes of the projects currently "on the drawing boards."

It is appropriate here to try to specify those characteristic or frequently encountered barriers that confounded the implementation process. Learning from the experience of the sixties and early seventies, today's R&D officer may be better able to anticipate whether a candidate technology being considered for development has its own "fatal flaw," virtually assuring implementation difficulties, if not failure.

The most critical barriers found in the case studies can be grouped in the following categories.

1. Interdependency of actors. Successful implementation requires cooperation between divisions, agencies, or levels of government; public and private sectors; labor and management.

2. Simultaneity of events. Implementation requires integration of component social and technical elements simultaneously; incremental evolution of technology/supply-system/consumer acceptance precluded by factors such as economies of scale.

3. Adverse impacts. Implementation requires costly side payments or mitigation to reduce the controversy or damage associated with adverse social, environmental, or economic impacts.

4. Uncertainty about technology cost. Costs cannot be estimated on the basis of current products; a pilot project or experimental project at a small scale is inadequate for cost assessment.

5. Uncertainty about development and demonstration costs.

6. Uncertainty about consumer acceptance or sales potential. Consumer reaction cannot be estimated on the basis of current product experience; a small pilot project provides an inadequate market test.

7. Sensitivity to exogenous economic factors. A project's probability of success is dependent on cyclic economic

factors such as rates of inflation and interest, etc.

8. Sensitivity to exogenous policy factors. Implementation requires program and budget continuity over a long time frame; implementation requires the introduction of economic incentives or regulatory penalties; the political commitment to budgets, incentives, or penalties is uncertain or problematic.

9. Improved technology performance is achieved at the penalty of higher cost.

10. Inability to price the technology in relation to cost of production because performance elements necessary to accomplishment of public policy objectives are not valued by the user of the technology—requires user-subsidy to achieve adoption; requires enforcement of regulatory standards or application of regulatory sanctions to achieve compliance.

11. Major or comprehensive change in consumer behavior. For adoption to occur, the consumer must change the way he or she uses forms of products or services.

12. Major or comprehensive change in supplier behavior. For adoption to occur, the delivery system must be altered vis-à-vis the way currently available products or services are produced.

13. Excessively costly technologies.

These barriers cannot, obviously, be anticipated with the certainty of clairvoyance, but they can be considered by R&D managers and can be raised as issues by policymakers. What is at issue here is a trade-off between risk and payoff. Each of the factors identified as barriers—interdependencies, uncertainties, cost, sensitivity to events beyond control, and the inertia of current ways of making and using things—add to the risk associated with R&D.

Assessing whether the payoff is worth the risk is a matter for management judgment; but more importantly, it is a matter for informed management evaluation, assessment, and then judgment. In the cases of implementation failure, it appears that R&D managers wished away or failed to thoroughly evaluate the barriers their technology might encounter downstream in the implementation process. In some cases, they seem to have viewed implementation as "none of my business."

The Case Findings and Chapter Five Hypotheses

The case studies have yielded a set of case-specific findings and a number of rather important generalizations about the reasons for the failure of federal research, development, and demonstration programs to produce technologies that fit market needs in local government and the private sector. They were:

1. Inadequate attention to problem definition, needs analysis, and market matching
2. Insufficient program continuity to permit development of the agency/supplier/market linkages necessary for adoption and diffusion of innovation
3. Excessively costly technologies
4. Conflict between the public interest and the goals of the technology delivery system
5. Insufficient effort to anticipate barriers to implementation

These seem to be the most important of the proximate causes for implementation failure found in the case studies.

The hypotheses in Chapter 5 go beyond proximate causes in an effort to plumb and explain the organizational dynamics behind the problems reported here.

In light of the case studies, we can restate and reformulate the Chapter 5 hypotheses as propositions that seek to explain the high failure rate of federally funded research, development, and demonstration. The cases, augmented by the technical literature reviewed in Chapters 1 through 4, lead us to think that the following propositions are reasonable explanations for the organizational and institutional dynamics of implementation failure. (We focus on organizational and institutional questions here because this is the realm of correctable action, whereas the intractability of a technology problem may mean that it is not susceptible to corrective action.)

1. Research, development, and demonstration (RD&D) teams have displayed a bias toward pure hardware solutions. As a consequence, "needs" have been defined in terms of technological systems rather than in terms of fitting hardware components into existing sociotechnical systems.

2. Many R&D managers are veterans of the space program and military procurement. They need to learn the political vagaries of the civil sector and marketing orientation of the private sector. The painful learning experience of the sixties is producing greater attention to implementation requirements in the seventies.

3. Project success has not been measured by technology adoption and diffusion. In fact, the reward and prestige structure of R&D agencies is still not tied to the success of implementation, but to reputation-makers such as size of budget, size of project, technical elegance of approach, and the challenge of the research problem.

4. Self-serving political demands can distort a project budget, timetable, and demonstration site in a fashion that distracts the project team from its concern with engineering performance or market impact.

5. There is a general lack of market information and marketing savvy in the federal R&D establishment. Since market analysis is not conducted early in the R&D process, it does not seem to influence the screening of candidate technologies. Similarly, cost analysis does not seem to be conducted in time to abort projects that are "certain" or "probable" losers. This is part and parcel of the technologist's belief that "implementation is somebody else's problem."

6. Lack of program continuity, in terms of personnel, funding levels, and policy priorities, is a source of implementation failure. Program continuity is necessary to develop the constellation of suppliers, developers, and return customers that make up a mature technology delivery system. This has not developed in the civilian sector. (Revenue sharing has substantially diminished the likelihood of the development of a vigorous social-industrial complex.)

7. Agencies with R&D missions are often not equipped with implementation authority. They rarely, for example, have authority to use penalties and incentives other than demonstration and information programs to encourage technology adoption. As a consequence, decisions about social policy, technology policy, and regulatory policy tend to be made disjointedly. Interagency cooperation in coordinating technology and regulatory policy is sporadic and seems to be frequently marked by interagency competition. This means that the coordinated planning of research and

intervention efforts necessary to motivate the technology delivery system is often lacking.

8. The failure of technology implementation is often a function of the shortcomings of standard setting as an incentive for innovation. Where market processes do not produce socially desirable results, the conventional federal approach has been to impose regulations. Regulation through the specification of minimum emission standards, minimum highway safety standards, and minimum job safety standards has proven difficult to enforce and is liable to legal challenge on the basis of capriciousness or anticompetitive impacts (i.e., antitrust law). Economic incentives such as tax deductions and "policy taxes" such as emission charges seem to offer a more promising opportunity to promote technological innovation by manufacturers themselves. Charges provide an incentive for the technology deployment system to adjust itself to new input prices and output costs in the most cost-effective manner, whether that be technological or managerial.

9. R&D efforts are undertaken in a context which is framed by economic and ideological conventions about the "appropriate" roles of the public and private sectors. These conventions include legal canons governing property rights, patents, licensing, and the recoupment of windfall profits that result from public investment. They shape and frame the R&D process in a fashion that has traditionally discouraged the public sector from engaging in "downstream" activities such as market analysis. Instead, federal efforts have been located far "upstream" where technology risks are higher and the probability of early commercial adoption lower.

These refinements of the hypotheses presented in Chapter 5 lead us to accept the general proposition that the critical challenge in technology innovation, adoption, and diffusion is matching policy push and market pull. Two strategies emerge as critically important: (1) the use of economic incentives such as pricing strategies and "policy taxes" to motivate cost-effective problem solving by those who know their business best (individual firms and localities) and (2) the treatment of research, development, and demonstration as a matching rather than a pure engineering problem. The challenge of "matching" is to engineer technologies to fit the demands of the technology manufacturer and user or to develop economic or regulatory incentives that motivate the delivery system to produce and accept new outcomes.

Notes

1. This notion of "markets" was also used by Dr. Harvey Brooks in hearings before the House Subcommittee on Science, Research and Development, 22 June 1971.
2. So-called "automated guideway systems" have proven disappointing in reducing labor costs because of the large number of highly paid personnel required for maintenance and software activities. PRT critics have noted that bus drivers perform many more functions than simply chauffeuring passengers. They are also an "official presence" that deters crime and a source of information about bus routing.
3. At the same time that the regs impose planning requirements, they also confer limited powers to implement that planning. The regs confer "shadow" programming and budgeting authority on the regional agencies by conditioning the investment of federal funds on the adoption of a regional capital improvement plan listing the projects proposed by all implementing agencies in the region. The federal intent is that conflicts over project priorities will be resolved at the regional scale.
4. The study contains a general discussion of the degree to which each Request for Proposal (RFP) objective was obtained and lists a number of questions which need to be answered before a more detailed assessment of the program's accomplishments can be made.
5. Multidisciplinary teams are frequently viewed as inefficient because they have no common language and no common problem concept. That is precisely their merit in this setting.

Bibliography

Brooks, Harvey. "Civilian Conversion of Research and Development." *Hearings on the Conversion Research and Education Act of 1971* before the Subcommittee on Science

Research and Development of the house Committee on Science and Astronautics. Washington, D.C.: GPO, 1971, pp. 22-26.

Huth, M.J. "Operation Breakthrough: A HUD Response to the Nation's Housing Shortage." Unpublished manuscript.

Jones, David W., Jr. "The Politics of Metropolitan Transportation Planning and Programming." Institute of Transportation Studies, University of California, Berkeley, 1976.

Moynihan, Daniel P. *Coping, On the Practice of Government.* New York: Vintage Books, 1975.

Rubel, John H. "The Aerospace Project Approach Applied to Building New Cities." In H.W. Eldridge, *Taming Megalopolis, Vol. II.* New York: Doubleday, Anchor Paperback, 1965.

Kaiser, Edgar F. "The Report of the President's Committee on Urban Housing—A Decent Home." Washington, D.C.: GPO, 1968.

The National Commission on Urban Problems. *Building the American City.* New York: Praeger Publishers, 1969.

Weidman et al. *Summary of Initial Assessment and Evaluation Study Design for Operation Breakthrough.* Washington, D.C.: The Urban Institute, n.d.

Note: References to the case studies can be found in the technical report.

7
Getting It Off the Shelf

In this chapter we move from description to prescription. Here we offer a methodology designed to bring policy push and market pull into closer alignment and consequently to improve the probability of implementing the products of publicly sponsored R&D. Our investigation of implementation and R&D management provides a background for making strategic recommendations about how it might be possible to orient federal R&D activities so implementation concerns are incorporated in management, budgeting, and design decisions. It is important to recognize that our methodology represents but one means by which the existing R&D management process could be refined in order to mitigate the implementation problems characterized and analyzed in the preceding chapters.

One apparent solution to the dilemma of nonimplementation—conducting federal research the way it is done by private industry—although a very appealing one in its straight-forwardness, is neither totally possible nor desirable given that much public research is initiated in response to the marketplace failure to produce a socially desired outcome. There are some aspects of private sector research, such as increased awareness of the end user and manufacturing requirements from the early stages of program planning and project design, that should become an integral part of public sector research as well. However, whereas the private sector is guided by market criteria and motivated by return on investment in its conduct of research, federal research agencies must satisfy a broader test of social welfare—one that is composed of a more diverse constituency and more complicated set of motivations than are found in the private sector.

Therefore, we have rejected the rather simplistic notion that making the federal research agencies operate like private industry will resolve the implementation problem. Rather, we have opted for an approach that is sensitive to the differences between the sectors. The generalized strategy we propose is designed to be both compatible with existing research management processes and suitable to a variety of research programs, each of which has its own unique character. This strategy, termed the Technology Implementation Plan (TIP), consists of incorporating implementation considerations (e.g., the end user, the supply system, technical feasibility, and barriers) into technology selection, project specification, program monitoring, and budget decisions.

Before detailing the components of TIP, it is necessary to define the types of research which it is appropriate to evaluate on the basis of implementation potential, and thereby the context for applying TIP.

Drawing a Distinction between Basic and Applied Research

Not all R&D should be judged by the test of implementation potential. In evaluating alternative research projects, it is important to distinguish between applied and basic research. The reason for drawing this distinction is that in the latter case, basic research, it is not appropriate to speak in terms of project implementation.

Basic research can be subdivided into two classes. One kind of basic research is purely exploratory and adds to our knowledge of behavioral causality. Its primary intent is to increase our ability to predict behavior, whether the relevant behavior is that of atoms, individuals, or social systems. A second kind of basic research is at the boundary between theoretical and empirical research. This area represents the bridge between theory and application. This area of basic research is concerned with concept testing rather than prototype testing or design engineering. Its conceptual and analytical orientation distinguishes it from the development, engineering, and testing activities that are at the center of applied research.

Basic research is not normally undertaken with the objective of producing a specific product in the same sense that we may expect a piece of hardware to emerge as a result of an applied research project. That this research will not immediately provide an implementable product is irrelevant; a contribution to the understanding of some scientific or social phenomenon is the end goal of the research. Moreover, it is inappropriate to apply the same evaluation criteria for judging the merits of basic and applied research. A basic research project that "fails" can provide as much insight into a problem as one that produces "successful" (i.e., expected) results. The concept of success or failure is more suitable to applied research where attempts are made to adapt knowledge into a useful and viable product.

Where the distinction between the different classes of research should be drawn is less clear. Just as it would be naive to say that all basic research is purely exploratory, it would also be unrealistic to assume that all federally funded applied research leads to an end product. For example, there are instances when funding for research programs is provided to insure that an ongoing effort is maintained in research areas considered to be of continuing or potential importance. At other times, research programs may be funded in response to a strong public demand for government intervention to ameliorate a perceived crisis.

For many agencies, experience has shown that Congress and OMB are reluctant to allocate large amounts of money to support basic research. This reluctance seems to be a product of the felt need to justify expenditures of public funds with an identifiable product. Consequently, agencies are tempted to package basic research as if it were an applied research project. The failure of this research to produce a product is then construed to be a failure in the project's execution and can jeopardize both the research program and the execution of legitimate applied research. If Congress and OMB were to formally recognize and legitimize basic research activities and provide adequate funding to support them, some of the problems associated with masquerading basic research projects and facilitating the control of applied research projects could be overcome.

In order to proceed with the ordered management of

research activities, an early assessment of the nature of the proposed R&D projects must be made. Once this is done, a relevant set of criteria can be used to evaluate the potential and performance of the project. Whereas basic research activities can be judged on the basis of their contribution to the general understanding of a problem, applied research activities should be judged on the basis of whether they are likely to lead to an implementable product.

Our strategy here is to address only those research projects that have passed beyond either of the basic research areas and that are ready to be used to solve a particular problem. The research manager or the group assembled to prepare or review a research proposal would have to differentiate between those projects that are still basic and those that are sufficiently proven to be applied to the solution of specific problems. It is the latter type of research to which we will now turn.

The Technology Implementation Plan

The R&D management process presented in Chapter 4 described the sequence of events commonly associated with moving from a legislative mandate to a tested prototype and technology transfer. The argument developed throughout this document has been that the process's failure to explicitly consider implementation issues has rendered this process ineffectual in dealing with the market or political demands initially prompting program authorization. The purpose of this section is to describe a methodology—called the Technology Implementation Plan (TIP)—designed to introduce implementation considerations in the research management process.

TIP is a procedure for explicitly considering, documenting, and monitoring the probability of implementation success. It is a strategic planning and research activity which is intended for incorporation in the annual cycle of program budgeting and the day-to-day activities of the research process. Its physical manifestation is a documentation and justification sheet.

TIP is designed for application at the program level where go/no-go and increase/decrease decisions about technology development budgets are made. It involves a continuing process of technology assessment based on implementation feasibility. Thus, TIP involves risk/payoff analysis that goes beyond technical feasibility to incorporate the likelihood of a technology's implementation success and user acceptance.

Since TIP is focused on implementation feasibility, it should be applied at the level of technological systems rather than at the level of technology components. For example, TIP's risk/payoff analysis would be conducted for turbine engines, but not for turbine ceramics. Similarly, risk/payoff analysis would be conducted for STOL aircraft, but not for the avionics or propulsion projects making up the STOL program.

The application of TIP at the program level is intended to lodge responsibility for considering implementation with the program manager rather than with the technical specialist. This level of responsibility is appropriate because it is here that the responsibility for making programming and budgeting decisions about competing technologies is lodged. As will become evident in the following pages, TIP will offer an information resource for the program manager who must determine the composition and mix of a technology development program. TIP is intended to inform budget decisions such as the relative expenditure for turbine versus rankine engine R&D. By implication, TIP will influence the resources committed to subprojects within the turbine and rankine engine master projects.

Beyond its program planning function, TIP is intended to provide the program manager or branch chief with a set of reference points for ongoing technology assessment. It is also intended as a means of introducing market wants as performance standards for use in technology design. The TIP justification sheet—the paperwork representation of a larger research and planning process—will serve to define the implementation path of a candidate technology and help in the anticipation of potential barriers to implementation. The implementation plan will include strategies for relaxing barriers to implementation through design improvements, regulatory strategies, or subsidy measures.

Finally, the TIP is designed to help the program manager reevalute the merits of technology systems each year as more conclusive information on performance, cost, and implementation barriers becomes available. Thus, TIP demands that the program manager work with staff technologists to develop evaluation milestones that stress not only technical feasibility but also questions of market acceptance and implementation path. The milestones component of TIP is designed for incorporation as an integral element of the annual review cycle and allows a form of zero-based budgeting in the selection of R&D priorities.

The components of TIP are outlined in Figure 7-1. The components include: (1) technology description, (2) product diffusion, (3) work program and research plan, (4) barrier identification, (5) intervention strategies, and (6) milestones and strategies for reducing uncertainties. Corresponding with these components, a "checklist" designed to draw the program manager's attention to the salient implementation issues is provided and will be described in the following section.

As the R&D manager progresses through the TIP documentation, it will probably become apparent that in some cases the implementation of technologies can be brought about by insuring that they meet the traditional market criteria and the test of profitability for their producers, but that in other cases, technologies will be unable to meet these tests, and intervention strategies will have to be developed to "rig" the market in favor of the adoption of the technology.

Use of the TIP will cover both of these cases. Where the question is one of insuring compatibility between the technology and the market, the completion of the TIP should be fairly straightforward (as should the implementation of the technology if the TIP is followed and not treated merely as one more form to complete).

In the second instance, where the implementation of the technology will only occur if introduced in conjunction with extraordinary incentives or penalties, the need for these incentives or penalties should become more clear as the TIP is prepared. These measures, which would be aimed at changing the incentives structure of the market (or, in a broader sense, the technology delivery system) might include subsidies, loans, regulatory standards, and tax deductions, depending upon the nature of the mismatch between policy objectives and market performance. If one or more of these options could realistically be employed to achieve public

FIGURE 7-1. TIP Flow Chart

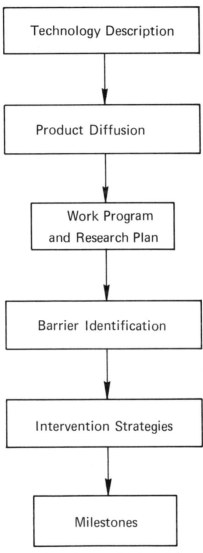

objectives, then assessing the method and impact of intervention should become a part of the overall research effort.

The philosophy behind the development of TIP is clear. It would be reckless to suggest that there exists a technique or research style which could force or guarantee implementation success. Instead, by making the treatment of implementation concerns an integral and explicit element of R&D management, it is hoped that the resulting products of research will be at least more suitable for end-use adoption and diffusion.

The strength of such a strategy lies in its conformity with existing procedures as well as its ability to provide a systematic approach to information gathering for decision making. TIP does not replace management judgments. Rather, it seeks to inform them through an explicit emphasis on implementation as a judgment criterion. Moreover, because TIP is not a deterministic technique, judgments play a central function in assessing and responding to the uncertainty associated with potential implementation risk and implementation payoff. The following subsections will detail the various components of TIP.

Preparation of a Technology Implementation Plan

The concept behind the TIP is to attack the implementation problem in a fashion that is compatible with the research management planning methodologies used in government today. With this in mind, we have designed a TIP form that would become a part of the total program documentation package and would follow it through the process of selection, development, and monitoring. The various components of the TIP—policy objective and end user, technology description, technical feasibility, production of the product, market and producer considerations, barriers anticipated, the research plan, and monitoring checkpoints—are all dealt with in some detail in the pages to follow. Of immediate importance is the fact that these various subcomponents are all combined on a form such as the one illustrated in Figure 7-2. Obviously, the amount of space allocated does not preordain the required inputs because additional pages can be appended. However, the form does allow the program managers to clearly identify the salient features of the proferred technology and suggests the probability of its being implemented by or for an end user.

In each section of this form, a number of questions are presented that can be used by program managers (or prospective contractors) to guide them in preparing a TIP. The

FIGURE 7-2. Technology Implementation Plan Justification Sheet

	Reference Number		
Program Element	Date:		
Resources Required	Branch:	Prepared by:	
Personnel	Division:	Approved by:	
Total Budget			
End User of Final Product:			
Technological Feasibility			
Market Assessment:			
Producers of the End Product:			
Work Program and Research Plan			
Barriers Identified:			
Intervention Strategies:			
Strategies for Reducing Uncertainty and Critical Decision Points:			

importance of any single question is likely to be a function of
the specific technology under consideration in conjunction
with the current policies of the agency sponsoring the
program. The step-by-step procedures in the preparation
and use of the TIP are considered next.

Component #1: Technology Description

In preparing the technology description, the R&D manager will examine the motivations behind and justifications for
pursuing a specific research program. There are two parts to
this component: (1) an assessment of the social problem or
personal need this research will resolve and (2) a technical
description of the technology.

The problem assessment is designed to ensure that the
proposed research is not a solution in search of a problem. It
begins with the policy objective or market deficiency to be
addressed by the technology and explores the different
approaches that might be taken to fill the need. The purpose
of this step is to ensure there is consensus on the issues since
there is not always unanimous agreement throughout any
agency on what the broad policy objectives set by the
Congress and the White House translate into at the program
level. Specifying particular facets of the problem permits
explicit agreement between the policy and program managers that the problem being addressed is both the right one
and a real one in terms of individual and social needs.

The second component of the technology description (the
technical description) sets forth the technical specifications
of the proposed end product along with an engineering
justification for its development. This description should
focus on the characteristics of the technology which indicate
that it is a response to a social or individual need.

The reason for putting such a description here is to force
program managers to consider not only whether the technology is the appropriate one for the end user group, but also
whether it has matured enough to assure it can be a viable
product. In short, this technical description should ensure
that the project is not really basic research still requiring
"proof of concept" before one can reasonably discuss its
advance to an application stage.

Figures 7-3 and 7-4 identify a variety of questions considered relevant to the technology description component of TIP.

Component #2: Product Diffusion

This element of the TIP addresses whether the proposed technology is compatible with the technology delivery and utilization system which produces and distributes currently available technologies with a similar function. There are two aspects to end-user identification: (1) a description of the existing market for the technology, and (2) an identification of the firms or industry that will ultimately manufacture and market the technology.

The market assessment provides a better understanding of the market characteristics for the new technology and an early warning if there is going to be dissonance between market pull and policy push. It cannot be assumed that satisfying an agency objective or filling a social need will translate into consumer demand for the candidate technology. Benefits that accrue to society will not necessarily be realized by the individual consumers who, based upon their purchase of the item, will determine its "success." If, on the other hand, there is a consumer demand for the product or technology, then it should be ascertained why industry, which is in the business of searching new ways to turn consumer demand into profits, has not undertaken the research necessary to develop, produce, and market the technology.

Competition with products the new technology would replace as well as those that could be used as a close substitute for it is another aspect of the market that should be described in this section. If the new technology is to succeed, it must equal or exceed its competitors in performance, and it must be able to do this at a lower or equal cost to the manufacturer or command a higher price from the consumer. Otherwise, the normal workings of the marketplace that would bring about implementation will be absent, and extraordinary measures will be required to make up for this lack of market pull. If the latter is the case, then it is important that ways to solve this market failure problem be explored before com-

FIGURE 7-3. TIP Supplement A

Questions for the Discussion of Program Objectives
and End Users

---

1. Describe the problem or deficiency that the proposed research would remedy.

2. Why is the proposed option the best solution to the problems?

3. Have alternative solutions been considered?

4. Why was this solution chosen over the alternatives?

5. Is there a non-technology solution available?

6. How would this research fit in with overall agency research objectives?

7. Where did the motivation for the research originate?

    a) Staff _____

    b) Congress _____

    c) Agency chiefs _____

    d) Other agency _____

    e) Manufacturer _____

    f) Individual entrepreneur _____

    g) Interest group _____

    h) Think tank/academia _____

8. If the end user is different from the actor identified in question 7, who are the likely producers and consumers of this technology?

9. Are the wants and preferences of these consumers and the manufacturability requirements of this technology known?

FIGURE 7-4. TIP Supplement B

Questions for the Discussion of Technical Feasibility

---

1. What is the technical justification for the development of the proposed technology?

2. What are the engineering specifications of the proposed end-product?

3. What is the evidence of technical feasibility?

mitting the agency to the research.

Attention to the second aspect of product diffusion, the economics of production, will help the research team focus on designs that are sensitive to production constraints when conducting the R&D. This should help eliminate the problem of developing a technology that is beyond industry's production capabilities.

The competitiveness of the producing industry should have some bearing on how a new technology will be commercialized. If a new product has a strong profit potential and the producing industry is highly competitive, then it is likely that individual manufacturers will be sufficiently motivated to commercialize the product in the near term to gain an advantage over competitors. When this is the case, the federal push for implementation can be minimal. On the other hand, if the industry is not highly competitive, the manufacturer might show little incentive to speed up the normal manufacturing cycle to acquire a competitive edge in commercialization.

It might be argued that most public managers do not have the expertise to adequately complete the following checklist. There is some evidence that, when this is the case, little real thought is given to implementation. It is suggested here that the exercise of having to actually think through these questions and do the research that might be required to resolve uncertainties not only results in a better research plan but also aids in sharpening the instincts of those who conduct program planning.

Figures 7-5 and 7-6 show those questions which are considered relevant to the product diffusion component of TIP.

Component #3: Work Program and Research Plan

As we noted above, the program manager or technologist confronted with questions about a technology's manufacturability, marketability, user acceptance, and probability of diffusion may be intimidated—or simply disinterested (reacting with "That's not my job"). Top-level agency concern over implementation feasibility and management

FIGURE 7-5. TIP Supplement C

Questions for the Discussion of Market Assessment

1. Is there a preexisting demand for the technology?

2. If so, why has it not been tapped by private vendors?

3. Is there a replacement market for this technology or will it be a one-purchase-only product?

4. Do channels now exist to reach this market, or will they have to be developed?

5. What products currently on the market will the new product compete with?

6. Are there any close substitutes for the new product?

7. If so, might these substitutes be altered to better compete with the new product at an equal or lower cost?

8. What are the technical advantages/disadvantages of the new product over the one it will replace?

9. Do these advantages/disadvantages accrue to the user or to the public at large?

10. What are the cost advantages/disadvantages of the new product over the one it will replace?

11. Can the benefits of the new technology command a higher price from the consumer than the one it will replace?

FIGURE 7-6. TIP Supplement D

Questions for the Discussion of the Producers of the End Product

1. Who will produce or manufacture the product?

2. If the product will be profitable for the manufacturer to produce and market, why is it necessary for the federal government to support the R&D?

3. Can the producing industry command the responses necessary for implementation?

4. Will production require substantial retooling?

5. If so, will the technology be ready at a point that fits the industry's retooling cycle?

6. Is the capability in place to service and maintain the technology once it is introduced?

commitment to the evaluation of technology planning efforts in light of implementability can resolve the problem of staff-level disinterest or resistance. But top-level commitment will be insufficient to resolve the problem faced by the program manager or branch chief who is unable to comply with the intent of TIP because of a lack of knowledge about issues such as manufacturing, markets, and consumer behavior. And top-level commitment to implementation is not sufficient to resolve the problems of uncertainty inherent in any advanced research venture.

What can the branch chief or program manager do when confronted with uncertainty over whether a technology will satisfy the wants and preferences of the potential consumer, whether it will be competitive, and whether it can be manufactured at a profit? How does the technologist anticipate barriers to adoption without a working knowledge of political behavior, industrial decision making, and consumer behavior?

The thrust of TIP is that this knowledge should be acquired through research before or coterminously with the process of technology development and design. This will mean conceiving research plans and work programs more broadly than has been the rule in technology R&D. Work programs are currently organized in terms of technology systems and subsystems. Research on STOL aircraft, for example, involved research on technology subsystems required for propulsion, guidance and lift. Research on some advanced automotive engines involves research on advanced ceramic materials.

It should not be surprising that specialists in externally blown flaps for STOL aircraft or ceramics for turbine engines are not interested or expert in matters of marketing, production scheduling, cost engineering, and the like. We do not propose that they should become experts in implementation.

Rather, we argue that the research manager in charge of the overall work plan for STOL aircraft or turbine engines should be concerned with obtaining information about the feasibility of implementation *in time to influence the process of technology development and in time to inform the prioritization of R&D expenditures.* In most instances, this will mean including research on manufacturability, marketability, user acceptance, and implementation barriers in the overall work plan of the branch or division.

If the program manager has been unable to answer the questions in Figures 7-3, 7-5 and 7-6 (questions about the manufacturability, marketability, and user acceptance of a technology), then the overall work plan for that technology system should be amended to incorporate research on the dimensions of implementation feasibility. Obtaining answers to these questions is likely to require expertise that is not available in-house. This information can be assembled through consulting contracts, but the formulation of the necessary research and the interpretation of consultant reports will require development of at least limited in-house staff capability in the areas of cost-analysis, market assessment, and implementation planning. For these specialists to command the respect of program managers and other technologists, it will be necessary for them to be supplied with top-level management support because their role is likely to be initially perceived as threatening.

It is expected that implementation concerns will be addressed at the program rather than the project level. Thus, TIP will concentrate on whole technological systems rather than component subsystems. This means that the program manager will be concerned about the implementability of STOL aircraft or turbine engines, but not the *implementability* of STOL avionics or turbine ceramics. Avionics and ceramics would remain questions of technological feasibility while STOL and turbine engines as technological systems are assessed in terms of the additional dimension of implementation feasibility.

In developing the overall work program, the program manager should work with in-house "implementation specialists" and potential manufacturers to develop a research plan that responds to the questions in Figure 7-7.

Component #4: Barrier Identification

In reporting the results of the case studies in Chapter 6, we identified several classes of barriers that can confound the adoption and diffusion of a candidate technology once it reaches the prototype stage. These included:

FIGURE 7-7. TIP Supplement E

Questions for the Preparation of Overall Work Plan
1. Are there critical unknowns or uncertainties about the manufacturability or user acceptance of this technology?
2. Is a clear implementation and diffusion path evident for this technology? Has it been delineated strategically? Whose resources and cooperation are necessary for implementation?
3. Are any barriers to implementation anticipated? If so, what are they? (See Components #4 and #5 in the text.)
4. How will these concerns be addressed in the allocation of the group's research budget? When will this information become available in relation to the multi-year budget targets for the development and testing of this technology? (See Component #6 in the text.)
5. Could implementation be jeopardized by the difficulty or risk of failure in engineering any of its subsystems?

1. The need to coordinate and orchestrate a multiplicity of agencies and actors
2. Costs, including adverse environmental and social effects
3. Uncertainty
4. Sensitivity of project success to events beyond agency control
5. The inertia of current ways of making and using things

We noted, for example, that the risk of implementation failure is likely to be increased where:

- Cooperation between multiple organizations is necessary for successful implementation, but decision-authority is fragmented
- Simultaneous introduction of separate project components is necessary for implementation success
- Implementation results in adverse social, environmental, or economic consequences
- The technology is likely to cost more than currently available products

- The technology's costs defy advanced estimation
- The potential consumer acceptance and sales potential of the technology are highly uncertain
- The program's success is dependent upon long-term program continuity or the strength of political commitments
- The program's success is dependent upon the state of the nation's economy and sensitive to fluctuations in the business cycle
- The benefits of the technology accrue to the public at large rather than to the user who must pay its purchase price
- The technology's adoption and diffusion would require a major or comprehensive change in the behavior or attitudes of consumers
- The technology's adoption and diffusion would require a major or comprehensive change in the methods, behavior, or structure of the industry which produces today's comparable product or service

This inventory of potential "sticking points" in the implementation process provides a useful starting point for the R&D manager faced with the problem of anticipating potential barriers to implementation. A more fine-grained set of questions designed to search and scan for potential barriers is provided in Figure 7-8.

If the searching and scanning process turns up certain or potential barriers, the R&D manager is faced with a series of trade-off judgments. Whether the barrier is fatal must be assessed, and, if it is, whether technology development should be aborted. Or, one might judge that the barrier is problematic but not fatal. In this instance, the R&D manager may determine that the payoff from successful implementation justifies the risk of a strategic effort to "hurdle" the barrier or "break the bottleneck."

This kind of judgment decision is not one that can be made using quantified costs, benefits, and risks. Rather, the approach here is intended to help the R&D manager make explicit but qualitative risk/payoff decisions. It is also intended to impose a discipline on the R&D manager based on the proposition that it is very much the business of the technology planner to be concerned about the probability of

FIGURE 7-8. TIP Supplement F

```
                Questions for the Discussion of Barriers Anticipated
```

Coordination and orchestration requirements:

Does successful implementation require coordination and cooperation between several agency divisions, different agencies, different levels of government, or between the public and private sector?

What are the indications that others are motivated to cooperate or commit their resources to the extent necessary to make the project a success?

Does successful implementation require <u>simultaneous</u> action on the part of independent actors? Is a staged or incremental implementation path available?

Costs:

Will implementation result in adverse economic, social, or environmental impacts? Can they be mitigated at a reasonable cost?

Will the technology cost more or less than the closest currently available substitute? How much will it cost to obtain a reliable estimate of cost and performance?

Will the benefits of the technology accrue to the user who pays for it?

Uncertainty:

Is there a basis for assessing the cost-competitiveness of this technology?

Is there a basis for assessing the potential sales volume and consumer acceptance of this technology?

Is there evidence of manufacturer interest in or antagonism to the project or technology?

Are the cost/performance characteristics that the technology must achieve to insure consumer acceptance known? Can they be achieved?

Are the manufacturability and imageability characteristics that the technology must possess known? Can they be achieved with this technology?

Sensitivity of project results to events beyond agency's control:

Is successful implementation dependent on budget continuity over an extended time frame?

Is successful implementation dependent on policy or personnel continuity over an extended time frame?

Does successful implementation require incentives or penalities that are not currently in force or to which there is questionable political commitment?

Is project success dependent on cyclic economic factors such as the rate of inflation or the cost of borrowed capital? Has this been considered in the project's timing?

Inertia in the ways of making and using things:

Would implementation require the development of a new or substantially modified technology delivery system?

Would the technology require any substantial change in the behavior or attitudes of users?

Would the technology require any substantial change in the behavior or structure of the industry that manufacturers and markets currently available products or services of this sort?

Would introducing the technology involve substantial start-up costs for a manufacturer? Are they sufficiently large to prevent or limit commercial penetration?

implementation failure as well as the means of increasing implementation success.

In making an initial risk/payoff assessment, the R&D manager will be engaging in a thought process that pursues the kinds of questions shown in Figure 7-9.

FIGURE 7-9. Risk/Payoff Assessment

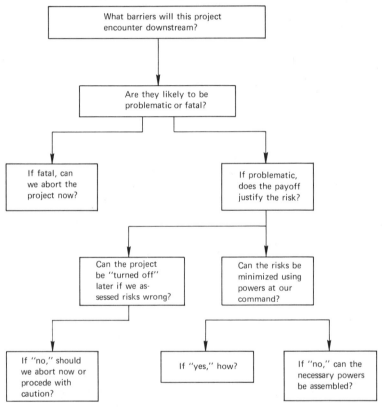

Two examples may be useful here. If a technology's large-scale adoption depends on a change in a federal standard or regulation (as is the case with diesel automobile engines and federal air pollution standards), then the R&D manager will probably perceive this barrier as problematic rather than fatal. Regulations are mutable, and Congress may be convinced to change them in order to achieve payoffs, such as a substantial improvement in fuel economy. But if another technology, an exotic new engine, for example, delivers lower performance at a higher cost to the user, it is unreasonable to expect the consumer to accept this product offering. In the first instance, the R&D manager may wish to accommodate risk by adjusting the size of the budget devoted to diesel R&D. In the second instance, it would be appropriate to view the barrier as fatal—and abort development of the technology.

Unfortunately, most decisions are not so clear-cut and easy as is the case of the engine costing more without working more efficiently. The more typical situation involves uncertainty about cost and performance. Here, the process of risk/payoff assessment involves establishing critical decision points in the development path where cost and performance will be reassessed in light of improving information. This process of establishing milestone points for barrier reassessment will be discussed later. We now turn to strategies for hurdling barriers.

Component #5: Strategies for Relaxing Barriers

We have argued that it is the technology planner's business to be concerned about barriers to implementation and the means of relaxing those barriers. One response to barriers is the design of technologies to fit the parameters of the marketplace. This means paying greater attention to cost and the dimensions of performance valued by the user as well as those dimensions of technology performance central to the agency's mission.

A technology, for example, that reduces pollution or conserves fuel, but costs more and is less reliable in operation, is not likely to receive an enthusiastic reception in the marketplace. This is a design challenge: to respond to those barriers associated with cost and consumer acceptance.

In many instances, however, an engineering response will be insufficient to achieve implementation success. In some cases, for example, it may be necessary to promote or catalyze the development of a new or substantially altered technology delivery system. In other cases, it may be necessary to motivate the current technology delivery system to perform in a new way. Grants, subsidies, tax incentives, regulatory penalties, and policy taxes, such as the fuel surcharges imposed in Europe, all represent strategies used to create markets and to motivate the behavior of local governments, private firms, and individual consumers.

The problem of motivating the technology delivery system is a particularly thorny one which involves questions of equity between firms and issues of anticompetitive impact. Issues of property rights, patents, licensing arrangements, the recoupment of windfall profits, and anticompetitive impacts are raised by public intervention in the marketplace and federal procurement of technological innovations. Unanticipated, these issues can erect irremediable barriers to the introduction of a new technology (as the Transbus case study illustrates most directly).

This argues very forcefully that technology planning should involve the mapping of an adoption and diffusion path in which issues of patent rights and competitive position are anticipated and resolved in parallel with technology development. The case studies indicate that these issues are extremely difficult to resolve when R&D is viewed as a procurement process or an adjunct of a regulatory process involving specification of a particular technology. The case studies also suggest the potential merit of economic incentives such as policy taxes as a method of motivating or rigging the marketplace without assuming a deterministic approach to the specifications of the technology that should be adopted and used. Economic incentives, such as "pollution taxes" and "full-cost pricing," offer a strategy for avoiding the problem of patents, licensing, and recoupment inherent in technology specification. In the presence of policy taxes, R&D can be used to "inform" rather than "dictate" market response to public policy objectives, thus avoiding the anticompetitive consequences of exclusive patents.

In the absence of economic or market incentives for the adoption of a new technology, the legal and anticompetitive issues associated with technology specification and governmental expenditures for R&D should be addressed as potential barriers requiring strategic anticipation and resolution.

In some cases, overcoming these barriers may demand the development of new forms of partnership between government and industry-wide associations rather than contract relationships with any one firm or supplier. This would mean the evolution of professional expertise extramural to each of the firms comprising an industry. But at the same time, it would leave research execution in the private sector as represented by an industry association or trade organization (for example, the Automotive Manufacturers Association). This may offer a strategy for gradually developing nonproprietary expertise and information in industries heavily colored with the public interest. Where such arrangements are unattainable and private firms are unwilling to undertake nonproprietary research, the development of public expertise as an aid to market entry by new firms may well be the appropriate last resort. This might mean, for example, the development of countervailing public expertise in extraordinary cases such as automotive pollution control and automotive safety.

It should be reiterated that two strategies for relaxing barriers are implied. The first is a design strategy: fit the technology to the dictates of the marketplace. The second is interventionist: rig or regulate the outputs of the marketplace. In the second instance, we are arguing that implementation may require an R&D strategy designed to increase the knowledge base in the public domain as an adjunct to regulatory or tax policy.

The second strategy is an explicit response to the problems of property rights, patents, and the potentially anticompetitive impacts of federally funded R&D undertaken by private firms. At the heart of this strategy is the notion that it may be necessary to conduct research wholly in the public sector or in contract relationships with industry associations rather than with individual firms as a means of ensuring that information is equitably available to all competitors and that regulatory efforts can be informed by publicly-held knowledge.

We recognize that this is not a strategy for "tip-toeing through the totems" of public/private relationships. It embodies the rather commonplace notion that the private and public welfare are not always identical and that private firms are not in the business of maximizing the public weal. In these cases, implementation may be most successfully directed through a long-term effort to develop expertise and information in the public domain. The intent of such a strategy would be to plan for an implementation path involving regulatory components or an incomes policy.

Such an approach would require viewing an industry rather than an individual firm as the implementation arena. This kind of approach will be difficult to accomplish in sectors of the economy where expertise is predominantly private rather than associational or public. This does not make the development of public domain expertise any less necessary as an ingredient of public-serving implementation efforts. In fact, it argues for early attention to the development of countervailing expertise.

There are costs associated with both intervention and design improvements. These should be assessed in the process of making the risk/payoff judgments raised by the consideration of barriers.

Figure 7-10 shows the kind of questions appropriate to the identification and assessment of strategies for relaxing barri-

FIGURE 7-10. TIP Supplement G

Questions for Assessing Intervention Strategies

1. Can the barrier identified be relaxed or removed by improvements or changes in technology design? If so, how? Are trade-offs implied?

2. Can the barrier be relaxed or removed through managerial effort or a firm commitment to a policy stance? If not, then:

3. What incentives or penalties does the agency command to motivate cooperation by other agencies or action on the part of producers or users?

   Are these incentives likely to be at least partially or limitedly effective in promoting adoption? Is the improved likelihood of implementation success worth the social, economic, and political cost of intervention?

4. What incentives or penalties could the agency bring to bear if it cooperated with other agencies or sought new authority?

5. Have the issues of proprietary information and anti-competitive impact been anticipated? Is there a short-term or long-term strategy for dealing with the industrywide diffusion of a technology as well as its adoption by an individual firm? Is this strategy consistent and compatible with the doctrine of competition?

ers. These questions deal with situations in which the primary barriers to technology adoption are questions of the mismatch between technology and marketplace.

But there is another class of barriers that frustrate implementation. These are the barriers associated with uncertainty. They can only be resolved over time by acquiring information which diminishes the uncertainty about a technology's cost, performance, and consumer acceptability. The cost and feasibility of acquiring the information necessary to reduce uncertainty is a strategic issue which should also inform the process of risk/payoff assessment. This is the subject we turn to next.

Component #6: Milestones and Strategies for Reducing Uncertainties

R&D efforts advancing the state of the art involve large degrees of uncertainty about the feasibility, cost, and performance of new technologies. How well the technology will perform and at what cost is rarely known at the beginning of R&D efforts. Often it is not known how well the technology must perform in order to achieve consumer acceptance or attract producer interest.

The case studies in Chapter 6 indicate that some R&D managers have used the magnitude of these uncertainties to disregard marketability issues and to avoid facing implementation barriers. The result is a fatalistic approach: "It will either work or it won't, and we can't tell in advance. Damn the barriers. Full speed ahead!"

We would argue that a more prudent and strategic approach is available. Market surveys can be conducted to narrow the range of uncertainty about consumer acceptance. These involve a relatively small front-end investment, given the scale of most R&D efforts. Their purpose would be to provide "procurement guidelines" that direct the engineering process toward a design target that is informed by consumer wants and needs.

More important, technologies involving intractable problems in cost analysis or requiring very large-scale demonstrations can be reduced in program priority. If technology cost and performance cannot be determined through laboratory testing or a limited and experimental approach to demonstration, it is probably unreasonable to expect a manufacturer to take the risk of implementation. It may be appropriate, therefore, to view the inability to anticipate cost, performance, and acceptance as a fatal barrier justifying project termination.

The more probable situation is that approximate costs and performance characteristics can be estimated in advance, but with a fairly substantial margin of error—especially early in the development process. Here, the issue is the development of milestones or critical points in a technology's development path at which the most recent information will be used to reassess the technology's likely performance in relation to each potential barrier. This process of reassessment requires the design of the R&D effort to produce the necessary information. It also requires a management commitment to reducing or eliminating expenditures on technologies at the earliest time they "go sour."

In short, the risk/payoff analysis implied by the TIP documentation is a continuing process that should occur concomitantly with an agency's annual planning and budgeting cycle, so that program priorities can be adjusted to reflect new information about the probability of implementation success as a technology matures. The monitoring and review feature of the TIP means that it is an ongoing process requiring reassessment during each budget cycle. It also means that any program office or agency that adopts such a methodology would be able to use it readily on projects that are just being formulated and on ones that are already underway.

The critical questions that should inform this process are shown in Figure 7-11.

It can be said emphatically that the R&D manager must be willing to establish go/no-go milestones based on the ability to overcome critical barriers if implementation concerns are to be successfully introduced in the process of federal R&D management. These milestones should be established as early as possible in the technology development process. New information or changing circumstances may dictate changing these milestones, and management judgment will always be required in making "accelerate/reduce/terminate" decisions. But the discipline of anticipating barriers and continually reassessing the probability of hurd-

FIGURE 7-11. TIP Supplement H

Questions for Reducing Uncertainties
1. When will the project produce reliable estimates of technology cost and performance?
2. Are reliable estimates obtainable on the basis of testing or a limited experimental demonstration?
3. What are critical go/no-go decision points in this technology's development and implementation path?

ling them is critical to the meaningful incorporation of commercialization and adoption concerns in the R&D process.

Implementing an Implementation Strategy

After all this research and analysis, the one final question to be addressed is, "How does one institutionalize a process like TIP and make it work?" There are fairly standard methods for instituting a new directive to be found in any text on public administration. The secret to implementing the TIP is to realize that, although it may appear straightforward, it represents a fairly fundamental change in the reward structure of R&D agencies. Specifically, good R&D managers are presently seen as people who are technically competent in the field(s) where they issue grants and contracts. Often these people are researchers themselves and attend professional meetings, give papers, and publish articles and books. The proclivity of such people is to do research that will further develop the state of the art. This motivates researchers to prove concepts rather than respond to problems. Still other monitors are of the engineering fraternity; they are trained to be problem solvers and would have little trouble evaluating the technical worth of projects.

Most of these people, however, are not interested in or qualified to assess the effective demand for the technology in the marketplace. Finally, management specialists in R&D positions have the obvious problem of not being able to evaluate and monitor the technical portions of the program. The happiest solution would be to hire people who are skilled in the technical aspects of the program, but who have had real-world marketing experience. These people are not available everywhere, and those that are so talented are often reluctant to leave lucrative positions in private industry. In the interim, some reliance will have to be put on teams of people who are willing to trade off their technical-marketing experiences with each other. The latter could be buttressed by contractor specialists when necessary.

A second change is attitudinal and requires a noticeable shift in the R&D reward structure. Most people would be willing to agree to a reasonable, clearly defined objective function as long as the shift were recognized by their superiors. This means that TIP and its stress on end users will have to be supported by people in positions of authority. It would help if all levels of administration endorsed the TIP because each level would support the one below it to an extent that the whole philosophy of research management responsibility would be established. For project managers, though, all that is required is that their managers support the TIP concept and make clear how it will be used to rank projects and judge personnel for advancement.

Summary and Retrospective

This study began with the concern that federal R&D programs have mistaken the engineering of technologies for the resolution of social ills and the satisfaction of personal needs. The objective function of federal R&D, we postulated, was establishing the technical feasibility of new technologies and pressing outward the boundaries of the technological state of the art. But was this objective suited to the development of technologies that perform a real problem-solving function? If technical feasibility were the driving concern of R&D managers, would they be likely to plan and design technology programs that resulted in implementation?

Asking and answering this question required an exhaustive literature search, extensive interviews with R&D managers, the development of hypotheses that explain implementation failure, and case studies to test and refine the hypotheses. At the end of this process, we were able to conclude with reasonable confidence that the problem of implementation is the problem of matching policy push and market pull, and that this problem was not being addressed early enough in the R&D process because many technology planners take the view that "implementation isn't my business."

We disagree. Implementation concerns should be within the scope of technology planning, and they should inform technology design. Why? Because the payoff from federal R&D expenditures is not realized at the point of technical feasibility but at the point of user adoption.

The last chapter in this report has been concerned with the incorporation of implementation concerns in the R&D management process. We concluded that increasing the likelihood of implementation will require federal agencies to focus (to an unprecedented degree) on the wants of individual consumers, the barriers to adoption and diffusion, and the costs of prototype technologies. And probably more important—and threatening—we concluded that increasing the probability and frequency of implementation success is going to require a commitment to continuing reassessment of the risks and payoffs associated with R&D efforts. In short, we are proposing an approach to R&D planning, screening, and management that is more responsive to the demands of consumers and more acutely sensitive to the "sticking points" and "bottlenecks" that complicate implementation.

This approach, we believe, would at minimum offer a strategy for cutting the losses associated with the "big project" that "goes sour." At best, it may serve to refocus the attention of applied R&D on problem solving rather than on technical feasibility.

But that is a tall order, and we are aware of the barriers to the implementation of a strategy like TIP.

- Because it is akin to zero-based budgeting in its insistence on the annual assessment of risks and payoffs, it

may be perceived as threatening to established lines
of research

- Because it would involve the public sector in downstream market analysis activities that are the traditional
  domain of the private sector, it is likely to be controversial
- Because it recognizes that programs can start from a
  misconception of "the problem" or "turn sour" over
  time, it may step on toes in both Congress and the
  research establishment
- And, because it would involve a new set of managerial
  and organizational skills, it may be resisted by the
  technologist who views implementation as a pure
  engineering problem (complicated by institutional ir-
  rationalities)

These problems are real, and, like any barrier to implementation, they cannot be wished away. But, we suspect,
addressing them explicitly should advance the probability
that TIP or something comparable can be introduced in the
management of federal R&D programs. Again, we empha-
size that it is not the specific form by which implementation
considerations are incorporated into the R&D management
process that is important. What is essential is that these
questions are recognized and addressed. Any methodology
will need to be adapted to respond to the specific requirements of individual agencies and their research programs.

TIP may well not be the "ultimate approach" to implementation. But it does, we believe, embody the right questions. Having posed these questions, we invite and challenge
R&D managers to strategize about managing the transition
to a new concern with the implementation payoff of R&D.